MORMONISM

Other books by the authors

Mormons Answered Verse by Verse
How to Rescue Your Loved One from Mormonism

MORMONISM

CHANGES,

CONTRADICTIONS,

AND ERRORS

JOHN R. FARKAS
and DAVID A. REED

Baker Books

A Division of Baker Book House Co
Grand Rapids, Michigan 49516

Published by Baker Books
a division of Baker Book House Company
P.O. Box 6287, Grand Rapids, MI 49516-6287

Printed in the United States of America

Library of Congress Cataloging-in-Publication Data

Farkas, John R.
    Mormonism : changes, contradictions, and errors / by John R. Farkas and David A. Reed.
        p. cm.
    Includes bibliographical references and indexes.
    ISBN 0-8010-3568-6
        1. Mormon Church—Controversial literature. 2. Church of Jesus Christ of Latter-day Saints—Controversial literature. I. Reed, David A. II. Title.
    BX8645.F37 1994
    289.3′32—dc20   94-28343

CONTENTS

ACKNOWLEDGMENTS

We would like to thank Phyllis Farkas for her insightful comments, corrections, and additions to the manuscript, and Penni Reed for her patient endurance.

Also, we give special thanks to the writers and researchers who went before us for making their information available for our use.

But above all we thank our Lord and Savior Jesus Christ for giving us this added opportunity to witness for the truth of his gospel.

HOW TO USE THIS BOOK

Do you want to share the gospel of Jesus Christ with Mormon relatives, friends, and acquaintances, and with those just getting interested in Mormonism? Then you will find this book useful as a tool for opening the door to such witnessing and to fruitful Bible discussion.

Mormons need the gospel message found in the Bible, but religious preconditioning blocks the way and prevents them from receiving it. Material such as that found in this book must first be presented to help members of the Church of Jesus Christ of Latter-day Saints come out from under the authority of their local and Salt Lake City leadership and become more receptive to Bible teachings. This book will also be useful for prospective converts who are just getting interested in Mormonism.

After you have read it yourself and have grasped the main points, open this book with your LDS acquaintance and read through the material together, preferably in the order in which it appears, beginning with the preface and then chapter 2, "The Basis for Evaluating Scripture Comparisons." He or she will see that Mormon sources are quoted and that Mormon standards are used to highlight the significance of contradictions, changes, and absurdities evident in these quotes.

Let the Mormon quotes do the talking, and Mormons, and others, will listen. (They may wish to verify some of the quotes by looking up original sources in Mormon libraries.) For more information on what *you* should say—and should avoid saying—during these discussions, please be sure to read our chapter on "Witnessing to Mormons" near the end of this book.

PREFACE

Since its beginning in 1830 the Church of Jesus Christ of Latter-day Saints (also called LDS or Mormon Church) has claimed through its top leaders and scriptures to be the one true church on the face of the whole earth. It claims to be the *only* true church, set up and established by the Lord Jesus Christ in 1830 through the Prophet Joseph Smith. It teaches that Joseph Smith had all the priesthood authority needed to do this given to him by Jesus Christ, and that priesthood authority has been handed down from prophet to prophet since then, residing now in the current Prophet. Examples of these claims are given below:

Joseph Smith a True Prophet, Mormons the Only Ones with True Gospel

Truly happy is that man, or woman, or that people, who enjoys the privileges of the Gospel of the Son of God, and who know how to appreciate his blessings. **Who is that person, or that people?**[*] We are ready to reply, '**The Latter-day Saints are the only people** on earth, that we have any knowledge of, to whom the everlasting Gospel has been given in these days; they are the **only people who are the heirs to it, with all its blessings and privileges.** Not

---

[*]Bold type and italics in all the quotes are added for emphasis. Items in brackets are given for additional information. Appendixes 1 and 2 have more details about the major references and their authors.

to our knowledge is there any other people on the face of this globe that enjoy this inestimable blessing. (President Brigham Young, February 20, 1853, *Journal of Discourses* 1:309)

The Only True Church

President Spencer W. Kimball said:

This is the only true church. . . . This is not a church. This is the Church of Jesus Christ. There are churches **of men** all over the land and they have great cathedrals, synagogues, and other houses of worship. . . . *(The Teachings of Spencer W. Kimball,* [President]** Spencer W. Kimball, 1982, p. 421)

President Ezra Taft Benson said:

This is not just another Church. This is not just one of a family of Christian churches. This is the **Church and kingdom of God,** the **only true Church upon the face of the earth,** according to the Lord's own words (see D&C [Doctrine and Covenants] 1:30). His Church—it bears His name and it is directed under the authority of His priesthood . . . is a message that will save and exalt the souls of the children of men. There is no other way, because **this is the only true message** and **the only true church upon the face of the whole earth.** Those are not my words; they are the words of the Lord Jesus Christ as found in the revelations. (D&C 1.) This gospel in its purity, now restored to the earth. . . . *(Teachings of Ezra Taft Benson,* [President] Ezra Taft Benson, 1988, pp. 164–65, 177)

God allegedly told Joseph Smith in 1820 that no other churches were right.

** When the position or office of a Mormon author (at the time of authorship) is not included in the work referenced, it is given in parentheses or brackets. When the position, or other description, is given on the title page of the referenced work, parentheses are not used. The office is given to show the authority of the author within the Mormon Church.

My [Joseph Smith's] object in going to inquire of the Lord was to know which of all the sects was right, that I might know which to join. No sooner, therefore, did I get possession of myself, so as to be able to speak, than **I asked** the Personages who stood above me in the light, **which of all the sects was right** (for at this time it had never entered into my heart that all were wrong)— and which I should join. **I was answered that** I must **join none of them**, for **they were all wrong**; and the Personage who addressed me said that all **their creeds were an abomination** in his sight; that those **professors were all corrupt**; that: "they draw near to me with their lips, but their hearts are far from me, they teach for doctrines the commandments of men, having a form of godliness, but they deny the power thereof.". . . I then said to my mother, "I have learned for myself that **Presbyterianism is not true**." (*Joseph Smith—History* 1:18–20, in Pearl of Great Price, a work viewed by Mormons as scripture)

God allegedly said that Mormonism is the only true and living church on the face of the earth.

And also those [Joseph Smith and others] to whom these commandments were given, might have power to lay the foundation of this church, and to bring it forth out of obscurity and out of darkness, **the only true and living church upon the face of the whole earth**, with which I, the Lord, am well pleased . . . (1831 [this is the date of the alleged revelation], Doctrine and Covenants [hereafter abbreviated D&C] 1:30; D&C is viewed by Mormons as scripture)

More Mormon Claims

The significance of the above references and their authors can be found in Appendixes 1 and 2. It is very important to understand that the statements made are not just "puffery" and/or enthusiasm presented in a salesman-like fashion to make the Mormon organization look good. The men saying these things were presidents and official spokesmen for the Church of Jesus Christ of Latter-day Saints. In a booklet published and copyrighted 1982 by the Corporation of the President of The Church of Jesus Christ of Latter-day Saints, it was said:

> The Lord provided that salvation should come through his gospel, functioning through his church. . . . But where is there such a church? How will we recognize it when we see it? . . . Is there such a church upon the earth? Until 1830 there was not. It had been lost through the falling away. . . . In 1830 the Almighty restored his church to earth again. . . . This restored church is known as The Church of Jesus Christ of Latter-day Saints, with headquarters in Salt Lake City. (*Which Church Is Right?* p. 17)

In recent years the Mormon missionaries have not given this message the same emphasis as in the past. It has not been changed; it just has not been given the strong focus, probably for public relations purposes. They have learned the old adage "You catch more flies with honey than vinegar."

The Mormon Challenge

But in any event the LDS message is significant, and the truth and validity of it needs to be established because, if it is true, we all need to know and yell it from the rooftops, so to speak. But if it is not true, we also need to know so that it is exposed for what it is. In fact, a past Mormon leader said:

> If Joseph Smith was a deceiver, . . . then he should be exposed; his claims should be refuted, and his doctrines shown to be false. . . . **If** his claims and declarations were built upon fraud and deceit, **there would appear many errors and contradictions**, which would be easy to detect. The doctrines of false teachers will not stand the test when tried by the accepted standards of measurement, the scriptures. (*Doctrines of Salvation*, [Apostle] Joseph Fielding Smith, 1954, 1:188)

We have taken up this challenge. What follows is the fruit of an in-depth study that compares Mormon scriptures on various subjects, compares statements of top LDS leaders on certain subjects, compares old editions and new editions of Mormon scriptures for changes, and then looks at absurdities taught by LDS Church leaders. We also look at the sect's own standards for determining the reliability of its scriptures and the reliability of statements by its top leaders.

In making this in-depth study, we have taken great care to be sure nothing has been taken out of context. The meaning of Mormon verses, allegedly from God, has been studied in the context of adjacent verses and adjacent chapters. Statements by top Mormon leaders have been examined in their context. Reliable sources, from a Mormon viewpoint, have been used—*most* of them are published and copyrighted by the Mormon Church or authorized by the First Presidency, and many of them feature teachings and sermons of Church presidents.

INTRODUCTION TO MORMONISM

A Brief History of Mormonism

1805   Joseph Smith, Jr., the founder of the organization now called the Church of Jesus Christ of Latter-day Saints (the Mormon Church), is born on December 23rd in Sharon, Vermont, the fourth child of Lucy Mack and Joseph Smith.

1816   The Smiths move to the Palmyra, New York, area (about forty miles east of Rochester).

1820   In the spring Joseph Smith, Jr., at the age of 14, allegedly receives a visit from God the Father and Jesus Christ, who tell him that all churches are wrong, their creeds are an abomination, and the professors of those creeds are corrupt.

1823   The angel Moroni allegedly visits Joseph in his bedroom three times one September night. These visits are the start of a series of lessons that results in Joseph's getting gold plates that were allegedly buried in Hill Cumorah, just a few miles south of Palmyra, in Manchester, New York.

1826   Court records of Chenango County, State of New York, *People v. Joseph Smith The Glass Looker*, March 20, 1826, reveal that Joseph Smith was brought to trial on charges of money digging, using a "peep stone" to locate buried treasure.

1827   Joseph allegedly receives from the angel Moroni the gold plates that were buried in Hill Cumorah. Written on them in "Re-

formed Egyptian" is the history of a previously unknown New
World people. With the help of God Joseph translates the writing into what is now the Book of Mormon.

1829   On May 15 John the Baptist allegedly gives the Aaronic Priesthood to Joseph Smith and his scribe Oliver Cowdery as part of
the restoration of God's Church on Earth—authority that had
been lost shortly after Jesus died.

1829   Probably in the summer, as a continuation of the restoration
of God's Church, the Apostles Peter, James, and John allegedly
give Joseph and Oliver the Melchizedek Priesthood.

1830   The Book of Mormon is printed by the Grandin Print Shop in
Palmyra, New York.

1830   On April 6, the Mormon Church is organized with a handful
of people as God's one true Church on Earth. At this time it is
named the Church of Christ.

1831   The Mormon Church moves to Kirtland, Ohio. At its peak in
the 1830s Kirtland reaches a population of around 3,200—about
equal to nearby Cleveland.

1832   Mormons start settlements in Missouri.

1833   A collection of sixty-five alleged revelations from God to Joseph
Smith is published as the *Book of Commandments*. Seventy-one
revelations have been given up to this date, but only sixty-five
are included, as the printing press and facilities at Zion (Independence, Missouri) are destroyed before the collection can be
completed.

1834   The name of the Church is changed to the Church of the Latter Day Saints.

1835   About this time the practice of polygamy starts in private but
is publicly denied.

1835   The 1833 *Book of Commandments* is updated with new revelations, and old ones are modified (with no indication they are
changed). The resulting new book, entitled Doctrine and
Covenants, has two parts. The first part is called "Theology on
the Doctrine of the Church of the Latter Day Saints" (better
known as the "Lectures on Faith").[1] The second part is named

"Covenants and Commandments." Section 101:4 forbids the practice of polygamy.

1838 Joseph leaves Kirtland and goes to Far West, Missouri, fleeing the wrath of the law and disgruntled members.

1838 The name of the Church is changed to the Church of Jesus Christ of Latter-day Saints.

1838 About nineteen Mormon men, women, and children are massacred by non-Mormons at Hauns Mill, Missouri.

1838–
1839 Mormons are driven out of Missouri due to conflicts between them and non-Mormons.

1839 Settlement of what is to become Nauvoo, Illinois, starts.

1840 The Mormon Church has about 17,000 members.[2]

1842–
1844 Joseph Smith, John Taylor, and other members of the community, in the Mormon Church newspaper, deny that polygamy is practiced, even though it is.

1843 The alleged revelation from God that allows the practice of polygamy is received, but is not formally announced until 1852, is not included in Mormon scripture until 1876, and is not voted on until 1880. (This is the present-day D&C 132, which says in its heading that Joseph had known the doctrine and principles since 1831.)

1844 The city of Nauvoo, Illinois, has a population of about 12,000; it is the second largest city in the state, after Chicago. Joseph Smith is the mayor and lieutenant-general of the Nauvoo legion.

1844 On June 7 William Law, Joseph Smith's second counselor, publishes *The Nauvoo Expositor*, which exposes the practice of polygamy in Nauvoo and the teaching by Joseph Smith that there is more than one God.

1844 On June 10, under the authority of Mayor Smith and the Nauvoo City Council, police led by Smith destroy the press, office, and papers of *The Nauvoo Expositor*.

1844 On June 25 Joseph Smith and Hyrum Smith are arrested for their part in the illegal destruction of *The Nauvoo Expositor* press and office and the calling out of the Nauvoo legion. Along with John Taylor and Dr. Willard Richards they are held in the jail in Carthage, Illinois. On June 27 a mob attacks the jail, killing Joseph and Hyrum in spite of Joseph's efforts at self-defense with a six-shooter. Two men in the mob are reported killed.

1846   Brigham Young, the second President of the LDS Church, leads the Mormon trek to what is then a portion of Mexico and will become Salt Lake City, Utah. They arrive there in 1847.

1850   Mormon Church membership numbers about 52,000.

1851   The first edition of the Pearl of Great Price is published. It is added to the Mormon scriptures in 1880.

1852   In August polygamy is announced for the first time at a public Mormon meeting.

1857   On September 11 a combined force of Indians and Mormon militia led by Mormon Bishop John D. Lee attacks and annihilates a wagon train of 120 non-Mormon men, women, and children in the infamous Mountain Meadows Massacre.

1860   The Reorganized Church of Jesus Christ of Latter-Day Saints is officially established at Amboy, Illinois, with Joseph Smith III as President and Prophet.

1860   Mormon Church membership reaches about 61,000.

1862   The Morrill Act prohibiting polygamy is passed by the U.S. Congress.

1876   D&C 132, which allows polygamy, is first printed in a volume of Mormon scripture.

1880   In October D&C 132, on polygamy, is first voted on by the Mormon membership.

1882   Congress passes the Edmunds Act, providing heavy penalties for practicing polygamy. The practice continues by many in hiding.

1887–
1890   The Edmunds-Tucker Act dissolves the Mormon Church corporation and seizes its property. The Idaho test oath law disenfranchises Mormon voters. A short time later the Supreme Court finds the Idaho test oath constitutional. Legislation is drafted to disenfranchise Mormons in Utah.

1890 On September 25 Mormon Church President Wilford Woodruff issues his Manifesto asking Mormons to stop the practice of polygamy. At a Mormon Church General Conference on October 6 this Manifesto, now called Official Declaration—1, is accepted by the general membership as "authoritative and binding." This does not reject the revelation allowing polygamy (D&C 132); it just puts the practice aside.

1890 Mormon Church membership is about 188,000.

1921 The first part of the Doctrine and Covenants, the "Lectures on Faith," are removed quietly without such removal ever being presented to the general membership for a vote.

1950 Mormon Church membership is about 1,111,000.

1967 The original papyri, allegedly written by the hand of the Old Testament Prophet Abraham and used by Joseph Smith to translate the Mormon scripture *Book of Abraham*, are rediscovered. (The document has since been shown to be an Egyptian funereal text called a "Book of Breathings," written some 1500 years after Abraham's day.)

1970 Mormon Church membership is about 2,931,000.

1978 On September 30 what is now Official Declaration—2, allowing all worthy males in the Mormon Church to hold the priesthood, is accepted by unanimous vote of the members. (Prior to this a man with any amount of African blood could not hold the priesthood.)

1980 Mormon Church has about 4,640,000 members.

1991 Mormon Church has about 8,100,000 members, about 267 mission centers, and about 43,000 missionaries in the field.

1993 Mormon Church has about 8,700,000 members.

A Brief Summary of the Doctrine Taught by the Mormon Church

This section focuses on the unique doctrine taught by the Mormon Church through its teaching manuals, scriptures, and talks by top Mormon leaders. Many of these items are not likely to be mentioned by Mormon missionaries or in Mormon Church advertising. Note that many of the theological terms are exactly the same as those used by Christians, but they have a different meaning for most Mormons.

Our intent here is not to provide a biblical answer to the Mormon teachings. That has already been done in our book *Mormons Answered Verse by Verse*. We outline the unique Mormon Church teachings to prepare the reader for the comparisons in the following chapters.

Aaronic Priesthood   This is called the lesser priesthood and is usually held by young men starting at the age of 12 to the age of about 18. It is also held for a short time by men who have just become members.

Adam-God   From April 1852 to at least February 1877 LDS Church President Brigham Young clearly taught that Adam of the Garden of Eden is the father of our spirits, that Adam is the father of the spirit of Jesus Christ and the literal father of his body, and that Adam is our God. This is not now taught by the Mormon Church, and many Mormons are not aware it once was; others claim Brigham Young is incorrectly quoted.

Afterlife   The Mormon afterlife is divided into four levels. The lowest is hell, and then there are three levels of heaven: the telestial, the terrestrial, and the place where God dwells, the celestial (also called the kingdom of God). The celestial is also divided, the highest level being exaltation, or becoming a God.

Apostles   The Mormon Church claims to have the same organization as the primitive church that Jesus set up. They also have twelve Apostles and sometimes use this as a proof of their divine appointment as the one true Church. But they actually have fifteen or more most of the time. The general practice has been for a new President, who is also an Apostle, to appoint counselors from the Quorum of the Twelve; then the openings left by the President and his counselors are filled, resulting in a total of fifteen.

Bible   The King James Version of the Bible is one of the canonized scriptures of the Mormon Church, but it is considered incomplete, incorrectly translated with parts missing. Joseph Smith rewrote it, but only the Reorganized Church of Jesus Christ of Latter-Day Saints regularly uses his version. They call it Joseph Smith's "New Translation" of the Bible. The Mormon Church in Salt Lake City calls it the Joseph Smith Translation. They feature some of it in the footnotes and appendix of their edition of the King James Bible.

Celestial Kingdom   See *Afterlife.*

Chapel   A local building where Mormons hold their worship services and other activities.

Eternal Progression   The teaching that each of us has the potential to become a God just like God the Father did. He was once a man capable of physical death, was resurrected, and progressed to become a God. We can take a similar path and get all the power, glory, dominion, and knowledge that the Father and Jesus Christ have. We then will be able to procreate spirit children who will worship us as we do God the Father.

Exaltation   Becoming a God in the highest level of the celestial kingdom. See *Eternal Progression.*

Excommunication   The highest disciplinary action that the Church can take against a member. Excommunicated persons lose their membership in the Church.

First Presidency   A collective name for the President of the Mormon Church and his counselors, usually two.

General Conference   An official meeting held twice per year, early in April and October, for general membership instruction, teaching, and announcements by the top leaders of the Mormon Church.

God   Within Mormonism, Gods, angels, people, and devils all have the same nature or substance but are at different stages along the line of progression to Godhood. God the Father was once a man like us, capable of physical death, and he progressed until he became a God. He has a body of flesh and bones, but no blood.

Heaven   See *Afterlife.*

Hell   A place of torment from which most nonbelievers are resurrected into the telestial kingdom; only a limited number remain in hell forever—the devil and the demons and apostates who consciously reject and work against Mormonism.

Jehovah   The name for the preincarnate Jesus Christ.

Jesus Christ   The spirit of Jesus Christ was the first spirit born to God the Father and his wife (Heavenly Mother), and he progressed to become a God under the Father. (The Father is also the literal father of Jesus' body in exactly the same way we were begotten by our earthly parents.) Jesus now has a body of flesh and bones, but no blood. He is the spirit brother of Satan, whose spirit was procreated in the same way as Jesus'.

Marriage   The Mormon Church teaches two types of marriage. One ends at death. The other is for "time and eternity." If a couple is married in a Mormon temple by someone with authority, it is believed they will stay married in the next life. This kind of marriage is needed if they are to progress, not only as husband and wife, but as God and Goddess.

Melchizedek Priesthood   The higher of two categories of ministry in the LDS Church, assigned primarily to seasoned members over the age of 18 and to males only.

Mother in Heaven   The wife of God the Father, the mother of his spirit children.

Polygamy   The practice of men having more than one wife was started by Joseph Smith in the early/mid 1830s and ostensibly ended in 1890. It is not now practiced within the Church of Jesus Christ of Latter-day Saints, the Mormon Church headquartered in Salt Lake City, Utah. Members found practicing it are excommunicated. While the practice was ended, the revelation teaching it is still in Mormon scripture (D&C 132). Some Mormon splinter groups believe the teaching was for eternity and still practice it. These modern-day polygamists (called fundamentalists) number in the 30,000–50,000 range.

Pre-existence   The Mormon teaching that our spirits (Mormons and non-Mormons) were procreated in a premortal life by God the Father and our Mother in Heaven, that our spirits were born and raised to maturity before coming to earth to obtain physical bodies, and that the spirit of Jesus Christ was the first one born to our heavenly parents.

Priesthood   A category of ministry in the LDS Church open to all worthy males 12 years of age or older, empowering them to act in God's name. See *Aaronic Priesthood* and *Melchizedek Priesthood.*

Prophet   The top leader of the Mormon Church is considered not only a Prophet but also a Seer and Revelator. He has the title "President." He is the only one who can speak for the whole church and receive new revelation for the whole church. When the existing Prophet dies, the most senior (in time as an Apostle, not in age) of the twelve Apostles, the President of the Quorum of the Twelve Apostles, becomes the new President. He can appoint counselors, who receive their authority from him.

Salvation   A word that Mormons qualify in one of three ways: *unconditional* or *general* salvation is simply resurrection from the dead, granted to all through Christ's atonement; *conditional* or *individual* salvation involves entering the celestial kingdom through works of Mormonism; *full* salvation means exaltation to become a God as a result of temple ceremonies and other works.

Satan   One of the spirit children of God. As a consequence of their rebellion, Satan and his angels cannot have mortal bodies; hence they cannot progress.

Scriptures   The Mormon Church has four documents it calls canonized scriptures: the Book of Mormon, Doctrine and Covenants, Pearl of Great Price, and the King James Version of the Holy Bible. See Appendix 1 for details.

Son of God   Besides Jesus Christ, all of us are viewed as the children of God, his literal spirit children. This makes us all—Mormons, non-Mormons, Jesus Christ, and Satan—spirit brothers and sisters. See *Pre-existence* and *Spirits.*

Spirits   Non-material beings allegedly procreated in the pre-existence by God the Father and his wife. Jesus Christ (and even we ourselves) was supposedly born and raised to maturity as a spirit before coming into a body on this earth. The spirit of Satan was also procreated in this way. This makes Satan and Jesus Christ spirit brothers. Jesus selected a righteous path; Satan selected the opposite.

Stake   A group of wards, similar to a Roman Catholic diocese.

Standard Works   The four canonized scriptures (see *Scriptures* above) used by the Mormon Church are called the *standard works*.

Temple   One of about four dozen large religious buildings around the world in which special ceremonies are performed for the living and the dead; off limits to nonmembers and even to Mormons who lack a "temple recommend" from their leaders.

Trinity   This word is used by Christians to summarize the biblical teaching that within the one true God are three persons: God the Father, God the Son, and God the Holy Ghost. They share the same nature or substance, so that there are not three Gods, but three persons in the one God.

Mormons say they also believe in the trinitarian concept of God. But what they really mean is that God the Father is a God, God the Son is another God, and God the Holy Ghost is a third God, and that they are "one God" because they are *"one in purpose."* Mormons often have an incorrect understanding of what Christians mean by the Trinity. They say Christians believe that the Father, Son, and Holy Ghost are one person (i.e., Monophysitism) or that God shows himself as the Father or the Son or the Holy Ghost (i.e., Modalism).

Virgin Birth   A concept negated by the view that God, a resurrected man with flesh and bones according to Mormon teachings, literally fathered Jesus in the flesh in the same way in which earthly men father their children.[3]

Ward   A local Mormon congregation. The building it meets in is called a chapel.

Word of Wisdom   The Mormon teaching requiring abstinence from tobacco, alcohol, and hot drinks (tea and coffee).

Authority in the Mormon Church

Within the Mormon Church authority flows from the top down. The organization is structured in what might be called a classical pyramid shape, with the point upward. The President of the Church (always a man), with his counselors (usually two, always men), together called the First Presidency, are at the point. The President also is called a Prophet, Seer, and Revelator. He is the only one in the Church who has full authority and "keys," and the only one who can speak for God and receive revelation for the Church. Bruce R. McConkie, in *Mormon Doctrine*, said: "He is the earthly head of the kingdom of God,[4] the supreme officer of the Church, the 'President of the High Priesthood of the Church. . . .' His duty is to preside over the whole church and to be like unto Moses . . ." (p. 591).

The men who are the top leaders in the Mormon Church under the Prophet are called the General Authorities,[5] and each gets his authority for assigned responsibilities from the President/Prophet.

The Quorum of the Twelve Apostles, twelve men, just under the Prophet, also have the same authority and "keys" as the President, but can only partially use them as authorized by the President. President Joseph F. Smith, in *Gospel Doctrine*, said: "What is a key? It is the right or privilege which belongs to and comes with the Priesthood, to have communication with God" (p. 142). They can be fully used by the Apostles only when there is no President, and that historically has seldom happened for long periods.

The Quorum of the Seventy forms the next level below the Apostles. As of this writing there are seventy-seven men in this body (quorum), but vacancies sometimes go unfilled for a period of time.

Within the Mormon Church only men can hold the priesthood. They are the only ones with the formal authority to act in God's name. (But the role of women can be considered significant in that the priesthood-holder cannot reach exaltation unless married to a woman in the temple for time and eternity.)

Apostle Bruce R. McConkie, in *Mormon Doctrine*, said: "... priest-hood is the power and authority of God delegated to man on earth to act in all things for the salvation of men" (p. 594).

At the local level is a Mormon congregation called a branch or a ward. A branch is a congregation, headed by a branch president, not large and/or stable enough to support all the usual activities. A ward is a congregation headed by a bishop and his two counselors and is the level at which the Mormon Church carries out most of its programs. Several branches and wards form a stake. A stake is similar to a diocese in the Catholic Church and is led by a stake president and his two counselors.

Authoritative Publications

There are many publications a person could read to ascertain the teachings of the Mormon Church. They include the canonized scriptures (Book of Mormon, Doctrine and Covenants, Pearl of Great Price, King James Version of the Bible)[6] and official sermons and talks by the President and other top leaders as found in official Church teaching manuals, books, magazines, and newspapers and in privately published newspapers, books, and papers. Most of the books are printed by the Mormon Church's publishing house, Deseret Book Company, or by private companies such as Bookcraft, Incorporated, of Salt Lake City. A wide range of materials is available from a wide range of sources. Pamphlets, tracts, audiotapes, and videos are usually directed at nonmembers and therefore do not get into deep Mormon doctrine. It is not possible to rank these publications in rigid order from most authoritative to least authoritative, but the above list does present them in that order in a general way.

Elder Boyd K. Packer of the Quorum of the Twelve Apostles, in speaking about the all-important Mormon priesthood, seemed to express the same ideas when he said:

> There are some things about the priesthood that every elder
> should know if he is to understand how the Church is governed.
> . . . There are principles and precepts and rules which are often
> overlooked and seldom taught. Some of these are found in the
> scriptures, others in the handbooks. Some of them are not found
> in either. They are found in the Church. You might call them
> traditions, but they are more than that. They are revelations
> which came when the Brethren of the past assembled themselves,
> agreed upon His word, and offered their prayers of faith. ("What
> Every Elder Should Know—and Every Sister as Well," *Ensign*,
> February 1993, p. 7)

The problem of determining the official position of the LDS
Church on a given subject is exacerbated by the fact that the Mormon scriptures, the *standard works*, while sometimes described
as the only source of doctrine, in many cases do *not* clearly present many of the unique Mormon teachings; in fact, there are instances where they teach just the opposite. For example, the Book
of Mormon says nothing about the vicarious work for the dead
carried on in Mormon temples; rather, it clearly teaches that salvation can be attained in this life only. There is also nothing on
eternal progression, the potential of men to progress to become
Gods. Nor does it teach anything about God the Father having
once been a man capable of physical death; rather, it teaches that
God is from all eternity to all eternity. You cannot get any idea
of the scope and importance of polygamy just by reading Doctrine and Covenants Section 132. But these ideas are presented
very clearly in teaching manuals published and copyrighted by
the Mormon Church and in talks by top leaders. Teaching manuals are in fact the best documents to use in determining official
teachings even though ostensibly they are not the top authority.
We think they are among the best sources because (1) such manuals many times explicitly spell out doctrines more clearly than
LDS scriptures; (2) in most cases they are published by the Mormon Church and copyrighted by the Corporation of the President of the Church of Jesus Christ of Latter-day Saints; and

(3) Mormons cannot deny that these books truly teach Mormon doctrine without opening the Mormon Church to the criticism of selling useless books.

Further confounding this issue are the assertions by Mormon Church Presidents that the President of the Church must be obeyed, *even if wrong*. (See our discussion of Mormon standards for following the top Mormon leaders in chapter 4.) Even Doctrine and Covenants 21:4–5 seems to support this idea: "... thou shalt give heed unto **all** his [the Prophet's] words and commandments which he shall give ... as if from my [Jesus Christ's] own mouth. ..."

Many collections of sermons and talks by top Mormon leaders have been published, including teachings by most of the Church Presidents. In addition, the largest collection of talks by early top leaders can be found in the twenty-six-volume *Journal of Discourses*. Started by the authority of Brigham Young in 1855, this collection covers the years from 1844 to 1886.

Key individuals and published works quoted herein are listed and discussed in Appendixes 1 and 2. It should be noted that the majority of the publications referenced are published and copyrighted by the Corporation of the President of the Church of Jesus Christ of Latter-day Saints, or are published under the sponsorship of the Mormon Church (like the periodicals and the *Journal of Discourses*), or consist of sermons and writings of presidents.

THE BASIS FOR EVALUATING SCRIPTURE COMPARISONS

Years ago the top leadership of the Mormon Church did not hesitate to challenge people to examine the teachings of their Church. Debates between top Mormon leadership and non-Mormons were not unusual. Today they are. Below are three examples of challenges by top Mormon leaders. Note that they say, "**convince us of our errors**," "**compare** the religion of the Latter-day Saints," and "if Joseph Smith was a deceiver . . . then **he should be exposed**." Particularly note the statement "there would appear **many errors and contradictions**." This book accepts this challenge by exposing such errors and contradictions.

> . . . **convince us of our errors of doctrine**, if we have any, by reason, by logical arguments, or by the word of God. . . . (*The Seer*, [Apostle] Orson Pratt, January 1853, p. 15)

> I say to the whole world, **receive the truth, no matter who presents it** to you. Take up the Bible, compare the religion of the Latter-day Saints with it, and **see if it will stand the test**. (President Brigham Young, May 1873, *Journal of Discourses* 16:46)

> **If Joseph Smith was a deceiver, . . . then he should be exposed**; his claims should be refuted, and his doctrines shown to be false. . . . If his claims and declarations were built upon fraud and deceit, **there would appear many errors and contradictions**, which would be easy to detect. The doctrines of false teachers will not stand the test when tried by the accepted standards of measure-

ment, the scriptures. (*Doctrines of Salvation*, [Apostle] Joseph
Fielding Smith, 1954, 1:188)

It is interesting to see this attitude of past leaders. This is not
the case now. *Church News*, a Mormon Church newspaper, for
the week ending June 6, 1992, contained an article compiled by
John L. Hart. He reported on an address to the October 1981
General Conference by Elder Carlos E. Asay of the Presidency of
the Seventy. The elder said:

> 1. Avoid those who would tear down your faith. Faith killers are
> to be shunned. . . . 4. **Do not contend or debate** over points of
> doctrine. . . . 6. Do not be swayed or diverted from the mission
> of the Church. There are those who would draw you off course
> and cause you to waste time and energies. . . .

From Acts 17:1–2, 17; 19:8–9 we learn that the Apostle Paul
did not hesitate to go into the marketplace and synagogue daily
and reason with people out of the Scriptures. Shouldn't we follow Paul's example? John 8:32 says: "Ye shall know the truth, and
the truth shall make you free."

In evaluating scriptures, some may want to apply their own
standards, perhaps those they use for the Bible. But in this book
we have chosen to use the criteria that the Mormon leadership
itself has established and what Mormon scriptures themselves
say. Even Mormons should find that fair.

Mormon Standards

What Did Joseph Smith Say?

The Prophet Joseph Smith was the founder and first President
of the Mormon Church and allegedly received by the power of
God over 95 percent of the present-day Mormon scriptures (except for the Bible). More information on Joseph Smith is found

in Appendix 2. Note in the following how he said, "there is no error in the revelations which I have taught." In other words, this man who was responsible for most of the Mormon scriptures claimed they have no errors.

> When did I [the Prophet Joseph Smith, May 1844] ever teach anything wrong from this stand? When was I ever confounded? I want to triumph in Israel before I depart hence and am no more seen. I never told you I was perfect but **there is no error in the revelations** which I have taught. Must I, then, be thrown away as a thing of naught? (*Teachings of the Prophet Joseph Smith*, compiled by Joseph Fielding Smith, p. 368)

On another occasion Joseph Smith said: "Why do not my enemies strike a blow at the doctrine? They cannot do it: **it is truth, and I defy all men to upset it**" (March 1844, *History of the Church* 6:273). So, in summary, the founder of the Mormon Church and the man responsible for 95 percent of its unique scriptures stated very clearly that there are no errors in them.

What Do Mormon Scriptures Say?

The first revelations that the Prophet Joseph Smith allegedly received from God were collected in 1833 into a book called the *Book of Commandments.* Chapter 1, verse 7 (hereafter written 1:7) says: "Search these commandments for they are **true and faithful. . . .**" A subsequent edition of this book was called Doctrine and Covenants (D&C) and was published in 1835. Section 1:7 of this edition is *exactly* the same as 1:7 in the *Book of Commandments.* (The present [1986] edition of the D&C has exactly the same wording as is found in the 1833 and 1835 editions under 1:7, but this passage is now numbered 1:37.) Later on in this book we will examine other verses that are in the *Book of Commandments* to see if they also are exactly the same in the 1835 edition. If they are "true and faithful" in the 1833 edition, one would expect no changes in the 1835 edition, and none in the 1986 edition. This is not to say that allowance will not be made for new "revelation." It is the old existing revelations that will be compared. It seems reasonable to expect that *no differences* would be observed, seeing that Joseph Smith said they have no error and that the revelation allegedly from God also said they are "true and faithful."

Another verse conveys a similar thought: "For God doth not walk in crooked paths, neither doth he turn to the right hand nor to the left, **neither doth he vary from that which he hath said**, therefore his paths are straight . . ." (July 1828, D&C 3:2). This was numbered 2:1 in the 1833 edition and 30:1 in the 1835 edition. Moreover, D&C 42:56 says: "Thou shalt ask, and my Scriptures shall be given as I have appointed, and **they shall be preserved** in safety." These all reinforce what Joseph Smith said, namely, that no errors should be expected in the revelations and that "they shall be preserved."

The Book of Mormon expresses similar ideas. In Alma 41:8 we find: "Now, the decrees of God are **unalterable** . . ."; and in Mormon 9:9 we have: "For do we not read that God is the same yesterday, today, and forever, and in him there is no variableness **neither shadow of changing?**" The Prophet Joseph Smith said the Book of Mormon was "the most correct of any book on earth and the keystone of our religion, and a man would get nearer to God by abiding by its precepts, than by any other book" (*History of the Church* 4:461). This quote is also found in the Introduction of the Book of Mormon and is reinforced in the April 1993 *Ensign*, page 74, in a letter from the First Presidency. The title page of the Book of Mormon says it came "forth by the gift and power of God." Doctrine and Covenants 17:6 has God saying the Book of Mormon "is true."

The Character of God

Some of the scriptures that are compared below speak of the character of God. In that connection it will be important to keep in mind this statement by Joseph Smith: "It is the first principle of

the gospel to **know for a *certainty* the character of God . . .**"
(*Search These Commandments*, 1984, p. 152, and *Journal of Discourses* 6:3). Joseph Smith said this at the April 6, 1844, Mormon Church General Conference in Nauvoo, Illinois. Note the key phrase "know for a certainty the character of God." As you go through the scripture comparisons on the character of God, note whether they reflect certainty or uncertainty.

Using Mormon Standards

It seems reasonable, then, to expect a high standard of quality in the Mormon scriptures, both in content and in the transmitted text. This should also mean no contradiction in teachings, if they are from God, for in 1 Corinthians 14:33 we learn that God is not the author of confusion. If there is confusion, then it seems reasonable to conclude that the scriptures must not be from God.

As you read and study the material below, keep in mind that we have taken great care not to take the references out of context. We have also consulted the Joseph Smith Translation (JST) of the Bible (also sometimes called the Inspired Version and the New Translation by the RLDS) to be sure we are representing Joseph Smith's thoughts in 1833 when he finished it. Joseph said that he started this translation of the Bible at the commandment of the Lord, and on January 10, 1832, he was told to continue the work until it was finished (D&C 73:3–4). On February 2, 1833, Joseph said: "I completed the translation and review of the **New Testament**, on the 2nd of February, 1833 and sealed it up no more to be opened till it arrived in Zion"[1] (*History of the Church* 1:324). On July 2, 1833, Joseph said: "We this day finished the translating of **the Scriptures**, for which we returned gratitude to our Heavenly Father. . . . Having finished the translation of the Bible, a few hours since . . ." (*History of the Church* 1:368–69). There is some debate if it was really finished then, but we will take Joseph at his word, seeing that he claimed the Lord commanded him to finish it (D&C 73:3–4) and said he had completed the New Testament and, later, the Bible. Where we use biblical verses to show a conflict with the other Mormon scriptures, except as noted,[2] the Joseph Smith Translation[3] agrees with the King James Version.

If indeed Mormonism is what it claims to be, then it must be measured by its own standards. These are clearly laid out in the preface and above.

MORMON SCRIPTURES COMPARED

In what area of the world did Adam live?
He lived in the Near East.

> ... the Lord God, caused a river to go out of Eden to water the garden ... and became into four heads.... The second ... that compasseth the whole land of Ethiopia.... Hiddekel; that which goeth toward the east of Assyria ... and the fourth river was the Euphrates. And I, the Lord God, took the man, and put him into the Garden of Eden, to dress it, and to keep it. (Moses 3:10, 13, 15)

> The LORD God planted a garden eastward in Eden.... And a river went out of Eden ... and became into four heads.... And the name of the third river is Hiddekel ... which goeth toward the east of Assyria. And the fourth river is Euphrates. (Genesis 2:8, 10, 14)

He lived in the New World, near Independence, Missouri.

> Spring Hill is named by the Lord Adam-ondi-Ahman....[1] (May 1838, D&C 116:1. From the heading of 116 we learn that Spring Hill is in Missouri, Daviess County, which is near Independence.)

> Adam-ondi-Ahman is named as the place where Adam dwelt. (March 1835, D&C 107:53 and July 1838, D&C 117:8)

> Let my servant Newel K. Whitney [a bishop in Kirtland, Ohio, 1831–?, D&C 72:8] ... come up to the land of Adam-ondi-Ahman, and be a bishop unto my people.... (July 1838, D&C 117:11)

When is a man baptized?
He is baptized after he has the priesthood.

> And now I speak concerning baptism. Behold, elders, priests, and
> teachers **were baptized**; and they **were not** baptized save they
> brought forth fruit meet that they were worthy of it. (Moroni 6:1)

He is baptized before he has the priesthood.

> ... [candidates] shall be received by baptism into his church. ...
> *The duty of the members after they are received by baptism.* ...
> (April 1830, D&C 20:37, 68. This is similar to Moroni 6:34, which
> also contradicts Moroni 6:1.)

Baptism is the ordinance for obtaining membership in the
present-day Mormon Church. Men must be baptized well *before*
they receive the priesthood and an office in it.

What words are used in a baptism?
Having been commissioned ...

> Having **been commissioned** of Jesus Christ, I baptize you in the
> name of the Father, and of the Son, and of the Holy Ghost. Amen.
> (April 1830, D&C 20:73)

These are the words now used by the Mormon Church, and
they must be said *word perfect* or the complete ceremony is repeated until it is done and said perfectly.

Having authority ...

> Having **authority given me** of Jesus Christ, I baptize you in the
> name of the Father, and of the Son, and of the Holy Ghost. Amen.
> (3 Nephi 11:25)

How do we receive the remission of our sins?
We receive it by having the Spirit of Christ.

And again, by way of commandment to the church concerning the manner of baptism.... take upon them the name of Jesus Christ, having a determination to serve him to the end, and truly manifest by their works that **they have received of the Spirit of Christ unto the remission of their sins**, shall be received by baptism into his church. (April 1830, D&C 20:37)

We receive it by baptism.

... baptism is unto repentance ... unto the remission of sins.... And the first fruits of repentance is baptism; and baptism cometh by faith unto the fulfilling the commandments; and the fulfilling the commandments bringeth remission of sins. (Moroni 8:11, 25)

Upon you my fellow servants, in the name of Messiah I confer the Priesthood of Aaron, which holds the keys of the ministering of angels, and of the gospel of repentance, and of **baptism by immersion for the remission of sins**; and this shall never be taken again from the earth, until the sons of Levi do offer again an offering unto the Lord in righteousness. (May 1829, D&C 13:1)

Yea, repent and **be baptized, every one of you, for a remission of your sins**; yea, be baptized even by water.... (October 1830, D&C 33:11)

... they who shall believe in your words, and come down into the depths of humility and **be baptized ... and shall receive a remission of their sins**. (3 Nephi 12:2)

Has Jesus Christ always been God?
No, he had a beginning.

And I, John, saw that he received not of the fulness at the first, but received grace for grace; And he received not of the fulness at first, but continued from grace to grace, until he received a fulness. And thus he was called the Son of God, because he received

not of the fulness at the first. . . . I was in the beginning with the
Father, and am the Firstborn. . . . (May 1833, D&C 93:12–14, 21)

. . . and mine Only Begotten is and shall be the Savior, for he is
full of grace and truth; **but there is no God beside me**, and all
things are present with me, for I know them all. (Moses 1:6)

This reference is saying that "mine Only Begotten" is the Savior but is *not* God. This is not taught by the Mormon Church,
yet this verse in their scripture clearly says this.

The first spirit born to our heavenly parents was Jesus Christ (see
D&C 93:21). (*Gospel Principles*, p. 9)

*Yes, Jesus—that is, Jehovah in the Old Testament—has al-
ways been God.*

By these things we know that there is a **God in heaven, who is infinite and eternal, from everlasting to everlasting**, the same unchangeable God, the framer of heaven and earth, and all things
which are in them. . . . Which Father, Son, and Holy Ghost are
one God, infinite and eternal, without end. Amen. (April 1830,
D&C 20:17, 28)

For behold, the time cometh, and is not far distant, that with power,
the Lord Omnipotent who reigneth, **who was, and is from all eternity to all eternity**, shall come down from heaven among the children of men, and shall dwell in a tabernacle of clay, and shall go
forth amongst men, working mighty miracles, such as healing the
sick, raising the dead, causing the lame to walk, the blind to receive
their sight, and the deaf to hear, and curing all manner of diseases. . . . And he shall be called Jesus Christ, the Son of God, the
Father of heaven and earth, the Creator of all things from the beginning; and his mother shall be called Mary. (Mosiah 3:5, 8)

Hearken and listen to the voice of him who is **from all eternity
to all eternity**, the Great I AM, **even Jesus Christ**. (January 1831,
D&C 39:1)

For behold, I am God. . . . I am the **same yesterday, today, and forever**. . . . I, the Lord your God, have created all men. . . . I am the **same yesterday, today, and forever**. . . . (2 Nephi 27:23; 29:7, 9)

In the KJV . . . and the name [Jehovah] is generally denoted by LORD or GOD, printed in small capitals. Jehovah is the premortal Jesus Christ. . . . (Bible Dictionary of the Mormon edition of the King James Bible, pp. 710–11)

For I am the **Lord** thy God. . . . My name is Jehovah. . . . (Abraham 2:7–8)

Before the mountains were brought forth, or ever thou hadst formed the earth and the world, even **from everlasting to everlasting**, thou art God. (Psalm 90:2)

Who formed the earth and the world? A footnote on Psalm 90:2 in the Mormon edition of the Bible refers to D&C 38:1, which refers to Jesus Christ.

Can men become Gods just like God the Father did?
God has not always been God; man can become a God like he did.

Then shall **they be gods**, because they have no end; therefore shall they be from everlasting to everlasting. . . . then shall they be above all, because all things are subject unto them. Then shall **they be gods**, because they have all power, and the angels are subject unto them. (July 1843, D&C 132:20)

We can become **Gods** like our Heavenly Father. This is exaltation. . . . They [people] will become gods . . . and will be able to have spirit children also. These spirit children will have the same relationship to them as we do to our Heavenly Father. They will be an eternal family. . . . They will have **everything** that our Heavenly Father and Jesus Christ have, all power, glory, dominion, and knowledge. (*Gospel Principles*, 1986 edition or older, p. 290)

As shown in this chapter, **our Father in heaven was once a man as we are now, capable of physical death**. . . . he progressed from one stage of life to another until he attained the state that we call exaltation or godhood. (*Achieving a Celestial Marriage*, 1976, 1992, p. 132)

President Joseph Fielding Smith said "Our Father in heaven, according to the Prophet, **had a Father**, and since there has been a condition of this kind through all eternity, **each Father had a Father**." (*Search These Commandments*, Melchizedek Priesthood Personal Study Guide,[2] 1984, p. 152)

I am going to tell you how God came to be God. We have **imagined and supposed** that God was God from all eternity. **I will refute that idea**, and take away the veil, so that you may see. (Joseph Smith, at the April 1844 conference of the Church, *Teachings of the Prophet Joseph Smith*, compiled by Joseph Fielding Smith, p. 345)

God the Father has always been God; there are no other Gods.

For I know that God is not a partial God, **neither a changeable being**; but he is **unchangeable from all eternity to all eternity**. (Moroni 8:18; also see 7:22)

For do we not read that God is the **same yesterday, today, and forever**, and in him there is no variableness neither shadow of changing? (Mormon 9:9; also see 9:19)

. . . the Lord Omnipotent who reigneth, who was, and is **from all eternity to all eternity**, shall come down from heaven among the children of men. (Mosiah 3:5)

By these things we know that there is a God in heaven, **who is infinite and eternal, from everlasting to everlasting**, the same unchangeable God, the framer of heaven and earth, and all things which are in them. . . . Which Father, Son, and Holy Ghost are one God, infinite and eternal, without end. (April 1830, D&C 20:17, 28)

. . . I am the Lord God Almighty, and Endless is my name; for I am **without beginning of days or end of years**; and is not this endless? (Moses 1:3)

. . . even **from everlasting to everlasting**, thou art God. (Psalm 90:2)

Ye are my witness, saith the LORD, and my servant whom I have chosen: that ye may know and believe me, and understand that I am he: **before me there was no God formed, neither shall there be after me**. (Isaiah 43:10)

Thus saith the LORD the King of Israel, and his redeemer the LORD of hosts; I am the first, and I am the last; and beside me there is no God. . . . fear ye not, neither be afraid: have not I told thee from that time, and have declared it? ye are even my witnesses. Is there a God beside me? **yea, there is no God**; I know not any. . . . Thus saith the LORD, thy redeemer, and he that formed thee from the womb, I am the LORD that maketh all things; that stretcheth forth the heavens **alone**; that spreadeth abroad the earth by **myself**. . . . (Isaiah 44:6, 8, 24)

On page 353 of *Gospel Principles* we find the following definitions:

ETERNAL: Everlasting, without beginning or end . . .
EVERLASTING: Lasting or enduring forever . . .
FOREVER: Always, no end, eternal.

The above definitions and Mormon scriptures clearly say that God the Father has always been God and that there *never* was a time when he was not God, so when was he a man like us, capable of physical death? In Isaiah 43:10; 44:6, 8, 24 the Lord, who would not lie to us and knows everything, does not know anything about any God before him or after him, or about his alleged father or grandfather or great-grandfather, etc. He tells us *he is all by himself!*

Does God the Father have a body of flesh and bones?
Yes, he does.

> The Father has a body of flesh and bones as tangible as man's; the Son also. . . . (April 1843, D&C 130:22)[3]

No, he does not; he is spirit.

> Holy, holy God; we believe that thou art God, and we believe that thou art holy, and that thou **wast a spirit**, and that **thou art a spirit**, and that thou **wilt be a spirit forever**. (Alma 31:15;[4] Alma 18:2–5, 26–28; 22:8–11 are similar)

> They are the Father and the Son: The Father being **a personage of spirit**, glory and power: possessing all perfection and fulness: The Son, who was in the bosom of the Father, a personage of tabernacle [a body]. . . . (1835 D&C, "Lecture Fifth of Faith" 5:2, p. 53. The "Lectures on Faith" were in the D&C from 1835 to 1920, when they were quietly removed.)

> God is a Spirit: and they that worship him must worship him in spirit and in truth. (John 4:24 in the Bible. The Joseph Smith Translation[5] changes this to read, "For unto such hath God promised his Spirit. And they who worship him, must worship in spirit and in truth." [John 4:26 JST. The numbering in the JST does not match the KJV.])

> . . . The Father and Son . . . are one God, yea, the very Eternal Father of heaven and earth. And thus **the flesh becoming subject to the Spirit, or the Son to the Father**, being one God. . . . (Mosiah 15:1–5)

> Ye were **also** in the beginning with **the Father; that which is Spirit**, even the Spirit of truth. . . . (May 1833, D&C 93:21)

How many Gods are there?
There is more than one God.

> The Father has a body of flesh and bones as tangible as man's; the Son also; but the Holy Ghost has not a body of flesh and bones, but is a personage of Spirit. Were it not so, the Holy Ghost could not dwell in us. (April 1843, D&C 130:22)

> . . . that is the Gods organized and formed the heavens and the earth. . . . and the Spirit of the Gods was brooding upon the face of the waters. (Abraham 4:1–2; also see vv. 3–31)

> I will preach on the plurality of Gods. I have selected this text for that express purpose. I wish to declare I have always and in all congregations when I preached on the subject of the Deity, it has been the **plurality of Gods**. It has been preached by the Elders for fifteen years. I have always declared God to be a distinct personage, Jesus Christ a separate and distinct personage from God the Father, and that the Holy Ghost was a distinct personage and a Spirit: and **these three constitute three distinct personages and three Gods**. If this is in accordance with the New Testament, lo and behold! **we have three Gods** anyhow, and they are plural; and who can contradict it? (*Teachings of the Prophet Joseph Smith*, compiled by [Apostle] Joseph Fielding Smith, 1976, p. 370. While this is not a Mormon scripture it provides an explanation by Joseph Smith of the two scriptures above.)

There is one God.

> And the honor be to the Father, and to the Son, and to the Holy Ghost, which is **one God**.[6] Amen. (Introduction of the Book of Mormon, the last sentence of the paragraph on the three witnesses)

> . . . be arraigned before the bar of Christ the Son, and God the Father, and the Holy Spirit, which is **one Eternal God**. . . . (Alma 11:44)

> . . . unto the Father, and unto the Son, and unto the Holy Ghost, which are **one God**. . . . (Mormon 7:7)

And after this manner shall ye baptize in my name; for behold, verily I say unto you, that the Father, and the Son, and the Holy Ghost **are one**; and I am in the Father, and the Father in me, and the Father and I **are one**. (3 Nephi 11:27)

. . . God himself shall come down. . . . because he dwelleth in flesh he shall be called the Son of God . . . being the Father and the Son-The Father, because he was conceived by the power of God; and the Son, because of the flesh; thus becoming the Father and Son-And **they are one God**, yea, the very Eternal Father of heaven and earth. And thus the flesh becoming subject to the Spirit, or the Son to the Father, being **one God**. . . . (Mosiah 15:1–5)

Can the Father and/or the Son dwell in your heart?
No, they cannot.

. . . the idea that the Father and the Son dwell in a man's heart is an old sectarian notion, and is **false**. (April 1843, D&C 130:3.[7] Verse 22 of this same reference gives the reason why: they both have bodies of flesh and bones.)

Yes, they can.

And this I know, because the Lord hath said he dwelleth not in unholy temples, **but in the hearts** of the righteous doth he dwell. . . . (Alma 34:36)

Jesus answered and said unto him, If a man love me, he will keep my words: and my Father will love him, and we will come unto him, and **make our abode** with him. (John 14:23)

. . . That Christ may **dwell in your hearts** by faith. . . . (Ephesians 3:17)

Know ye not your own selves, how that **Jesus Christ is in you**, except ye be reprobates? (2 Corinthians 13:5. The JST did not change this verse.)

Are vicarious ordinances for the dead effective?

Yes, they are.

> Else what shall they do which are baptized for the dead, if the dead rise not at all? Why are they then baptized for the dead? (1 Corinthians 15:29)[8]

> The heavens were opened upon us, and I beheld the celestial kingdom of God. . . . I saw . . . the Father and the Son. . . . I saw Father Adam and Abraham; and my father and my mother; my brother Alvin [he died in 1823, before the Mormon Church was organized], that has long since slept; Thus came the voice of the Lord unto me, saying: All who have died without a knowledge of this gospel, who would have received it if they had been permitted to tarry, shall be **heirs of the celestial kingdom** of God. . . . (January 1836, D&C 137:1–5)

These passages, along with others, are the reasons the Mormon Church teaches that vicarious sacred ordinances for the dead must be done *on earth* in Mormon temples for those who have died, so they may have the choice to accept the benefits of such work in the spirit world.

No, they are not.

> And, in fine, wo unto all those **who die in their sins**; for they shall return to God [for judgment?], and behold his face, and **remain in their sins**. (2 Nephi 9:38)

> . . . he that persists in his own carnal nature, and goes on in the ways of sin and rebellion against God, **remaineth in his fallen state** and the devil hath **all power** over him. . . . if they be evil, to the resurrection of endless damnation, being delivered up to the devil, who hath subjected them, which is damnation. (Mosiah 16:5, 11)

... for behold, **now is the time** and the day of your salvation. ...
for behold, **this life** is the time for men to prepare to meet God. ...
this life is the day for men to perform their labors. ... then cometh
the night of darkness wherein there can be no labor performed. ...
for the **same spirit** which doth possess your bodies at the time
that ye go out of this life, that same spirit will have power to possess your body in that eternal world. For behold, if ye have pro-
crastinated the day of your repentance even until death, behold,
ye have become **subjected to the spirit of the devil**, and he doth
seal you his. ... (Alma 34:31–35)

What is the doctrine of Jesus Christ?
It is more than faith, repentance, and baptism.

Most of the items listed above and the items in "A Brief Summary of the Doctrine Taught by the Mormon Church" in chapter 1 demonstrate the detailed, unique doctrine taught by the
Mormon Church. Obviously it is more than faith, repentance,
and baptism.

It is only faith, repentance, and baptism.

Behold, verily, verily, I say unto you, **I will declare unto you my
doctrine**. And **this is my doctrine**, and it is the doctrine which
the Father hath given unto me; and I bear record of the Father,
and the Father beareth record of me, and the Holy Ghost beareth
record of the Father and me; and I bear record that the Father
commandeth all men, everywhere, to repent and believe in me.
And whoso believeth in me, and is baptized, the same shall be
saved; and they are they who shall inherit the kingdom of God. ...
Verily, verily, I say unto you, that this is my doctrine, and whoso
buildeth upon this buildeth upon my rock, and the gates of hell
shall not prevail against them. **And whoso shall declare more or
less than this, and establish it for my doctrine, the same cometh
of evil,** and is not built upon my rock; but he buildeth upon a
sandy foundation, and the gates of hell stand open to receive such
when the floods come and the winds beat upon them. (3 Nephi
11:31–33, 39–40)

Say **nothing but** repentance unto this generation; keep my commandments, and assist to bring forth my work, according to my commandments, and you shall be blessed. (April 1829, D&C 6:9)

Behold, this is my doctrine—whosoever repenteth and cometh unto me, the same is my church. **Whosoever declareth more** or less than this, the same is not of me, but is against me; therefore he is not of my church. (1828, D&C 10:67–68)

Has God let his scriptures be tampered with?
Yes, he has.

They have taken away from the gospel of the Lamb many parts which are plain and most precious. . . . there are many plain and precious things taken away from the book [the Bible] which is the book of the Lamb of God. (1 Nephi 13:26, 28)

We believe the Bible to be the word of God as far as it is translated correctly. . . . (*Articles of Faith* #8, in Pearl of Great Price)

The most reliable way to measure the accuracy of any biblical passage is not by comparing different texts, but by comparison with the Book of Mormon and modern day revelation. (An open letter from the First Presidency [Presidents Benson, Hinckley, and Monson] dated May 22, 1992, to all members of the church, in *Church News*, June 20, 1992, p. 3)

No, he has not.

Neither pray I for these alone, but for them also which shall believe on me **through their word**. (John 17:20)

If Mormonism is correct, then this prayer of Jesus Christ was of no effect for about 1800 years. Incredible! Jesus prayed for those who would believe in him through the word of his disciples. It is not logical that he (Jesus) would let his disciples' word be lost and diluted.

> ... by the word of God, which liveth and abideth **for ever**. ...
> But the word of the Lord endureth **for ever**. And this is the word which by the gospel is preached unto you. (1 Peter 1:23–25)

> And take the helmet of salvation, and the sword of the Spirit, which is the Word of God. (Ephesians 6:17)

Would the apostle Paul tell us to take up a defective sword, a defective Word of God? We don't think so.

> The Book of Mormon ... contains, as does the Bible, the fulness of the everlasting gospel. (Introduction of the Book of Mormon, first paragraph)

The fulness of the everlasting gospel (according to Mormon teachings) is that information from God that, if we accept it and live by it, will lead us to exaltation (becoming a God) in the celestial kingdom of God.[9] So, considering this, even by this Mormon standard there cannot be too much wrong with the Bible. Then why do we need anything besides the Bible?

> What I the Lord have spoken, I have spoken, and I excuse not myself; and though the heavens and the earth pass away, my word shall **not** pass away. ... (November 1831, D&C 1:38)

Is polygamy acceptable to God?
It is acceptable to God.

> Laws governing the plurality of wives are set forth. (D&C 132, heading summary for verses 58–66)

> David also received many wives and concubines, and also Solomon and Moses my servants, also many others of my servants, from the beginning of creation until this time; and **in nothing did they**

sin save in those things which they received not of me. David's wives and concubines were given unto him of me, by the hand of Nathan, my servant, and others of the prophets who had the keys of this power; and in **none** of these things **did he sin** against me. . . . And again, as pertaining to the law of the priesthood— if any man espouse a virgin, and desire to espouse another, and the first give her consent, and if he espouse the second, and they are virgins, and have vowed to no other man, then is he justified; **he cannot commit adultery** for they are given unto him; **for he cannot commit adultery** with that that belongeth unto him and to no one else. And **if he have ten virgins** given unto him by this law, **he cannot commit adultery**, for they belong to him, and they are given unto him; therefore is he justified. (July 1843, D&C 132:38–39, 61–62)

It is not acceptable to God.

Behold, David and Solomon truly had many wives and concubines, which thing was **abominable** before me, saith the Lord. Wherefore, my brethren, hear me, and hearken to the word of the Lord: For there shall not any man among you have save it be **one wife**; and concubines he shall have none. . . . Behold, the Lamanites your brethren, whom ye hate because of their filthiness and the cursing which hath come upon their skins, are more righteous than you; for they have not forgotten the commandment of the Lord, which was given unto our father ["fathers" in 1977 edition]—that they should have save it were **one wife**, and concubines they should have none. . . . (Jacob 2:24, 27; 3:5)

. . . he [King Noah] did **not** keep the commandments of God, but he did walk after the desires of his own heart. And he had **many wives** and concubines. (Mosiah 11:2)

. . . Riplakish did not do that which was right in the sight of the Lord, for he did have **many wives** and concubines. . . . (Ether 10:5)

In as much as this church of Christ has been reproached with the crime of fornication, and **polygamy**: we declare that we believe, that **one man should have one wife**; and one woman, but one husband. . . . (1835 D&C 101:4, p. 251)

This was in the D&C from 1835 to 1876, yet polygamy was practiced from about 1832 to 1890, when it was ostensibly ended.

A bishop then must be blameless, the husband of **one wife**. . . . Let the deacons be the husbands of **one wife**. . . . (1 Timothy 3:2, 12)

Who created light?
God did.

And I, God, said: Let there be light; and there was light. (Moses 2:3)

See also the rest of chapter 2 and 3 in Moses; God, with his Only Begotten (2:1, 26), did the creation. But see the next topic below for the answer to: Who Is the Only Begotten of the Father?

The Gods did.

And they [the Gods] said: Let there be light; and there was light. (Abraham 4:3)

And the Gods called the light day. . . . (Abraham 4:5)

Also see the rest of chapter 4 and 5 in Abraham: "the God*s*" did the creation.

Who is the Only Begotten of the Father?
The Holy Ghost is.

And in that day the Holy Ghost fell upon Adam, which beareth record of the Father and the Son, saying: I am the **Only Begotten**[10] of the Father from the beginning, henceforth and forever, that as thou hast fallen thou mayest be redeemed, and all mankind, even as many as will. (1830–1831, Moses 5:9)

In this reference the Holy Ghost says: "I am the Only Begotten." According to Mormon teachings, Jesus Christ is the Only Begotten.

The Savior Jesus Christ is.

All these had departed the mortal life, firm in the hope of a glorious resurrection, through the grace of God the Father and his **Only Begotten** Son, Jesus Christ. (October 1918, D&C 138:14)

And I, John, bear record that I beheld his glory, as the glory of the **Only Begotten** of the Father, full of grace and truth, even the Spirit of truth, which came and dwelt in the flesh, and dwelt among us. (May 1833, D&C 93:11)

And I have a work for thee, Moses my son; and thou art in the similitude of mine **Only Begotten**; and mine **Only Begotten** is and shall be the Savior, for he is full of grace and truth; but there is no God beside me, and all things are present with me, for I know them all. (1830–1831, Moses 1:6)

Is murder and/or killing forgivable?
No, it is not.

And now, behold, I speak unto the church. Thou **shalt not kill**; and he that kills shall **not** have forgiveness in this world, nor in the world to come. . . . And again, I say, thou **shalt not kill**; but he that killeth shall die. . . . And it shall come to pass, that if any persons among you shall kill they shall be delivered up and dealt with according to the laws of the land; for remember that he hath no forgiveness; and it shall be proved according to the laws of the land. (February 1831, D&C 42:18–19, 79)

. . . and in none of these things did he [King David] sin against me save in the case of Uriah and his wife; and, therefore he **hath**

fallen from his exaltation, and received his portion; and he shall not inherit them out of the world, for I gave them unto another, saith the Lord. (July 1843, D&C 132:39)

. . . able to find forgiveness, **except** in the murder of Uriah. . . . David is still unforgiven, but he received a promise that the Lord would not leave his soul in hell. He will be resurrected at the end of the Millennium. (Bible Dictionary, p. 654, found in the King James edition of the Bible published by the Mormon Church)

And David said unto Nathan, I have sinned against the Lord. And Nathan said unto David, The Lord also **hath not** put away thy sin; thou shalt not die. (2 Samuel 12:13 JST)

In other words, King David *has not been forgiven* for murdering Uriah and taking his wife. He will not become a God in the celestial kingdom.

Yes, it is.

And I also thank my God, yea, my great God, that he hath granted unto us that we might repent of these things, and also that he hath **forgiven us** of those our many sins and **murders** which we have committed. . . . (Alma 24:10)

Yea, I would tell you these things if ye were capable of hearkening unto them; yea, I would tell you concerning that awful hell that awaits to receive such **murderers** as thou and thy brother have been, **except** ye repent. . . . (Alma 54:7)

Turn, all ye Gentiles, from your wicked ways; and repent of your evil doings . . . and of your **murders** . . . and come unto me, and be baptized in my name . . . that ye may be numbered with my people who are of the house of Israel. (3 Nephi 30:2)

And David said unto Nathan, I have sinned against the LORD. And Nathan said unto David, The LORD also **hath** put away thy sin; thou shalt not die. (2 Samuel 12:13)

What did Joseph Smith think before he went to pray?
He wondered whether all the churches could be wrong.

> In the midst of this war of words and tumult of opinions, I **often** said to myself: What is to be done? Who of all these parties are right; **or, are they all wrong together**? If any one of them be right, which is it, and how shall I know it? (*Joseph Smith—History* 1:10)

He never thought they could all be wrong.

> My object in going to inquire of the Lord was to know which of all the sects was right, that I might know which to join. No sooner, therefore, did I get possession of myself, so as to be able to speak, than I asked the Personages who stood above me in the light, which of all the sects was right (**for at this time it had *never entered into my heart* that all were wrong**)—and which I should join. (*Joseph Smith—History* 1:18)

Was Joseph Smith to be killed?
He was to be protected.

> And as for the perils which I [Joseph Smith] am called to pass through. . . . I feel, like Paul, to glory in tribulation; for to this day has the God of my fathers delivered me **out of them all**, and **will deliver me from henceforth**; for behold, and lo, I shall triumph over all my enemies, for the Lord God hath spoken it. (September 1842, D&C 127:2)

> Behold, that seer [Joseph Smith according to the section heading] will the Lord bless; and they that seek to destroy him **shall be confounded**. . . . (2 Nephi 3:14, supposedly written about 580 B.C.)

Joseph Smith was killed.

> To seal the testimony of this book and the Book of Mormon, we announce the **martyrdom** of Joseph Smith the Prophet. . . . They

were shot [dead] in Carthage jail, on the 27th of June, 1844.[11]
(June 1844, D&C 135:1)

Is intelligence (our spirit) eternal or was it created when we were?[12]

Intelligence (spirit) is eternal.

> Ye were also in the beginning with the Father; **that which is Spirit,** even the Spirit of truth. . . . Man was also in the beginning with God. **Intelligence,** or the light of truth, **was not created** or made, neither indeed can be. (May 1833, D&C 93:23, 29)

> . . . if there be **two spirits,** and one shall be more intelligent than the other, yet these two spirits, notwithstanding one is more intelligent than the other, **have no beginning;** they existed before, they shall have no end, they shall exist after, **they are gnolaum, or eternal.** . . . (Abraham 3:18–19)

Intelligence (spirit) was created.

> For behold, by the power of his word man came upon the face of the earth, which earth was created by the power of his word. Wherefore, if God being able to speak and the world was, and to speak and **man was created.** . . . (Jacob 4:9)

> . . . Adam your father, whom I **created.** (September 1830, D&C 29:34)

> Who shall say that it was not a miracle that by his word the heaven and the earth should be; and by the power of his word **man was created** of the dust of the earth; and by the power of his word have miracles been wrought? (Mormon 9:17)

> . . . the LORD, which stretcheth forth the heavens, and layeth the foundation of the earth, and **formeth the spirit of man within him.** (Zechariah 12:1)

Then shall the dust return to the earth as it was: and the **spirit shall return unto God who gave it**. (Ecclesiastes 12:7)

How many levels are there in heaven?
There are three levels.

> These are they whose bodies are **celestial**. . . . even the glory of God. . . . these are they who are of the **terrestrial**. . . . These are they who receive of the presence of the Son, but not of the fulness of the Father. Wherefore, they are bodies **terrestrial**, and not bodies celestial, and differ in glory as the moon differs from the sun. . . . we saw the glory of the **telestial**, which glory is that of the lesser. . . . These are they who are thrust down to **hell**. . . . (February 1832, D&C 76:70–107)

This scripture describes *four levels* in the Mormon afterlife; they are hell, telestial, terrestrial, and celestial. Only those in the celestial kingdom will be in the presence of the Father for eternity. Those in the terrestrial level will be visited by the Son but not the Father (D&C 76:77–78).

There is one level.

> And there is a place prepared, yea, even that awful hell of which I have spoken, and the devil is the preparator[13] of it; wherefore the final state of the souls of men is to **dwell** in the kingdom of God [the celestial kingdom], **or** to be **cast out** because of that justice of which I have spoken. Wherefore, the wicked are rejected from the righteous, and also from that tree of life, whose fruit is most precious and most desirable above all other fruits; yea, and it **is the greatest** of all the gifts of God. . . . (1 Nephi 15:35–36)

> And I would that all men might be saved. But we read that in the great and last day there are some who shall be cast out, yea, who shall be cast off **from the presence** of the Lord; Yea, who shall be consigned to a state of endless misery, fulfilling the words which say: They that have done good shall have everlasting life; and they

that have done evil shall have everlasting damnation. And thus
it is. . . . (Helaman 12:25–26)

And whoso believeth in me, and is baptized, the same **shall be
saved**; and they are they who shall **inherit the kingdom of God**.
And whoso believeth **not** in me, and is **not** baptized, **shall be
damned**. (3 Nephi 11:33–34)

The following are very similar: Mormon 9:23; Ether 4:18; Helaman 14:18–19; Alma 3:26; 40:26; 41:4; Mosiah 16:11; 2 Nephi
2:28–29; 9:16; 28:21–22; 3 Nephi 27:11, 17. The Book of Mormon describes an afterlife of only two levels, spending eternity
in the presence of God or with the Devil.

What are the proper ingredients for the sacrament?
Wine and bread are to be used.

Matthew 26:26–29 and Luke 22:17–19 clearly show that Jesus
used bread and wine.

> . . . bless and sanctify this **wine**. . . . (Moroni 4:3, 5:2)

> . . . bless and sanctify this **wine**. . . . (April 1830, D&C 20:77, 79;
> February 1833, D&C 89:5–6 and 3 Nephi 18:1–8 support this also.)

Water and bread are to be used.

> . . . it mattereth not what ye shall eat or what ye shall drink when
> ye partake of the sacrament. . . . you shall **not** purchase wine nei-
> ther strong drink of your enemies. . . . (August 1830, D&C 27:2–4)

The present-day Mormon Church uses water instead of wine
in its sacrament service. One has to wonder why the Church continues to use water, if wine was acceptable to the Book of Mormon people with all their disruptions from wars, and if Jesus in
the Bible said we should use wine, and if the Mormon community is no longer engulfed in problems with its neighbors as it

was in its early years. And why would God, four months after telling the Mormons to use wine, change his command?

Should the Church pay its workers?
No, they should not be paid.[14]

> But the laborer in Zion shall labor for Zion; for if they labor for money they shall perish. (2 Nephi 26:31)

> Yea, and all their priests and teachers should labor with their **own hands** for their support, in all cases save it were in sickness, or in much want; and doing these things, they did abound in the grace of God. (Mosiah 27:5)

Yes, they should be paid.

> D&C 24:18–19; 42:70–73; 51:13–14; 75:24–25; 84:78–79, 86–89; and 119:1–2 all show that it is okay for Mormon members and leaders to be paid or supported by their church for church activity.

> In 1 Corinthians 9:1–14 the Apostle Paul says it is okay to be supported for gospel work.

> I robbed other churches, taking wages of them, to do you service. . . . for that which was lacking to me the brethren which came from Macedonia supplied. . . . (2 Corinthians 11:8–9; also see Numbers 18:21; 3 John 6–8; Matthew 10:9–10)

Should you curse your enemy?
Yes, you should.

> . . . ye have brought before me [God] against them, **ye [Joseph Smith] shall curse them**; And whomsoever ye curse, I will curse, and ye shall avenge me of mine enemies. (February 1834, D&C 103:24–25)[15]

> But if he trespass against thee [Church members] the fourth time thou **shalt not forgive him**, but shalt bring these testimonies be-

fore the Lord; and they shall not be blotted out until he repent and reward thee four-fold in all things wherewith he has trespassed against thee. (August 1833, D&C 98:44)

No, you should not. You must forgive him.

And behold it is written also, that thou shalt love thy neighbor and hate thine enemy; But behold I say unto you [Christ's Church in the New World], **love** your enemies, **bless** them that curse you, do **good** to them that hate you, and **pray** for them who despitefully use you and persecute you. . . . (3 Nephi 12:43–44)

Wherefore, I say unto you [elders of the Church], that ye ought to forgive one another. . . . I, the Lord, will forgive whom I will forgive, but of you it is **required** to **forgive all men**. (September 1831, D&C 64:9–10)

Are the three Nephites still alive on earth now?
Yes, they are.

What is it that ye desire of me, after that I am gone to the Father? And when he had spoken unto them, he turned himself unto the three, and said unto them: What will ye that I should do unto you, when I am gone unto the Father? And he said unto them: Behold, I know your thoughts, and ye have desired the thing which John, my beloved, who was with me in my ministry, before that I was lifted up by the Jews, desired of me. Therefore, more blessed are ye, **for ye shall never taste of death**; but ye shall live to behold all the doings of the Father unto the children of men, **even until all things shall be fulfilled according to the will of the Father, when I shall come in my glory with the powers of heaven. And ye shall never endure the pains of death; but when I shall come in my glory ye shall be changed in the twinkling of an eye from mortality to immortality**; and then shall ye be blessed in the kingdom of my Father. (3 Nephi 28:1, 4, 6–8)

Note that it is Jesus Christ speaking here and that it is not a contingent statement or promise. It is a clear promise, without any "strings attached." The three Nephites are promised they will be on the earth until Jesus comes in his glory.

No, they are not.

> **The three Nephites are taken away** (heading of Mormon chapter 1).

> But wickedness did prevail upon the face of the whole land, in- somuch that the **Lord did take away his beloved disciples**, and the work of miracles and of healing did cease. . . . (Book of Mormon, Mormon 1:13)

How Might Mormons Respond?

Some Mormons might respond: "The same thing you've done here with the unique Mormon scriptures (Book of Mormon, Doctrine and Covenants, Pearl of Great Price) could also be done with the Bible." We would agree that you can make the Bible appear to say anything you want by pulling verses out of context.[16] But we have not done this with the Mormon scriptures. We have not misrepresented verses by ignoring context.

The reader must also understand where most Mormons are coming from, what is their point of reference. To most Mormons the Bible is an incomplete document, and that is why their other scriptures are needed. To them it ranks below these other scriptures in reliability and completeness. Some Mormons may not want to admit at first that they hold this view of the Bible, but if you demonstrate your knowledge of the subject, some will soon confess that this is their view. The LDS position on the Bible is illustrated in the following references.

> The most reliable way to measure the accuracy of any biblical passage is not by comparing different texts, but by comparison

with the Book of Mormon and modern-day revelations. (An open letter from the First Presidency [Presidents Benson, Hinckley, and Monson] dated May 22, 1992, to all members of the Church, in *Church News*, June 20, 1992, p. 3)

We believe the Bible to be the word of God as far as it is translated correctly.... (*Articles of Faith* #8, in the Pearl of Great Price)

And after they go forth by the hand of the twelve apostles of the Lamb, from the Jews unto the Gentiles, thou seest the formation of a great and abominable church, which is most abominable above all other churches; for behold, they have **taken away** from the gospel of the Lamb many parts which are plain and most precious; and also many covenants of the Lord have they taken away. ... because of the plain and most precious parts of the gospel of the Lamb which have been **kept back** by that abominable church, whose formation thou hast seen. ... because of the most plain and precious parts of the gospel of the Lamb which have been **kept back** by that abominable church, which is the mother of harlots, saith the Lamb.... (1 Nephi 13:26, 32, 34)

Mormons who hold the Bible in lower esteem can more easily conceive of its having contradictions than their own unique scriptures.

In addition to proper consideration for context, the Mormon scripture comparisons must also be evaluated in light of statements by top Mormon leaders and Mormon scriptures. As quoted in detail in the preface and in chapter 2, these statements are as follows:

If Joseph Smith was a deceiver ... then he should be exposed.... **there would appear many errors and contradictions.** (*Doctrines of Salvation*, [Apostle] Joseph Fielding Smith, 1954, 1:188)

... there is no error in the revelations.... (*Teachings of the Prophet Joseph Smith*, compiled by Joseph Fielding Smith, p. 368)

Why do not my enemies strike a blow at the doctrine? They cannot do it: it is truth, and I defy all men to upset it. (Joseph Smith, March 1844, *History of the Church*, 6:273)

Search these commandments for they are true and faithful. (November 1831, D&C 1:37)

... my Scriptures ... shall be preserved in safety. (February 1831, D&C 42:56)

The decrees of God are unalterable. (Alma 41:8)

... God is the same yesterday, today, and forever, and in him there is no variableness neither shadow of changing. (Mormon 9:9)

The Doctrine and Covenants are from Jesus Christ. (November 1831, D&C 1:6)

The Prophet Joseph Smith said the Book of Mormon was "the most correct of any book on earth and the keystone of our religion, and a man would get nearer to God by abiding by its precepts, than by any other book." (*History of the Church* 4:461)

The title page of the Book of Mormon says it was translated "by the gift and power of God."

D&C 17:6 has God saying the Book of Mormon "is true."

These last three statements are quoted and reinforced in the April 1993 *Ensign*, page 74, in a letter from the First Presidency.

If indeed Mormonism is what it claims to be, then it must be measured *by its own standards* as summarized here. These should be applied in evaluating the scripture comparisons. It is reasonable to expect that imperfections of man will show up in anything he does. But these should be relatively few and should have little or no impact on Mormon doctrine, assuming God is in charge, as claimed by the Mormon Church. It seems reasonable to expect that the contradictions outlined above would *not* be there if the real God were truly the founder of the Mormon Church and the author of its unique scriptures (Book of Mormon, Doctrine and Covenants, Pearl of Great Price).

The unique Mormon scriptures attest to this. Statements summarized above to the effect that the decrees of God are unalterable, that there is no variableness neither shadow of changing, that we should search these commandments for they are true and faithful argue against the thought that such a large number of conflicting scriptures would come from the real God. He is not the author of confusion, as he says in the Bible: "For God is not the author of confusion, but of peace, as in all churches of the saints" (1 Corinthians 14:33). Even a Mormon verse echoes this teaching: "Behold, mine house is a house of order, saith the Lord God, and not a house of confusion" (D&C 132:8).

Because of its importance we will also repeat another item that was said earlier. We have also consulted the *Joseph Smith Translation* of the Bible (it is also sometimes called the *Inspired Version* and the *New Translation* by the RLDS) to be sure the Bible verses we used represented Joseph Smith's thoughts in 1833 when he finished it. On July 2, 1833 Joseph said:

> We this day finished the translating of the Scriptures, for which we returned gratitude to our Heavenly Father. . . . Having finished the translation of the Bible, a few hours since. . . . (*History of the Church*, 1:368–69)

Where we did use biblical verses to show a conflict with the other Mormon scriptures, except as noted, the Joseph Smith Translation (JST) agreed with the King James Version used.

But scripture conflicts are not the only examples of the confusion within Mormonism. Conflicts of a similar nature exist just as much with the teachings of the top Mormon leaders.

MORMON PRESIDENTS COMPARED

The President of the Mormon Church is the highest leader in what is claimed to be the one true Church that Jesus Christ "restored" in 1830 through Joseph Smith. Including Smith, a total of fourteen men have held the office. They have been the only ones with "authority" to receive revelation for the Church and to instruct the Church.[1] In order to understand the importance and status of the position, let us examine what some of these thirteen men, other top Mormon leaders, official Mormon Church publications, and Mormon scriptures say about the importance of listening to what the President says.[2]

Mormon Standards for Following Top Mormon Leaders

The Importance of the Teachings by Mormon Prophets

The first five items are from *Search These Commandments*, Melchizedek Priesthood Personal Study Guide, published and copyrighted (1984) by the Mormon Church. It is a teaching manual for Mormon men. The sixth item is from a similar 1983 manual titled *Come Follow Me*.

The words of the President are more than the advice of man.

Elder George Albert Smith noted: "When we are instructed by the President of this Church, we believe he tells us what the Lord would have us do. **To us it is something more than just the advice of man**" (in Conference Report, Oct. 1930, p. 66). (p. 272)

We have our marching orders.

President Ezra Taft Benson has said, "Therefore, the most important reading we can do is any of the words of the Prophet contained each week in the Church Section of the *Deseret News* and any words of the Prophet contained each month in our Church magazines. Our **marching orders** for each six months are found in the general conference addresses which are printed in the *Ensign* magazine" ("Fourteen Fundamentals in Following the Prophets," *1980 Devotional Speeches of the Year* [Provo, Utah: Brigham Young University Press, 1981], p. 27). (p. 273)

We have God's will for us.

President Ezra Taft Benson has pointed out that "the most important prophet, so far as you and I are concerned, is the one living in our day and age to whom the Lord is currently revealing **His will for us**" ("Fourteen Fundamentals in Following the Prophets," *1980 Devotional Speeches of the Year* [Provo, Utah: Brigham Young University Press, 1981], p. 27). (p. 275)

The Lord will never permit the President to lead us astray.

President Wilford Woodruff gave the following assurance, "I say ... the Lord **will never permit** me nor any other man who stands as the President of this Church, to lead you astray" (*The Discourses of Wilford Woodruff*, p. 212). (p. 276)

Our eternal life depends on his word.

At the conclusion of one general conference, President Kimball said: "Now as we conclude this general conference, let us all give heed to what was said to us. Let us assume the counsel given applies to·*us*, to me. Let us hearken to those we sustain as prophets and seers, as well as **the other brethren**, as if our eternal life depended upon it, **because it does!**" (Spencer W. Kimball, in *Conference Report,* April 1978, p. 117; or *Ensign,* May 1978, p. 77). (p. 276)

The Prophets speak the mind, will, and voice of the Lord and the power of God unto salvation.

President Harold B. Lee [he was the President and Prophet of the Mormon Church at the time] once said at the close of a general conference, "If you want to know what the Lord has for this people at the present time, I would admonish you to get and read the discourses that have been delivered at this conference; for what these brethren[3] have spoken by the power of the Holy Ghost **is the mind of the Lord, the will of the Lord, the voice of the Lord, and the power of God unto salvation**" (in Conference Report, April 1973, p. 176; or *Ensign,* July 1973, p. 121). (p. 11)

Wilford Woodruff, Harold B. Lee, and Spencer W. Kimball were Presidents of the Church when they made these statements. The other two men were Apostles, the level just below the President of the Church, when they made their statements, and became President of the Church at a later date.

More Teachings from the Top Leaders

Follow the President even if what he says is wrong.

And President Harold B. Lee stated that "President Grant used to say to us . . . 'Brethren, keep your eye on the President of this Church. **If he tells you to do anything and it is wrong and you do it**, the Lord will bless you for it. But you don't need to worry; the Lord will **never** let his mouthpiece lead this people astray.'" (*The Ensign*, October 1972)

When the leaders speak, the thinking has been done.

When our leaders speak the thinking has been done. When they propose a plan—it is God's plan. When they point the way, there is no other which is safe. When they give direction, it should mark the end of controversy. (*The Improvement Era*, under "Ward Teacher's Message for June 1945," p. 354; also in *Deseret News*, Church Section, May 26, 1945, p. 5)

The words of the living Prophets become scripture to us.

The words of our living prophets are also accepted as scripture. . . . In addition to these four books of scripture, the inspired words of our living prophets **become scripture** to us. Their words come to us through conferences, Church publications, and instructions to local priesthood leaders. (*Gospel Principles*, pp. 49, 51–52)

Mormon Scriptures Say the Following:

Give heed to all the Prophet's words and commandments.

Wherefore, meaning the church, thou shalt give heed unto **all** his [the Prophet's] words and commandments which he shall give unto you as he receiveth them, walking in all holiness before me. . . . (April 6, 1830, D&C 21:4)

When elders are moved by the Holy Ghost, it shall be scripture.

And this is the ensample unto them, that they [the elders, see verse 7] shall speak as they are moved upon by the Holy Ghost. And whatsoever they [the elders] shall speak when moved upon by the Holy Ghost **shall be scripture,** shall be the will of the Lord, shall be the mind of the Lord, shall be the word of the Lord, shall be the voice of the Lord, and the power of God unto salvation. (November 1831, D&C 68:3–4)

The Lord will do nothing without telling the Prophet.

Surely the Lord GOD will do nothing, but he revealeth his secret unto his servants the prophets. (Amos 3:7)[4]

What Did Others Say?

No one can say I ever gave wrong counsel.

> I see around me a great people. Joseph Smith was called of God, and sent to lay the foundation of this latter-day kingdom. He presided over this people fourteen years. Then he was martyred. Since that time your humble servant has presided over and counselled this people. . . . For the space of twenty-four years he has watched over their interests. . . . What man or woman on the earth, what spirit in the spirit-world can say truthfully that **I ever gave a wrong word of counsel, or a word of advice that could not be sanctioned by the heavens**? The success which has attended me in my presidency is owing to the blessings and mercy of the Almighty. (President Brigham Young, December 29, 1867, *Journal of Discourses* 12:127)

My words when approved by me are as good as scripture.

> Brother Orson Hyde referred to a few who complained about not getting revelations. I will make a statement here that has been brought against me as a crime, perhaps, or as a fault in my life. Not here, I do not allude to anything of the kind in this place, but in the councils of the nations—that Brigham Young has said "when he sends forth his discourses to the world they may call them Scripture." I say now, when they are **copied and approved by me they are as good Scripture as is couched in this Bible**, and if you want to read revelation read the sayings of him who knows the mind of God, without any special command to one man to go here, and to another to go yonder, or to do this or that, or to go and settle here or there. (President Brigham Young, at General Conference, October 6, 1870, *Journal of Discourses* 13:264)

I have never preached a sermon they may not call scripture.

The Lord is in our midst. He teaches the people continually. I have **never** yet preached a sermon and sent it out to the children of men, that they may not call **Scripture**. Let me have the privilege of correcting a sermon, and it is as good Scripture as they deserve. The people have the oracles of God continually. (President Brigham Young, January 2, 1870, *Journal of Discourses* 13:95)

There is more scripture than in the standard works.

Millions feel that what is written in the Bible is the total of the revelations of the Lord, in spite of John's statement that if all that Jesus did were recorded, there would be numerous books. Some Latter-day Saints also make a similar error and feel that what is written in the *standard works* constitutes the sum total of the revelations in this dispensation. To this error George Q. Cannon, a member of the First Presidency, speaks:

"Some have deceived themselves with the idea that because revelations have not been written and published, therefore, there has been a lessening of power in the Church of Christ. This is a very great mistake. . . . the servants of the Lord **do receive revelations, and they are as binding upon the people as though they were printed and published throughout all the Stakes of Zion.** The oracles of God are here, and He speaks through His servant whom He has chosen to hold the keys. . . . We have been blessed as a people with an abundance of revelation. Have this people ever seen the day when the counsel of God's servants has not been sufficient to guide them in the midst of difficulties? No. We never have. **There has not been a single minute that this people has been left without the voice of God**; there has not been a single minute since this church was founded to this time that the power of God has not been plainly manifested in our midst . . . (*Gospel Truth*, p. 332)." The day of revelation has never passed; the Lord continues to communicate with his servants in our own day *as always*. (*Faith Precedes the Miracle*, [President] Spencer W. Kimball, pp. 21–22)

The Lord's will also comes from the Prophet.

We are to give heed to the words of eternal life. In other words, we must understand and live by the revelations the Lord has granted to His prophets. These are contained in the four *standard works* **and the written and public declarations of our current prophet**. ("Three Imperative Responsibilities," London England Area Conference, 19–20 June 1976.) (*Teachings of Ezra Taft Benson*, [President] Ezra Taft Benson, pp. 404–5)

Only the President can teach doctrine not in the standard works, *but it cannot contradict what is already there.*

We have the standard Church works. Why do we call them standard? If there is any teacher who teaches a doctrine that can't be substantiated from the standard church works—and I make one qualification, and that is **unless that one be the President of the Church**, who alone has the right to declare **new doctrine**—.... **The President of the Church alone may declare the mind and will of God to His people**. No officer nor any other church in the world has this high and lofty prerogative. **When the President proclaims any such *new doctrine,* he will declare it to be a revelation from the Lord**.... It is not to be thought that every word spoken by the General Authorities is inspired, or that they are moved upon by the Holy Ghost in everything they write. I don't care what his position is, if he writes something or speaks something that goes beyond anything that you can find in the standard church works, ***unless*** that one be the prophet, seer, and revelator—please note that one exception—you may immediately say, "Well, that is his own idea." **And if he says something that contradicts what is found in the standard church works, you may know by that same token that it is false, regardless of the position of the man who says it.** We can know or have the assurance that they are speaking under inspiration if we so live that we can have a witness that what they are speaking is the word of the Lord. There is only one safety, and that is that we shall live to have the witness to know. President Brigham Young said something to the effect that "the greatest fear I have is that the people of this Church will accept what we say as the will of the Lord without first praying about it and getting the witness within their own hearts that what we say is the word of the Lord." (*Stand Ye in Holy Places,* [President] Harold B. Lee, pp. 109–10, 162–63)

It is important to understand this concept taught by President Lee. He is saying that only the President of the Church, the Prophet, can teach new doctrine that is not in the *standard works.* But even his teachings, if they conflict with what is already in the *standard works,* can be ignored.

But Not All Seem to Agree

But other Mormon voices have at times sounded a cautionary note, calling for current pronouncements to be subjected to the test of being in agreement with the *standard works.* Consider, for example, these words of Apostle Joseph Fielding Smith:

STANDARD WORKS JUDGE TEACHINGS OF ALL MEN.
It makes no difference what is written or what **anyone** has said, if what has been said is in conflict with what the Lord has revealed, we can set it aside. My words, and the teaching of **any other** member of the Church, **high or low,** if they do not square with the revelations, we need not accept them. Let us have this matter clear. We have accepted the four *standard works* as the measuring yardsticks, or balances, by which we measure every man's doctrine.
You cannot accept the books written by the authorities of the Church as standards in doctrine, only in so far as they accord with the revealed word in the standard works. (*Doctrines of Salvation,* [Apostle] Joseph Fielding Smith, 3:203)

ALL TEACHINGS MUST CONFORM TO REVELATIONS.
It is not to be supposed from this that all that has been written outside of the standard works of the Church is discarded and rejected, for these things are profitable as helps in the government of the Church, and to promote faith in the members. The point is this, if in these books mistakes are found, "they are the mistakes of men," and the Church as an organization is not to be held accountable for them, but for that which is received from time to

time by vote of the Church, as it comes through the President of the High Priesthood. When the Lord reveals his mind and will, it is to be received, "whether by mine own voice or by the voice of my servants, it is the same," **but we are not to be judged by unauthorized sayings or deeds**. (*Doctrines of Salvation*, 1:322–23)

These cautionary words concerning new teachings are clearly in the minority—an exception to what other Mormon leaders have traditionally said—and they come from Joseph Fielding Smith at a time (prior to 1956) when he was an Apostle, not when he spoke as President (1970–1972). In addition, his words are not supported by scripture and actual past practice, hence they are really his own personal opinion. Moreover, even he expressed himself on other occasions in full agreement with the more prevalent view:

WHAT IS SCRIPTURE?
When one of the brethren stands before a congregation of the people today, and the inspiration of the Lord is upon him, he speaks that which the Lord would have him speak. It is just as much scripture as anything you will find written in any of these records, and yet we call these the *standard works* of the Church. We depend, of course, upon the guidance of the brethren who are entitled to inspiration. (*Doctrines of Salvation*, 1:186)

All of the quotes presented so far in this chapter combine to establish the weighty significance Mormons attach to statements by their leaders, particularly statements by LDS Church Presidents. This authoritative nature of presidential pronouncements should be kept in mind as we now make some comparisons among them.

The Comparisons

Is the Bible a Mormon standard for evaluating Mormonism?
Yes, use the Bible to test Mormonism.

I say to the whole world, receive the truth, no matter who presents it to you. **Take up the Bible**, compare the religion of the Latter-day Saints with it, and see if it will stand the test. (President Brigham Young, May 1873, *Journal of Discourses* 16:46)

If Joseph Smith was a deceiver . . . then he should be exposed; his claims should be refuted, and his doctrines shown to be false. . . . If his claims and declarations were built upon fraud and deceit, there would appear many errors and contradictions, which would be easy to detect. The doctrines of false teachers will not stand the test **when tried by the accepted standards of measurement, the scriptures**. (*Doctrines of Salvation*, [Apostle] Joseph Fielding Smith, 1954, 1:188)

. . . convince us of our errors of doctrine, if we have any, by reason, by logical arguments, or by **the word of God**. . . . (*The Seer*, [Apostle] Orson Pratt, January 1853, p. 15)

No, it is not reliable; parts are missing.

The most reliable way to measure the accuracy of any biblical passage is not by comparing different texts, but by comparison with the Book of Mormon and modern-day revelations. (Letter from the First Presidency [Presidents Benson, Hinckley, and Monson] to all members of the Church, dated May 22, 1992, in *Church News*, June 20, 1992, p. 3)

Unlike the Bible, which passed through generations of copyists, translators, and **corrupt religionists who tampered with the text**, the Book of Mormon came from writer to reader in just one inspired step of translation. (*Ensign*, January 1992, p. 5)

We believe the Bible to be the word of God **as far as it is translated correctly**. . . . (*Articles of Faith* #8, in Pearl of Great Price)

And after they go forth by the hand of the twelve apostles of the Lamb, from the Jews unto the Gentiles, thou seest the formation of a great and abominable church, which is most abominable above all other churches; for behold, they have **taken away** from the gospel of the Lamb many parts which are plain and most precious; and also many covenants of the Lord have they taken away. . . . because of the plain and most precious parts of the gospel of the Lamb which have been **kept back** by that abominable church, whose formation thou hast seen. . . . because of the most plain and precious parts of the gospel of the Lamb which have been **kept back** by that abominable church, which is the mother of harlots, saith the Lamb. . . . (1 Nephi 13:26, 32, 34)

The challenge by the top Mormon leaders makes sense only if we assume they were addressing non-Mormons. Brigham Young said to use the Bible, Joseph Fielding Smith the scriptures, and Orson Pratt the word of God. They said to compare the teachings of the Mormon Church with the Bible. Why would they make such a challenge in light of the third and fourth references, which they should have known? Most Mormons, including the ones in 1853, 1873, and 1954, consider the Bible to have parts missing or to be translated wrong. Were these Mormon leaders just making verbal "smoke" to sound good for their audience?

What is the greatest commandment?
Labor for the dead.

Each of us should make sure that temple work is done for ourselves and our own ancestors. The Prophet Joseph Smith taught that the **greatest responsibility** we have in this world is to identify our ancestors and go to the temple in their behalf (see *Teachings of the Prophet Joseph Smith,* p. 356). Another modern prophet, Joseph Fielding Smith, said: "Some may feel that if they pay their tithing, attend their regular meetings and duties, give of their substances to the poor, . . . spend one, two, or more years preaching the gospel in the world, that they are [free] from further duty. But the **greatest and grandest duty** of all is to labor for the dead" (see *Doctrines of Salvation,* 2:149). (*Gospel Principles,* p. 248)

. . . yet the **greatest commandment** given us, and made obligatory, is the temple work in our own behalf and in behalf of our dead. (*Doctrines of Salvation,* [Apostle] Joseph Fielding Smith, 2:149)

Love the Lord thy God.

Then one of them, which was a lawyer, asked him a question, tempting him, and saying, Master, which is the **great commandment** in the law? Jesus said unto him, Thou shalt love the Lord thy God with all thy heart, and with all thy soul, and with all thy mind. **This is the first and great commandment**. And the second is like unto it, Thou shalt love thy neighbour as thyself. (Matthew 22:35–39)

And Jesus answered him, The **first of all the commandments** is, Hear, O Israel; The Lord our God is one Lord: And thou shalt love the Lord thy God with all thy heart, and with all thy soul, and with all thy mind, and with all thy strength: this is the first commandment. And the second is like, namely this, Thou shalt love thy neighbour as thyself. **There is none other commandment greater** than these. (Mark 12:29–31)

The Mormon Church considers Jesus Christ the ultimate head of the Church he supposedly restored in 1830 (see *Joseph Smith— History* 1:17–19; 1 Nephi 14:10; D&C 1:6, 30; *Gospel Principles,* p. 106). Matthew 13:57; 21:11; Mark 6:4; Luke 24:19; John 4:44; 6:14 show that Jesus accepted the title of prophet. Indeed, in a sense, he is the chief prophet. So in Mark 12 and Matthew 22 we have the chief prophet telling us what the greatest commandment is. In Joseph Smith's translation of the Bible, except for numbering, all the Bible references above are essentially unchanged. Which prophet will you believe?

The gospel of Jesus Christ is the law of love, and love of God with the whole heart and mind **is the greatest commandment,** and the next is like unto it: love thy neighbor as thyself. (*Gospel Doc-*

trine, a priesthood study manual in 1919, [President] Joseph F. Smith, 1939 edition, p. 274)

What is the first principle of the gospel?
Faith in God, in Jesus Christ, is the first principle.

Faith a Gift of God. . . . Although **faith** is called the first principle of the Gospel of Christ, though it be in fact the foundation of religious life. . . . (*Articles of Faith* [the book], [Apostle] James E. Talmage, p. 107)

The first principle of the Gospel is **faith in God**—faith in a Supreme Being. (*Discourses of Brigham Young,* President Brigham Young, p. 154. This is also in July 1869, *Journal of Discourses* 13:142.)

We believe that the first principles and ordinances of the Gospel are: first, **Faith** in the Lord Jesus Christ; second, Repentance; third, Baptism by immersion for the remission of sins; fourth, Laying on of hands for the gift of the Holy Ghost. (*Articles of Faith* #4, in the Pearl of Great Price)

The first principle of the gospel is **faith** in the Lord Jesus Christ; and of course we are not going to have faith in the Lord Jesus Christ without having faith in his Father. (*Doctrines of Salvation,* [Apostle] Joseph Fielding Smith, 2:303)

The first principle is to know the character of God.

These are incomprehensible ideas to some, but they are simple. It is the first principle of the gospel to **know for a certainty the character of God,** and to know that we may converse with Him as one man converses with another, and that He was once a man like us; yea, that God himself, the Father of us all, dwelt on an earth, the same as Jesus Christ Himself did; and I will show it from the Bible. (President Joseph Smith, at General Conference, April 7, 1844, *History of the Church* 6:305)

Who is the first man?
Adam is the first man.

> ... Adam, who is the first man ... (September 1832, D&C 84:16)

> And **worlds without number** have I **created**; and I also **created** them for mine own purpose; and by the Son I created them, which is mine Only Begotten. And the **first man of all men have I called Adam**. . . . (1830–1831, Moses 1:33–34; and in *History of the Church* 1:100)

> And so it is written, The **first man Adam** was made a living soul; the last Adam was made a quickening spirit. (1 Cor. 15:45)

God the Father is the first man.

> I have learned by experience that there is but one God that pertains to this people, and He is the God that pertains to this earth—**the first man. That first man sent his own Son** to redeem the world, to redeem his brethren; his life was taken, his blood shed, that our sins might be remitted. (Heber C. Kimball, first counselor to Brigham Young, June 29, 1856, *Journal of Discourses* 4:1)

> **God himself is the First Man**[5] and the Father of all men. In the pure language, spoken by Adam, the name of the Father is Man of Holiness. . . . (*The Mortal Messiah*, [Apostle] Bruce R. McConkie, 1979–1981, 1:21)

Did Brigham Young teach Adam-God doctrine and call it revelation?
Yes, he did, for over nineteen years.

> How much unbelief exists in the minds of the Latter-day Saints in regard to one particular **doctrine** which I revealed to them, and which **God revealed to me**—namely that **Adam is our father and God**. . . . Our Father Adam is the man who stands at the gate and holds the keys of everlasting life and salvation to all his children who have or who ever will come upon the earth.

(President Brigham Young, June 8, 1873, *Deseret News*, June 14, 1873, p. 308)

Who was the savior begotten by? . . . Who did beget him? His Father, and his father is our God, and the Father of our spirits, and he is the framer of the body, the God and Father of our Lord Jesus Christ. **Who is he? He is Father Adam; Michael; the Ancient of Days**[6] (President Brigham Young, February 19, 1854, *Brigham Young Collection*, LDS Archives)

When we can see that very character (Michael) and talk and live with him in our tabernacles. . . . and **he is the father of our Lord Jesus Christ and of our spirits**. . . . I tell you this as my belief about that personage who is called the Ancient of days, the Prince. . . . I did not understand so until my mind became enlightened with the spirit and **by revelations of God**; neither will you understand until our Father in Heaven reveals all things unto you. (President Brigham Young, April 25, 1855, *Manuscript Addresses of Brigham Young*)

I will give you **a few words of doctrine**. . . . I advanced **a doctrine with regard to Adam being our father and God**. . . . (President Brigham Young, at General Conference, October 8, 1864, *Brigham Young Collection*, LDS Archives)

Additional references are given just below in the first part of "Was Adam made from the dust of this earth?" These references are just a small sample of the many that could be given. Two books are recommended to learn more on this subject: *Adam-God* by Craig L. Tholson and *The Adam-God Maze* by Culley K. Christensen, M.D.

It is only alleged that he taught it; it is false doctrine.

We warn you against the dissemination of doctrines which are not according to the scriptures and which are **alleged to have been taught** by some of the General Authorities [Brigham Young was a General Authority] of past generations. Such, for instance is the Adam-God theory. We **denounce** that theory and hope that everyone will be cautioned against this and other kinds of **false doctrine**. (President Spencer W. Kimball, *Deseret News*, October 9, 1976, p. 11; and *Ensign*, November 1976, p. 77) '

Did Brigham Young consider his Adam-God teachings a "theory" or doctrine revealed by God?

Was Adam made from the dust of this earth?
Adam was made from the dust of another earth; he is a resurrected person.

> **You believe Adam was made of the dust of this earth. This I do not believe**, though it is supposed that it is so written in the Bible; but it is not, to my understanding. You can write that information to the States, if you please—that I have publicly declared that I do not believe that portion of the Bible.... (President Brigham Young, October 23, 1853, *Journal of Discourses* 2:6)

> **Adam was made from the dust of an earth, but *not* from the dust of this earth.** He was made as you and I are made, and no person was ever made upon any other principle. (President Brigham Young, April 20, 1856, *Journal of Discourses* 3:319)

> I tell you more, **Adam is the father of our spirits. He had lived upon an earth**; he did abide his creation, and did honor to his calling and priesthood, and obeyed his master or Lord, and probably many of his wives did the same and they lived, and died upon an earth and then were resurrected again; to immortality and eternal life.... I reckon that **Father Adam was a resurrected being,** with his wives and posterity.... (Brigham Young at General Conference, October 8, 1854, *Brigham Young Papers*, October 8, 1854, call number Ms. D 1234, Church Historian's Office)

Apostle Wilford Woodruff (he became the fourth President of the Mormon Church in 1889), who was present at the above talk, said in his journal under October 8, 1854, that the "General

Conference commenced this morning. . . . President Young preached to a congregation of several thousand, out of door and I believe that he preached the greatest sermon that ever was delivered to the Latter-day Saints since they have become a people."

Adam was made from the dust of this earth.

> *The Book of Mormon*, the *Bible*, the *Doctrine and Covenants*, and the *Pearl of Great Price* [these four are Mormon scriptures] all declare that Adam's body was created from the dust of the ground, that is, **from the dust of *this ground, this earth*.** . . . We hear a lot of people talk about Adam passing through mortality and the resurrection on another earth and then coming here to live and die again. . . . **Adam had *not* passed through a resurrection when he was in the Garden of Eden.** . . . (*Doctrines of Salvation*, [Apostle] Joseph Fielding Smith, 1954, 1:90–91)

Is God progressing in knowledge, power, and dominion?

Yes, he is.

> God himself is increasing and progressing **in knowledge**, power, and dominion, and will do so, worlds without end. It is just so with us. (Apostle Wilford Woodruff, December 6, 1857, *Journal of Discourses* 6:120)

> . . . the very Eternal Father is a progressive Being. . . . (*Articles of Faith* [the book], Apostle James E. Talmage, 1988 edition, p. 530)

No, he is not.

> It seems very strange to me that members of the church will hold to the doctrine, "God increases in knowledge as time goes on." . . . Where has the Lord ever revealed to us that he is lacking **in knowledge**? That he is still learning new truth; discovering new laws that are unknown to him? I think this kind of doctrine is very dangerous. I don't know where the Lord has ever declared

such a thing. (*Doctrines of Salvation*, [Apostle] Joseph Fielding Smith, 1954, 1:7–8)

Is God omnipresent, that is, can he be in all places at once?

Yes, he is omnipresent.

> We here observe that God is the only supreme governor, and independent being, in whom all fulness and perfection dwells; who is omnipotent, **omnipresent**, and omniscient; without beginning of days or end of life. . . .
> Q. How do you prove that God has faith in himself independently?
> A. Because he is omnipotent, **omnipresent**, and omniscient; without beginning of days or end of life. . . . (1835 D&C, "Lecture Second of Faith" 2:2, pp. 17 and 26, and the question-and-answer section after verse 56)

The immediate context of these verses, and the remainder of the book, in no way changes their meaning. *Omnipresent* in 1835 had the same meaning it does today.[7]

No, he is not. He can be in only one place at a time.

What follows just below is the use of the above 1835 "Lecture Second of Faith" 2:2 quoted in a present-day teaching manual published by the LDS Church.

> God is the only supreme governor[8] and independent being in whom all fullness and perfection dwell; who is omnipotent, **omnipresent** and omniscient. . . . (Joseph Smith, Lectures on Faith 2:2). . . . Accordingly they all think, act, speak, and are alike in all things. . . . (*Doctrines of the Gospel*, Student Manual, Religion 231 and 232, p. 8)

Now read below another part of this same page 8 (and p. 11) to see how *omnipresent* is redefined.

... they are three separate and distinct entities [Father, Son, and Holy Ghost]. Each occupies space and is and cannot be in but one place at one time.... The Holy Ghost as a personage of Spirit can no more be omnipresent in person than can the Father or the Son.... (*Doctrines of the Gospel,* Student Manual, Religion 231 and 232, pp. 8 and 11; also in *Mormon Doctrine,* [Apostle] Bruce R. McConkie, p. 319)

Who is Jehovah?
The Son is Jehovah.

Jehovah ... In the KJV ... and the name is generally denoted by LORD or GOD, printed in small capitals. Jehovah is the premortal Jesus Christ and came to earth being born of Mary. (Bible Dictionary, in the Mormon edition of the King James Bible, p. 711)

... Jehovah who is Jesus Christ the Son of Elohim.... That Jesus Christ, whom we also know as Jehovah, was the executive of the Father, Elohim.... (*Articles of Faith* [the book], James E. Talmage, 1987 edition, p. 467. A Doctrinal Exposition[9] dated June 30, 1916, by the First Presidency and the Council of the Twelve Apostles)

The Lord God is Jehovah; the Son is someone else.

... I lifted up my voice unto the Lord my God, and the Lord ... heard ... behold **my name is Jehovah** ... I have heard thee.... For **I am the Lord thy God**.... **my name is Jehovah**.... if there be two spirits, and one shall be more intelligent than the other. ... **I am the Lord thy God, I am more intelligent than they *all*.** Now the Lord had shown unto me, Abraham, the intelligences that were organized before the world was; and among all these there were many of the noble and great ones; And God saw these souls that they were good.... And there stood one among them that was like unto God.... And the Lord said: Whom shall I send? And one answered like unto the **Son of Man** [Jesus Christ].... (*Abraham* 1:15–16; 2:7–8; 3:18–19, 22–24, 27)

The Son is the Father.

> Now Zeezrom saith again unto him: Is the Son of God the **very Eternal Father**? And Amulek said unto him: Yea, he is the **very Eternal Father**. (Alma 11:38–39)

> . . . God himself shall come down. . . . he shall be called the Son of God. . . . **being the Father and the Son**—The Father, because he was conceived by the power of God; and the Son, because of the flesh; thus becoming the Father and Son—And they are one God, yea, the **very Eternal Father** of heaven and earth. And thus the flesh becoming subject to the Spirit, or the Son to the Father, **being one God**. . . . (Mosiah 15:1–5)

> Behold, I am he who was prepared from the foundation of the world to redeem my people. Behold, I am Jesus Christ. I am the **Father and the Son**. . . . he that will not believe me will not believe the Father who sent me. **For behold, I am the Father**. . . . (Ether 3:14; 4:12)

> For unto us a child is born, unto us a son is given; and the government shall be upon his shoulder; and his name shall be called, Wonderful, Counselor, The **Mighty God,** The **Everlasting Father**, The Prince of Peace.[10] (2 Nephi 19:6; also see 2 Nephi 22:2; 26:12; Mosiah 7:27; 16:15; Ether 3:14)

> . . . trusting in the arm of **Jehovah,**[11] **the Eloheim** [*sic*], who sits enthroned in the heavens. . . . (Joseph Smith, letter of August 14, 1842, in *History of the Church* 5:94)

Was Mary, the mother of Jesus Christ, a virgin after his birth?
Yes, she was.

> His message delivered, Gabriel departed, leaving the chosen Virgin of Nazareth to ponder over her wondrous experience. Mary's promised Son was to be "The Only Begotten" of the Father in the flesh; so it had been both positively and abundantly predicted.

True, the event was unprecedented; true also it has never been paralleled; but that the **virgin birth** would be unique was as truly essential to the fulfillment of prophecy as that it should occur at all. That Child to be born of Mary was **begotten of Elohim, the Eternal Father.** . . . *(Jesus the Christ,* Apostle James E. Talmage, 1962 edition, p. 81)

Our Lord is the only mortal person ever **born to a virgin,** because he is the **only person who ever had an immortal Father.** Mary, his mother, "was carried away in the Spirit" (1 Ne. 11:13–21), was "overshadowed" by the Holy Ghost, and the conception which took place "by the power of the Holy Ghost" resulted in the bringing forth of the **literal and personal Son of God** the Father. (Alma 7:10; 2 Ne. 17:14; Isaiah 7:14; Matt. 1:18–25; Luke 1:26–38) **Christ is not the Son of the Holy Ghost, but of the Father.** (*Doctrines of Salvation,* vol. 1, pp. 18–20) Modernistic teachings denying the virgin birth are utterly and completely apostate and false. (*Mormon Doctrine,* [Apostle] Bruce R. McConkie, 1979, p. 822, under "Virgin Birth")

He was the Only Begotten Son of our Heavenly Father in the flesh—the only child whose mortal body was begotten by our Heavenly Father. His mortal mother, Mary, was called a virgin, **both before and after** she gave birth. (See 1 Nephi 11:20.) ("Joy in Christ," *Ensign* 16, March 1986: 3–4) (*Teachings of Ezra Taft Benson,* President Ezra Taft Benson, Bookcraft, 1988, p. 7)

The Book of Mormon provides a second witness of the mission of Jesus Christ to the Bible. Book of Mormon prophets testified hundreds of years before the birth of Jesus that He would be **born of a virgin** named Mary and that His name would be Jesus Christ. Long before Jesus was born these prophets outlined His public ministry, that He would work mighty miracles, such as "healing the sick, raising the dead, causing the lame to walk, the blind to receive their sight, the deaf to hear, and curing all manner of diseases" (Mosiah 3:5). (*Teachings of Ezra Taft Benson,* p. 54)

No, she was not.

These name-titles all signify that our Lord is the only Son of the Father in the flesh. Each of the words is to be understood literally. Only means only; Begotten means begotten; and Son means son. Christ was begotten by an Immortal Father **in the same way** that mortal men are begotten by mortal fathers. (*Mormon Doctrine*, p. 546, under "Only Begotten Son")

God the Father is a perfected, glorified, holy Man, an immortal Personage. And Christ was born into the world as the literal Son of this Holy Being; he was born in the same personal, real, and literal sense that any mortal son is born to a mortal father. There is nothing figurative about his paternity; **he was begotten, conceived and born in the normal and natural course of events**, for he is the Son of God, and that designation means what it says (1 Ne. 11). (*Mormon Doctrine*, 1979, p. 742, under "Son of God")

"I want the little folks to hear what I am going to tell you. I am going to tell you a **simple truth**, yet it is one of the **greatest truths** and one of the most **simple facts ever revealed** to the children of men.

"You all know that your fathers are indeed your fathers and that your mothers are indeed your mothers—you all know that don't you? You cannot deny it. Now, we are told in scriptures that Jesus Christ is the only begotten Son of God in the flesh. Well, now for the benefit of the older ones, **how are children begotten? I answer just as Jesus Christ was begotten of his father**. . . . We must come down to simple fact that God Almighty was the Father of His Son Jesus Christ. . . . Now, my little friends, I will repeat again in words as simple as I can, and you talk to your parents about it, that God the Eternal Father, **is literally** the father of Jesus Christ" (Joseph F. Smith, Box Elder Stake Conference Dec. 20, 1914 as quoted in *Brigham City Box Elder News,* 28 Jan. 1915, pp. 1–2.) (President Joseph F. Smith, speaking to young children at an official Mormon Church Stake Conference in 1914, quoted in *Family Home Evening, Personal Commitment,* 1972, p. 125)

From D&C 130:22 we learn that "the Father has a body of flesh and bones as tangible as man's." And from the above references we learn that, **by Mormon teachings**, Jesus Christ was begotten, conceived, and born in the *same way* we were, and just as little children are. This could only mean that the Father, *according to Mormon teachings,* used his physical body to perform a sexual act with Mary. If this were the case, then how could she remain a virgin? *Webster's New Collegiate Dictionary* has several meanings for *virgin.* The third meaning is: "One who has not had sexual intercourse." While Bruce R. McConkie on page 822 of *Mormon Doctrine* calls Mary a virgin, in other parts of his book, on pages 546 and 742, he says something totally different. The only conclusion we can speculate on is that a virgin to this Mormon Apostle has one of the other meanings. Or maybe a virgin is a person that has not had sex with a mortal man, but sex with an immortal God still leaves a person a virgin.

What will the impact be if you use coffee, tea, tobacco, or alcohol?

You cannot hold office, and you will not go to the celestial kingdom.

To be sent greeting; **not by commandment or constraint**, but by revelation and the word of wisdom, showing forth the order and will of God in the temporal salvation of all saints in the last days—.... That inasmuch as any man drinketh wine or strong drink among you, behold it is not good, neither meet in the sight of your Father, only in assembling yourselves together to offer up your sacraments before him. And, behold, this should be wine, yea, pure wine of the grape of the vine, of your own make. And, again, strong drinks are not for the belly, but for the washing of your bodies. And again, tobacco is not for the body, neither for the belly, and is not good for man, but is an herb for bruises and all sick cattle, to be used with judgment and skill. And again, hot drinks are not for the body or belly. (February 1833, D&C 89:2, 5–9)

These are the key verses in what is called the "Word of Wisdom," a health law of the Mormon Church.

> **We must obey the Word of Wisdom to be worthy to enter the temple.** If we do not live the Word of Wisdom, the Lord's Spirit may not dwell with us. . . . WE ARE COMMANDED **NOT** TO TAKE CERTAIN THINGS INTO OUR BODIES. The Lord commands us not to use wine and strong drinks, meaning drinks containing alcohol. . . . The Lord also counsels us against the use of "hot drinks." The leaders of the Church have said that this means coffee and tea. (*Gospel Principles*, pp. 181–82)

> . . . if you drink coffee or tea, or take tobacco, are you letting a cup of tea or a little tobacco stand in the road and bar you from the celestial kingdom of God? . . . God is not going to save every man and woman in the celestial kingdom. . . . Now if we want to become heirs, joint-heirs with Jesus Christ, possessing the blessings of the kingdom, there is only one thing required of you and of me, and that is that we keep the *whole law*, not a part of it only. (*Doctrines of Salvation*, [Apostle] Joseph Fielding Smith, 1955, 2:16–17, 37)

> I notice in the observance of the Word of Wisdom, a manifestation of the Holy Spirit connected with it. Whenever a person has failed to observe it, and becomes a slave to his appetite in these simple things, he gradually grows cold in his religion. . . . (George A. Smith, first counselor to President Brigham Young, August 13, 1871, *Journal of Discourses* 14:212)

> After a free and full discussion, Joseph Smith the Prophet gave the following decision which was unanimously accepted by the council [1834]: "No official member in this Church **is worthy to hold an office** after having the Word of Wisdom [February 1833, D&C 89] properly taught him, and he, the official member, neglecting to comply with and obey it."[12] (*Teachings of the Prophet Joseph Smith*, Joseph Fielding Smith, p. 117, see footnote; also see *Mormon Doctrine*, [Apostle] Bruce R. McConkie, 1966, p. 846, under "Word of Wisdom")

People *cannot* now become members of the Mormon Church if they do not observe and practice the Word of Wisdom, and when they become members they *cannot* obtain a temple recommend if they are breaking it, i.e., using coffee or tea or alcohol or tobacco. Such people lose their chance to become Gods with all the power, authority, and dominion the Father and Son have.

Joseph Smith and other leaders did not adhere to the Word of Wisdom.

Wednesday, 3rd—called at the office and drank a glass of wine with Sister Jeneta Richards made by her mother in England. . . . (Joseph Smith, May 3, 1843, *History of the Church* 5:380)

Elders Orson Hyde, Luke S. Johnson, and Warren Parrish, then presented the Presidency with three servers of **glasses filled with wine**, to bless. And it fell to my [Joseph Smith's] lot to attend to this duty, which I cheerfully discharged. It was then passed round in order, the cake in the same order; and suffice it to say, our hearts were made glad while partaking of the bounty of earth which was presented, **until we had taken our fill**; and joy filled every bosom, and the countenances of old and young seemed to bloom alike with cheerfulness and smiles of youth. . . . (Joseph Smith, at a wedding reception, January 1836, *History of the Church* 2:378)

Sometime after dinner **we sent for some wine**. It has been reported by some that this was taken as a sacrament. It was no such thing; our spirits were generally dull and heavy, and it was sent for to revive us. . . . I believe we all drank of the wine, and gave some to one or two of the prison guards. (Apostle John Taylor [who later became the third President of the Mormon Church], June 1844, *History of the Church* 7:101)

He is describing an event just shortly before the assassination of Joseph Smith while they were in jail together. In *History of the Church* 6:616 he provides more information on the same event:

> The guard immediately **sent for a bottle of wine, pipes, and two small papers of tobacco**; and one of the guards brought them into the jail soon after the jailor went out. Dr. Richards uncorked the bottle, and presented a glass to Joseph [Smith], who tasted, as also Brother Taylor and the doctor, and the bottle was then given to the guard. . . .

There is no indication that the wine referenced above was juice, non-alcoholic. Noah Webster's 1828 dictionary has as the first definition for wine "The fermented juice of grapes."

> Then went to John P. Greene's and paid him and another brother $200. **Drank a glass of beer at Moessers.** Called at William Clayton's. . . . (Joseph Smith, on Saturday, June 1, 1844, *Millennial Star* 23:720, under "History of Joseph Smith)[13]

> *Ordinance on the Personal Sale of Liquors.* Section 1. Be it ordained by the City Council of Nauvoo, that the Mayor [Joseph Smith] of the city be and is hereby authorized to sell or give spirits of any quantity as he in his wisdom shall judge to be for the health and comfort, or convenience of such travelers or other persons as shall visit his house from time to time. Passed December 12, 1843. Joseph Smith, Mayor. Willard Richards, Recorder. (*History of the Church* 6:111)[14]

What was the character of Joseph Smith?
His character was as good as any in the Bible.

> Well, now, examine the character of the Savior, and examine the characters of those who have written the Old and New Testaments; and then compare them with the character of Joseph Smith, the founder of this work.[15] . . . and you will find that his character stands as fair as that of any man's mentioned in the Bible. We can find no person who presents a **better character** to the world when the facts are known than Joseph Smith, jun., the prophet, and his brother Hyrum Smith, who was murdered with him. (President Brigham Young, 1871, *Journal of Discourses* 14:203)

He was a boaster—more stood by him than Jesus.

> Come on! ye prosecutors! ye false swearers! All hell, boil over! Ye burning mountains, roll down your lava! for I will come out on the top at last. I have more to boast of than ever any man had. I am the **only** man that has ever been able to keep a whole church together since the days of Adam. A large majority of the whole have stood by me. Neither Paul, John, Peter, **nor Jesus ever did it. I boast** that **no man** ever did such a work as I. The followers of Jesus ran away from Him; but the Latter-day Saints never ran away from me yet. . . . I love to hear the wolves howl! **When they can get rid of me, the devil will also go.** (Joseph Smith, May 26, 1844, *History of the Church* 6:408–9, the footnote)

Joseph Smith said this about himself in a public address several weeks before he was killed in Carthage Jail.

When will black men hold the priesthood?
The first that were cursed will be the last to get the priesthood.

> He [Cain] killed his brother. The Lord put a mark on him; and there are some of his children in this room. When all the other children of Adam have had the privilege of receiving the Priesthood, and of coming into the kingdom of God, and of being redeemed from the four quarters of the earth, and have received their resurrection from the dead, then it will be time enough to remove the curse from Cain and his posterity. . . . **he is the last to share the joys of the kingdom of God.** (President Brigham Young, December 3, 1854, *Journal of Discourses* 2:143)

> . . . the children of Cain cannot receive the first ordinances of the Priesthood. They were the first that were cursed, and they will be the **last** from whom the curse will be removed. When the residue of the family of Adam come up and receive their blessings, then the curse will be removed from the seed of Cain, and they will receive blessings in like proportion. (President Brigham Young, at General Conference, October 9, 1859, *Journal of Discourses* 7:290)

They can now hold the Mormon priesthood; the ban was lifted in 1978.

> . . . by revelation has confirmed that the long-promised day has come when every faithful, worthy man in the Church may receive the holy priesthood, with power to exercise its divine authority. . . . (A letter from the First Presidency, *Church News*, June 17, 1978, p. 3)

This is now found at the end of the D&C as Official Declaration—2. As of this date black men could hold the Mormon priesthood.

How many times should we be baptized?
By revelation, we can be baptized more than once.

> I will here state that Martin Harris, when he came to this Territory a few years ago, was **rebaptized**, the **same as every member** of the Church from distant parts is on arriving here. That seems to be a kind of standing ordinance for all Latter-day Saints who emigrate here, from the First Presidency down; **all are rebaptized** and set out anew by renewing their covenants. (Apostle Orson Pratt, July 18, 1875, *Journal of Discourses* 18:160)

> I know that in my traveling and preaching, many a time, I have stopped by beautiful streams of clear, pure water, and have said to myself, "How delightful it would be to me to go into this, to be baptized for the remission of my sins." When I got home Joseph [Smith] told me it was my privilege. At this time came **a revelation**, that the Saints could be baptized and **rebaptized** when they chose, and then that we could be baptized for our dear friends. . . . (President Brigham Young, June 23, 1874, *Journal of Discourses* 18:241)

We should be baptized only once.

> It is unnecessary, however, to rebaptize persons merely as a renewal of their covenants every time they transgress in order that they may obtain forgiveness, for this would greatly cheapen this

sacred ordinance and weaken its effectiveness. (*Doctrines of Salvation*, Joseph Fielding Smith, 1955 edition, 2:335)

But Brigham Young said that Joseph Smith received a revelation saying that baptism could be done when a person wanted it done. The present practice of the Mormon Church is to rebaptize only if a person has committed a major transgression and has been excommunicated and has then qualified to become a member again.

Was blood atonement ever practiced in the Mormon Church?

It was taught and practiced.

> There are sins that men commit for which they cannot receive forgiveness in this world, or in that which is to come, and if they had their eyes open to see their true condition, they would be perfectly willing to have their blood spilt upon the ground, that the smoke thereof might ascend to heaven as an offering for their sins; and the smoking incense would atone for their sins, whereas, if such is not the case, they will stick to them and remain upon them in the spirit world. . . . I know that there are transgressors, who, if they knew themselves, and the only condition upon which they can obtain forgiveness would beg of their brethren to shed their blood, that the smoke thereof might ascend to God. . . . It is true that the blood of the Son of God was shed for sins through the fall and those committed by men, yet men can commit sins which it can never remit. . . . (President Brigham Young, *Deseret News*, September 21, 1856, p. 235 [285?]; very similar to *Journal of Discourses* 4:53–54)

> Suppose you found your brother in bed with your wife, and put a javelin through both of them, you would be justified, and **they would atone for their sins, and be received into the kingdom of God.**[16] I would at once do so in such a case; and under such circumstances, I have no wife whom I love so well that I would not put a javelin through her heart, and I would do it with clean hands. (President Brigham Young, March 16, 1856, *Journal of Discourses* 3:247)

I could refer you to plenty of instances where men have been righteously slain, in order to atone for their sins.[17] I have seen scores and hundreds of people for whom there would have been a chance (in the last resurrection there will be) if their lives had been taken and their blood spilled on the ground as a smoking incense to the Almighty, but who are now angels to the devil, until our elder brother Jesus Christ raises them up—conquers death, hell, and the grave. I have known a great many men who have left this Church for whom there is no chance whatever for exaltation, **but if their blood had been spilled, it would have been better for them**. (President Brigham Young, February 8, 1857, *Journal of Discourses* 4:220)

No, it was not. Not a single individual was ever blood atoned.

But that the Church practices "Blood Atonement" on apostates or any others, which is preached by ministers of the "Reorganization" [the RLDS] is a damnable falsehood for which the accusers must answer. . . . Church Never Practiced Blood Atonement. Your report says: "This doctrine was introduced by Brigham Young" and that it meant "Death to anyone who left the Church. . . . That the apostate whose throat was cut from ear to ear . . . saved his soul." . . . but were you not aware that it was but the repetition of the *ravings of enemies of the Church, without one grain of truth?* Did you not know that *not a single individual was ever "blood atoned,"* as you are pleased to call it, for apostasy or **any other cause**? (*Doctrines of Salvation*, [Apostle] Joseph Fielding Smith, 1:136–37)

What was the name of the messenger from God that showed Joseph Smith the gold plates?
His name was Moroni.

He called me by name, and said unto me that he was a messenger sent from the presence of God to me, and that **his name was Moroni**; that God had a work for me to do; and that my name should be had for good and evil among all nations, kindreds, and tongues, or that it should be both good and evil spoken of among all people. (*Joseph Smith—History* 1:33)[18]

His name was Nephi.

He called me by name, and said unto me that he was a messenger sent from the presence of God to me, and that **his name was Nephi**; that God had a work for me to do; and that my name should be had for good and evil among all nations, kindreds, and tongues, or that it should be both good and evil spoken of among all people. (This same wording, with slight differences in punctuation, is in the first edition of the Pearl of Great Price[19] [1851] and the April 15, 1842, *Times and Seasons* 3:753, under "History of Joseph Smith."[20])

When was the religious revival that affected Joseph Smith?

It happened when he was age 14, in the spring of 1820.

Some time in the second year after our removal to Manchester,[21] there was in the place where we lived an unusual excitement on the subject of religion. It commenced with the Methodists, **but soon became general among all the sects in that region of country**. Indeed, the whole district of country seemed affected by it, and great multitudes united themselves to the different religious parties, which created no small stir and division amongst the people, some crying "Lo, here!" and others, "Lo, there!" Some were contending for the Methodist faith, some for the Presbyterian, and some for the Baptist. . . .

I was at this time in my **fifteenth year**.[22] My father's family were proselyted to the Presbyterian faith. . . . So, in accordance with this, my determination to ask of God, I retired to the woods to make the attempt. It was on the morning of a beautiful, clear day, **early in the spring of eighteen hundred and twenty**. . . . (*Joseph Smith—History* 1:5, 7, 14; the heading has "Extracts from the History of Joseph Smith, the Prophet, *History of the Church, Vol. 1, Chapters 1–5*")

This official version was not written until 1838, eighteen years after the alleged event.

> You will recollect that I informed you, in my letter published in the first No. of the *Messenger and Advocate*, that this history would necessarily embrace the life and character of our esteemed friend and brother, J. (Joseph) Smith, Jr. one of the presidents of this church, and for information on that part of the subject, I refer you to his communication of the same, published in this paper [p. 40]. I shall, therefore, pass over that, **till I come to the 15th year of his life**.
>
> It is necessary to premise this account by relating the situation of the public mind relative to religion, at this time: One Mr. Lane,[23] a presiding Elder of the Methodist church, visited Palmyra, and vicinity.... There was a great awakening, or excitement raised on the subject of religion, and much enquiry for the word of life. **Large additions were made** to the Methodist, Presbyterian, and Baptist churches.[24] ... and in common with others, our brother's mind became awakened. . . .[25] (*Letter III, Messenger and Advocate*, Oliver Cowdery, editor, December 1834, Vol. 1, p. 42)

It happened when he was age 17, in 1823.

Two months later Oliver Cowdery corrected his previous statement on the age of Joseph Smith when he said:

> You will recollect that I mentioned the time of a religious excitement, in Palmyra and vicinity to have been in the 15th year of our brother J. (Joseph) Smith Jr's, age—**that was an *error* in the type—it should have been in the 17th**.—You will please remember this correction, as it will be necessary for the full understanding of what will follow in time. This would **bring the date down to the year 1823**. . . .[26] (*Letter IV, Messenger and Advocate*, Oliver Cowdery, editor, February 1835, Vol. 1, No. 5, p. 78–79)[27]

Who or what did Joseph Smith see in his First Vision?
He saw the Father and the Son.

When the light rested upon me **I [Joseph Smith] saw two Personages**, whose brightness and glory defy all description, standing above me in the air. One of them spake unto me, calling me by name and said, pointing to the other—*This is My Beloved Son. Hear Him!* My object in going to inquire of the Lord was to know which of all the sects was right, that I might know which to join. No sooner, therefore, did I get possession of myself, so as to be able to speak, than I asked the **Personages** who stood above me in the light, which of all the sects was right . . . and which I should join. I was answered that I must join none of them, for they were all wrong; and the **Personage** who addressed me said that all their creeds were an abomination in his sight; that those professors were all corrupt; that: "they draw near to me with their lips, but their hearts are far from me, they teach for doctrines the commandments of men. . . ." (*Joseph Smith—History* 1:18; this is the official version)[28]

He saw the Lord only.

. . . and while in the attitude of calling upon the Lord a pillar of light above the brightness of the sun at noon day came down from above and rested upon me and I was filled with the spirit of God and the Lord opened the heavens upon me and **I saw the Lord** and he spake unto me saying Joseph my Son thy Sins are forgiven thee, go thy way, walk in my statutes. . . . (Joseph Smith's diary in his own hand, 1832, p. 3, as quoted in *Ensign,* December 1984, pp. 24–26 and January 1985, p. 11)

He saw two personages and angels.

. . . I kneeled again, my mouth was opened and my toung liberated, and I called on the Lord in mighty prayer, a pillar of fire appeared above my head. . . . **a person appeared** in the midst of this pillar of flame. . . . **another personage soon appeared** like unto the first, he said unto me thy sins are forgiven thee, he testifyed unto me that Jesus Christ is the Son of God; and **I saw many angels** in this vision. I was about 14 years old when I received this first communication. . . . (Joseph Smith's diary, 1835, as quoted in *Joseph Smith's First Vision,* Milton V. Backman, Jr., Appendix B. Spelling in this last reference, as in all references, is as in the original. Both the above references can also be found in *The Personal Writings of Joseph Smith,* compiled and edited by Dean C. Jessee, Deseret Book Co., 1984.)

He saw only angels.

But He did send His angel to this same obscure person, Joseph Smith jun., who afterwards became a Prophet, Seer and Revelator, and informed him that he should not join any of the religious sects of the day, for they were all wrong; that they were following the precepts of men instead of the Lord Jesus. . . . (President Brigham Young, February 1855, *Journal of Discourses* 2:171)

He [Joseph Smith] sought the Lord by day and by night, and was enlightened by the vision of **an holy angel**. When this personage appeared to him, one of his first inquiries was, "Which of the denominations of Christians in the vicinity was right?" (George A. Smith, first counselor to President Brigham Young, June 20, 1869, *Journal of Discourses* 13:78)

Has the angel flown through the midst of heaven and delivered the Gospel to the children of men? Yes, we believe all this. Do we believe that the Lord **sent his messengers** to Joseph Smith, and commanded him to refrain from joining any Christian church, and to refrain from the wickedness he saw in the churches? . . . (President Brigham Young, June 23, 1874, *Journal of Discourses* 18:239)

. . . just as it was when the Prophet Joseph asked **the angel** which of the sects was right that he might join it. (Apostle John Taylor, March 2, 1879, *Journal of Discourses* 20:167)

Were our spirits created, procreated, or eternally in existence?
Our spirits were not created; they are from eternity.

The Spirit of man is not a created being: it existed from eternity, and will exist to eternity. Anything created cannot be eternal.... (President Joseph Smith, June 2, 1839, *History of the Church* 3:387; *Journal of Discourses* 6:238; both read the same)

... namely, the soul, the mind of man, **the immortal spirit**. Where did it come from? All learned men and doctors of divinity say that God created it in the beginning. But it is not so.... I do not believe the doctrine.... The mind or the intelligence which man possesses is coequal with God himself. I know that my testimony is true.... I am dwelling on the immortality of the spirit of man.... **The intelligence of spirits had no beginning**, neither will it have an end.... **There never was a time when there were not spirits**; for they are coequal with our Father in heaven. (Prophet Joseph Smith, at General Conference, April 6, 1844, *History of the Church* 6:310–11; *Journal of Discourses* 6:6; both are the same)[29]

Our spirits were begotten and born in the pre-existence.[30]

God is not only our ruler and our creator; he is also our Heavenly Father. "All men and women are ... literally the sons and daughters of Deity.... Man, as a spirit, was **begotten and born** of heavenly parents, and reared to maturity in the eternal mansions of the Father, prior to coming upon the earth in a temporal (physical) body" (Joseph F. Smith, "The Origin of Man," *Improvement Era,* Nov. 1909, pp. 78, 80).... The **first spirit born** to our heavenly parents was Jesus Christ.[31] ... Our spirits resemble our heavenly parents although they have resurrected bodies. (*Gospel Principles,* 1986 or older edition, p. 9)

Is the New Testament Apostle John a resurrected being?
Yes, he is.

Then came John the Baptist who had been beheaded by the king in a moment of weakness.... [then] **Peter, James and John now resurrected**. (*The Teachings of Spencer W. Kimball,* [President] Spencer W. Kimball, p. 456)

When a person passes behind the vail, he can only officiate in the spirit-world; but when he is resurrected **he officiates as a resurrected being, and not as a mortal being**. You read in the revelation that Joseph was ordained, as it is written. When he received the Melchizedek Priesthood, he had another revelation. **Peter, James, and John came to him.** (President Brigham Young, May 7, 1861, *Journal of Discourses* 9:88–89)

No, he is not; he is still alive on earth.

John the Beloved **shall live until the Lord comes.** . . . And the Lord said unto me: John, my beloved, what desirest thou? For if you shall ask what you will, it shall be granted unto you. . . . I say unto thee, because thou desirest this **thou shalt tarry until I come in my glory**, and shalt prophesy before nations, kindreds, tongues and people. . . . I will give this power and the keys of this ministry until I come. (April 1829, D&C heading of section 7; 7:1, 3, 7)

Was polygamy practiced by the Mormons between 1835 and 1850?

No, it was not.

Inasmuch as the public mind has been unjustly abused through the fallacy of Dr. [John Cook] Bennett's letters, we make an extract on the subject of marriage, showing the rule of the church on this important matter. The extract is from the Book of Doctrine and Covenants, and is the **only rule** allowed by the church. ". . . Inasmuch as this church of Christ has been reproached with the crime of fornication, and polygamy: we declare that we believe, that one man should have one wife; and one woman, but one husband, except in case of death. . . ." (*Times and Seasons*, [President] Joseph Smith, editor, September 1, 1842, Vol. 3, p. 909; this quote is from section 101:4 in the 1835 D&C)

All of 1835 D&C 101:1–4, which includes the verse just above, is quoted in the article. The article then goes on with: "We have given the above rule of marriage as the **only one** practiced in this church. . . ." (*Times and Seasons,* October 1, 1842, Vol. 3, pp. 939–40)

The names of twelve men are at the end of the article, the notable ones being (Apostle) John Taylor and W. Woodruff. Nineteen women also signed this same article, the most notable being Joseph's first wife, Emma Smith, Eliza R. Snow, and Jane Law, wife of William Law, Joseph Smith's second counselor.[32]

> NOTICE. As we have lately been credibly informed, that an Elder of the Church of Jesus Christ, of Latter-day Saints, by the name of Hiram Brown, has been preaching Polygamy, and other false and corrupt doctrines. . . . This is to notify him and the Church in general, that he has been cut off from the church, for his iniquity; and he is further notified to appear at the Special Conference, on the 6th of April next to make answer to these charges. Joseph Smith, Hyrum Smith,[33] Presidents of said Church. (*Times and Seasons,* [Apostle] John Taylor, editor, February 1, 1844, Vol. 5, p. 423)

> Nauvoo, March 15, 1844 . . . Richard Hewitt has called on me today, to know my views concerning some doctrines that are preached in your place, and states to me that some of your elders say, that a man *having a certain priesthood,* may have as many wives as he pleased, and the doctrince [*sic*] is taught here: I say unto you that man teaches *false doctrine,* **for there is no such doctrine taught here**; neither is there any such thing practiced here. (*Times and Seasons,* [Apostle] John Taylor, editor, March 15, 1844, Vol. 5, p. 474)

In 1850, in France at Boulogne-sur-Mer, Apostle John Taylor entered into a public debate with three ministers. In his own report of the event he said:

> "We are accused here of **polygamy**, and actions the most indelicate, obscene, and disgusting, such that none but a corrupt and depraved heart could have contrived. These things are too outrageous to admit of belief. . . ."[34] In refutation, he read the Church's official attitude toward marriage, from the 1835 Doctrine and

Covenants, Section 101. . . . (*The John Taylor Papers*, Samuel W. Taylor and Raymond W. Taylor, Taylor Trust Publisher, 1984, 1:159. This is also found on page 151 of *The Kingdom or Nothing*, Samuel W. Taylor, Macmillan, 1976. Both references also report that Apostle Taylor had ten wives at the time of the debate.)

Yes, it was practiced.

To put this matter more correctly before you, I here declare that the principle of plural marriage was not first revealed on the 12th day of July, 1843. It was written for the first time on that date, but it had been revealed to the Prophet many years before that, perhaps as early as 1832. . . . It need scarcely be said that the Prophet found no one any more willing to lead out in this matter in righteousness than he was himself. . . . but none excelled, or even matched the courage of the Prophet himself. (Joseph F. Smith, July 7, 1878, *Journal of Discourses* 20:29)

I was baptized when eight years old. I always tried to bear a good name and follow the teachings of my parents and those whose right it was to rule over me. In the spring of forty-four (1844), plural marriage was introduced to me by my parents from Joseph Smith, asking their consent and a request to me to be his wife. Imagine if you can my feelings, to be a plural wife, something I never thought I ever could. I knew nothing of such religion and could not accept it. Neither did I. ("Cordelia Morley Cox Autobiography and Biography of Isaac Morley," holograph, BYU-S,[35] p. 4)

About the first of April, 1843, the Prophet with some of the Twelve and others came to Macedonia to hold a meeting, which was to convene in a large cabinet shop owned by Brother Joseph E. and myself, and as usual he put up at my house. Early on Sunday morning he said, "Come Brother Bennie, let us have a walk." I took his arm and he led the way into a by-place in the edge of the woods surrounded by tall brush and trees. Here, as we sat down upon a log he began to tell me that the Lord had revealed to him that plural or patriarchal marriage was according to His law; and that the Lord had not only revealed it to him but had commanded him to obey it; that he was required to take other wives; and that he wanted my Sister Almira for one of them, and wished me to see and talk to her upon the subject. If a thunderbolt had fallen at my feet I could hardly have been more shocked or amazed. He saw the struggle in my mind and went on to explain. But the shock was too great for me to comprehend anything. . . . (*Benjamin Franklin Johnson, My Life's Review*, Independence, Mo., Zion's,[36] 1947, pp. 93–95)

And now to your question, "How early did the Prophet Joseph practice polygamy?" I hardly know how wisely to reply, **for the truth at times may be better withheld**; but as what I am writing is to be published only under strict scrutiny of the wisest, I will say, that the revelation [D&C 132] to the Church at Nauvoo, July 21, 1843, on the Eternity of the Marriage Covenant and the Law of Plural Marriage, was **not the first** revelation of the law **received and practiced** by the Prophet. In 1835, at Kirtland, I learned from my sister's husband, Lyman R. Sherman, who was close to the Prophet, and received it from him, "that the ancient order of Plural Marriage was again to be practiced by the Church." This at the time, did not impress my mind deeply, although there then lived with his family a neighbor's daughter, Fannie Alger,[37] a very nice and comely young woman about my own age, toward whom not only myself, but every one, seemed partial for the amiability of her character; and it was whispered even then that Joseph loved her. After this, there was some trouble with Jared Carter, and through Brother Sherman I learned that "as he had built himself a new house, he now wanted another wife," which Joseph would not permit. (Benjamin Franklin Johnson, letter to George S. Gibbs, 1903; Church Archives, in E. Dale LeBaron, comp. M.A. thesis, BYU, 1967, p. 334)

In the year 1842, President Joseph Smith sought an interview with me [Lucy Walker], and said: "I have a message for you. I have been commanded of God to take another wife, and you are the woman." My astonishment knew no bounds. This announcement was indeed a thunderbolt to me. He asked me if I believed him to be a prophet of God. "Most assuredly I do," I replied.

(Lyman Omer Littlefield, *Reminiscences of Latter-day Saints*, Logan, Utah: Utah Journal Co., 1888, pp. 46–47)

I now come to that part of my story that you will be most likely interested in, which regards the doctrine taught by the Prophet Joseph Smith in regard to the plural marriage system. At first the doctrine was taught in private, the first I knew about it was in John Higbee's family; he lived close to us and being well acquainted with him and family I discovered he had two wives. The next I noticed when in company with the young folks the girls were calling one another spirituals. Now the reason why the young folks was [*sic*] in advance of me, my work was in the machine shop 22 miles above Nauvoo where I spent nearly all my time. But when at Nauvoo in the winter of 1841 and 1842, I became fully initiated. ("Orange L. Wight Autobiography, 1823–1903," typescript, BYU-A,[38] p. 8)

That Joseph Smith actually was the person who introduced plural marriage into the Church and that he practiced it himself are amply proved by existing facts.

The revelation known as section one hundred thirty-two in the Doctrine and Covenants, which contains the doctrine of celestial marriage and also the practice of plural marriage, was dictated to his scribe, William Clayton, by Joseph Smith on July 12, 1843, a year before the martyrdom of the Prophet. It had been received by the Prophet some years before, and taught to many, but was not reduced to writing until 1843. . . .[39] (Andrew Jenson, Historical Record, Volume VI, pp. 225, 226). (*Evidences and Reconciliations*, Apostle John A. Widtsoe, 1943, p. 340)[40]

Was polygamy practiced with official sanction after the 1890 Manifesto?

No, it was not.

Inasmuch as laws have been enacted by Congress **forbidding plural marriages** which laws have been pronounced constitutional by the court of last resort, I hereby declare my intention to **submit to those laws,** and to use my influence with the members of the Church over which I preside to have them do likewise. (D&C Official Declaration—1, found at the end of the D&C, given by President Wilford Woodruff in 1890)

On October 6, 1890, at a General Conference the full declaration, which includes the above quote, was accepted as authoritative and binding by a unanimous vote. With this the Mormon Church supposedly stopped the practice of polygamy. Today the Church excommunicates any member found practicing it.

PRESIDENT JOSEPH F. SMITH'S MANIFESTO AT APRIL ANNUAL CONFERENCE OF 1904: "Inasmuch as there are numerous reports in circulation that plural marriages have been entered into contrary to the official declaration of President Woodruff, of September 26, 1890, commonly called the Manifesto, which was issued by President Woodruff and adopted by the church at its general conference, October 6, 1890, which forbade any marriages violative of the law of the land, I, Joseph F. Smith, president of the Church of Jesus Christ of Latter-day Saints, do hereby affirm and declare that **no such marriages have been solemnized** with the sanction, consent, or knowledge of the Church of Jesus Christ of Latter-day Saints; and I hereby announce that all such marriages are prohibited, and if any officer or member of the church shall assume to solemnize or enter into any such marriage he will be deemed in transgression against the church, and will be liable to be dealt with according to the rules and regulations thereof and excommunicated therefrom.

(Signed) "JOSEPH F. SMITH," President of the Church of Jesus Christ of Latter-day Saints. (*A Comprehensive History of the Church of Jesus Christ of Latter-day Saints,* B. H. Roberts, 6:401)

It is important to note that in both of the above Manifestos D&C 132 was not rejected or removed from Mormon scriptures; only the practice was ended. The question should also be asked: Why was a second Manifesto even needed? The following references should answer this question.

Yes, it was practiced.

UNITED STATES SENATE
Washington, D. C., Dec. 15, 1899.

Hon. B. H. Roberts,

Dear Sir: In relation to the appointments of John C. Graham as postmaster at Provo [Utah] and Orson Smith as postmaster at Logan [Utah], I remember it was stated in the public press of Utah that protests against these men had been signed and forwarded to the president charging them with living in polygamy, that these men were generally reputed to be polygamists. That afterwards the names of these men were sent to the senate by the president. That while the matter of their confirmation was pending in the senate I was informed by my colleague, Senator Cannon, that affidavits charging them with living in polygamy had been presented to the president, and laid before the committee of the senate or post offices and post boards.

Respectfully,
(Signed) "J. L. RAWLINS"

(*A Comprehensive History of the Church of Jesus Christ of Latter-day Saints,* B. H. Roberts, 6:372–73)

See also Rawlins' *Washington Post* interview, of Nov. 29th, 1898. Thirty-one of the 107 members of the Utah constitutional convention, were in the status of polygamy, and were elected and served without protest from any quarter. (See tabulation of the convention in respect to this matter in proceedings in the Smoot Case, vol. iv, pp. 136–37). (*A Comprehensive History of the Church of Jesus Christ of Latter-day Saints,* B. H. Roberts, 6:373, footnote)

Not until 22 October 1904, did the First Presidency send a letter to [Apostle] John W. Taylor in Canada and to [Apostle] George Teasdale in Mexico informing them of the decision of the First Presidency and Quorum of the Twelve on 26 September to withdraw the authority that "President Woodruff and President Snow, each in his time, authorized some of the Apostles, and perhaps others to perform sealings for time and eternity" in places other than the temples. ("LDS Church Authority and New Plural Marriages, 1890–1904," *Dialogue: A Journal of Mormon Thought*, D. Michael Quinn, Spring 1985, p. 103)[41]

Many of the polygamous marriages took place outside the United States. Apostle John W. Taylor was excommunicated March 1911 for continuing the practice. Many Mormons then and now felt that D&C 132, the new and everlasting covenant, was given for eternity and hence could not be put aside. There are 30,000–50,000 people now practicing polygamy, primarily in the southwest of the United States, basing their lifestyle on past Mormon teachings.

Though the number of plural marriages sanctioned after statehood was small compared to pre-1890 practices, the conflict between **church leaders' endorsement of new polygamy** and their anti-polygamy public assurances began to cause increased difficulties. . . . Joseph F. Smith, who in 1906 would plead guilty to violating the Utah state anti-polygamy law, became sixth president of the church on 17 October 1901. Smith had not only been aware of authorized post-Manifesto marriages as evidenced by his 1890 advice to Byron Harvey Allred, Sr., and his 11 April 1911 telegram to Reed Smoot—but he had personally performed at least one such marriage prior to becoming church president. . . . The more than three thousand pages of testimony from witnesses, including President Joseph F. Smith and several apostles, placed the church in an extremely bad light. Senator-elect Smoot summarized the Mormon position of acute embarrassment in a 22 March 1904 letter: "(W)e have not as a people, at all times, lived strictly to our agreements with the Government, and this lack of sincerity on our part goes farther to condemn us in the eyes of the public men of the nation than the mere fact of a few new polygamy cases . . ." (Smoot to Jesse M. Smith). (*Mormon Polygamy—A History*, Richard S. Van Wagoner, pp. 162, 164, and 167)

Many historians have arrived at a similar conclusion. During the period from 1890 to roughly 1905 top Mormon leaders were saying the practice of polygamy had ended while privately they continued it.[42] This is exactly what happened in Nauvoo, Illinois, in the 1839–1846 period. Were these truly men of God?

Will polygamy ever be denied?
It will never be denied.

> **The only men who become Gods,** even the Sons of God, **are those who enter into polygamy.** . . . Do you think that we shall ever be admitted as a state into the Union without denying the principle of polygamy? If we are not admitted until then, we shall **never** be admitted, these things will be just as the Lord will. (Brigham Young, August 19, 1866, *Journal of Discourses* 11:269)

It was ended in 1890.

> Inasmuch as laws have been enacted by Congress **forbidding plural marriages** which laws have been pronounced constitutional by the court of last resort, I hereby declare my intention to **submit to those laws,** and to use my influence with the members of the Church over which I preside to have them do likewise. (D&C Official Declaration—1, found at the end of the D&C, given by President Wilford Woodruff in 1890)

On October 6, 1890, at a General Conference the full declaration, which the above quote is part of, was accepted as authoritative and binding by a unanimous vote. With this the Mormon Church supposedly stopped (though it was actually tolerated for another ten to fifteen years) the practice of polygamy. Today it excommunicates any member found practicing polygamy. Utah was admitted as a state on January 4, 1896.

The book *Gospel Principles* (1986 and older editions), on pp. 290–91, describes what becoming a God (exaltation) means and what the requirements are. *Nothing* is said about practicing polygamy.

Are children who die resurrected as children or as adults?

They are resurrected as children.

> A question has been asked—"Will mothers have their children in eternity?" Yes! yes! Mothers, you shall have your children; for they shall have eternal life. . . . **But as the child dies, so shall it rise from the dead**, and be for ever living in the learning of God. **It will never grow**; it will still be the child, in the same precise form as it appeared before it died out of its mother's arms, **but possessing all the intelligence of a God** . . . but appear in the same form as when on earth . . . with not one cubit added to [its] stature. (Joseph Smith, at General Conference, April 1844, *Journal of Discourses* 6:10)

The same idea is expressed in *Messages for Exaltation* (published by Deseret Sunday School, copyright by Deseret Sunday School Union, 1976), on page 384. The title page says: "For the Sunday Schools of The Church of Jesus Christ of Latter-day Saints, Gospel Doctrine Class."

They are resurrected as adults.

> All spirits are in adult form. They were adults before their mortal existence, and they are in adult form after death, even if they die as infants or children (see Joseph F. Smith, *Gospel Doctrine*, p. 455). (*Gospel Principles*, p. 278; also see p. 9)

Who is speaking in tongues for?

It is for the benefit of unbelievers.

> TONGUES were given for the purpose of preaching among those whose language is not understood; as on the day of Pentecost, etc., and it is not necessary for tongues to be taught to the Church particularly, for any man that has the Holy Ghost, can speak of the things of God in his own tongue as well as to speak in another; for faith comes not by signs, but by hearing the word of

God. (Instruction from the Prophet Joseph Smith, June 1839, *History of the Church* 3:379)

Sunday, 26—The public meeting of the Saints was at my [Joseph Smith's] house this evening, and after Patriarch Hyrum Smith and Elder Brigham Young had spoken on the principles of faith, and the gifts of the Spirit, I [Joseph Smith] read the 13th chapter of First Corinthians, also a part of the 14th chapter, and remarked that the **gift of tongues was necessary in the Church**; but that if Satan could not speak in tongues, he could not tempt a Dutchman, or any other nation, but the English, for he can tempt the Englishman, for he has tempted me, and I am an Englishman; but **the gift of tongues** by the power of the Holy Ghost in the Church, **is for the benefit of the servants of God *to preach to unbelievers*,** as on the day of Pentecost. When devout men from every nation shall assemble to hear the things of God, let the Elders preach to them in their own mother tongue, whether it is German, French, Spanish or "Irish," or any other, and let those interpret who understand the language spoken, in their own mother tongue, and this is what the Apostle meant in First Corinthians xiv: 27.[43] (December 1841, *History of the Church* 4:485–86)

It is for active Mormons singing and praying with each other and for a Mormon prophet and his wife.

After the dancing had continued about an hour, several excellent songs were sung, in which several of the brethren and sisters joined. The "Upper California" was sung by Erastus Snow, after which I [Brigham Young] called upon **Sister Whitney who stood up and invoking the gift of tongues, sang a beautiful song of Zion in tongues**. The interpretation was given by her husband, Bishop Whitney, and me, it related to our efforts to build this house to the privilege we now have of meeting in it, our departure shortly to the country of the Lamanites [to end up in what is now Salt Lake City], their rejoicing when they hear the gospel and of the ingathering of Israel. (December 1845, *History of the Church* 7:557–58)

This event was in the Nauvoo temple after the death of Joseph Smith.

> . . . my wife . . . waiting for me, and she started to lecture me, saying that I was breaking the Word of Wisdom. She suddenly stopped, and **by the gift of tongues** she gave me a most remarkable and wonderful blessing and promised me that I should live to pay off all my debts, which I did live to do. . . . Unless the **gift of tongues** and the interpretation thereof are enjoyed by the Saints in our day, then we are lacking one of the evidences of the true faith.—YWJ [*Young Women's Journal*], 16:128. (*Gospel Standards*, [President] Heber J. Grant (1870–1945), pp. 11–12, describing a personal experience)

When will the heathen come from the grave?
They will come from the grave in the first resurrection.

> . . . the heathen . . . they who knew no law shall have part **in the resurrection which to us is known as the first**. (*Doctrines of Salvation*, [Apostle] Joseph Fielding Smith, 1:86; also see D&C 45:54)

> As stated, the heathen whose sins are those of ignorance are to come forth with the just **in the first resurrection**. . . .[44] (*Articles of Faith* [the book], [Apostle] James E. Talmage, p. 404)

They will come from the grave in the second resurrection.

> **With certainty** we know only that the righteous will come forth from their graves **first**. (*Evidences and Reconciliations*, [Apostle] John A. Widtsoe, p. 203)

> The bodies of the **Saints will come forth in the first resurrection**, and those of **the unbelieving, etc., in the second, or last**. (*Gospel Doctrine*, [President] Joseph F. Smith, p. 18)

Is the Mormon temple endowment ceremony revelation from God, and has it been changed without membership vote?

It is revelation, and common consent (a vote) is required to change it.

... there is not a man living in the world outside of this Church who could perform the first ceremony in a Temple of the Lord of Hosts, and we would not ourselves have been in possession of that knowledge had God not **revealed** it to us. (Apostle John Taylor, November 1882, *Journal of Discourses* 23:324–25)

The temple ceremony was given by a wise Heavenly Father to help us become more Christlike. The endowment was revealed **by revelation** and can be understood only by revelation. (*Teachings of Ezra Taft Benson*, [President] Ezra Taft Benson, 1988, p. 250)

And **all things shall be done by common consent** in the church, by much prayer and faith, for all things you shall receive by faith. Amen. (July 1830, D&C 26:2)

For **all things must be done in order, and by common consent** in the church, by the prayer of faith. (1830, D&C 28:13)

Behold, mine house is **a house of order**, saith the Lord God, and **not a house of confusion**. (July 1843, D&C 132:8)

It has been changed, and it was not voted on.

The Mormon Church has changed some of its most sacred rituals, eliminating parts of the largely secret ceremonies that have been viewed as offensive to women and to members of some other faiths.... Church officials have confirmed that changes went into effect in mid-April [1990].... "because the temple ceremony is sacred to us we don't speak about it except in the general terms,"[45] said Beverly Campbell, the East Coast director for public communications for the Church.... ("Mormons Drop Rites Opposed by Women," *New York Times*, Peter Steinfels, May 3, 1990, p. 1)

The central temple ceremony in the Mormon Church has been changed to eliminate the woman's vow to obey her husband....

("Mormons Modify Temple Rites," *Los Angeles Times*, John Dart, May 5, 1990, p. F–20)

Most Mormon Church members quoted last month in news stories about revisions in the church's confidential temple ceremony have been summoned for interviews by church officials. . . . one man said he was "reprimanded." . . . another man, who did not wish to be identified, was asked to relinquish his temple privileges, but that matter is still pending, he said. . . .[46] ("Mormons Summon Those Who Spoke to Media of Temple Rites," *Los Angeles Times*, John Dart, June 2, 1990, p. F–12)

The changes in the Temple Endowment Ceremony are seen as a move to bring the secret ceremony closer to mainstream Christianity. The changes are the most drastic revisions of the century, rivaled only by the church's removal at the turn of the century of an oath to avenge the killers of church founder Joseph Smith, according to Mormon insiders. ("Mormon Temple Rite Gets Major Revision," *Arizona Republic*, Kim Sue Lia Perkes, Religion Editor, April 28, 1990, p. A-1)

In this same time period there were also articles in *Time* magazine and *U.S. News and World Report.*

From the first part of this item we can see that the Mormon temple endowment ceremony was allegedly given by revelation from God. It has from its beginning been changed many times (see *Evolution of the Mormon Temple Ceremony: 1842–1990,* Jerald and Sandra Tanner, 1990; and "The Development of the Mormon Temple Endowment Ceremony," by David John Buerger, *Dialogue, A Journal of Mormon Thought*, Vol. 20, No. 4, Winter 1987, pp. 33–76). The most recent change was in April 1990. There is no record of any membership vote taken to approve these changes, the same as required to add to or subtract from the *standard works* (the four Mormon scriptures). If it were revelation from God, why would it have to be changed in **any way** and why is it secret? Luke 8:17 says: "Nothing is secret, that shall not be made manifest; neither any thing hid, that shall not be known and come abroad." And in 1 Corinthians 14:33 we read: "**God is not the author of confusion**, but of peace, as in all churches of the saints."

How old is a deacon?[47]
He is married with children.

> When you have got your Bishop, he needs assistants, and **he ordains Counsellors, Priests, Teachers, and Deacons**, and calls them to help him; and he wishes **men** of his own heart and hand to do this. Says he, "I dare not even call a man to be a Deacon, to assist me in my calling, **unless he has a family.**" **It is not the business of an ignorant young man**, of no experience in family matters, to inquire into the circumstances of families, and know the wants of every person. Some may want medicine and nourishment, and to be looked after, and **it is not the business of boys to do this; but select a man who has got a family to be a Deacon, whose wife can go with him, and assist him in administering to the needy in the ward**. . . . I will venture to say the view I take of the matter **is not to be disputed or disproved by Scripture or reason**. (President Brigham Young, at General Conference, October 6, 1854, *Journal of Discourses* 2:89)[48]

> Let the deacons be the **husbands of one wife, ruling their children** and their **own houses** well. (1 Timothy 3:12)

He is twelve years old.

> When **a boy** has been baptized and confirmed a member of the Church and is worthy, **he may be ordained to the office of deacon when he is twelve years old**. . . . A worthy boy may be ordained a teacher when he is fourteen years old or older. (*Gospel Principles*, p. 81)

Few or none of these young men are married, have children, or have their own household at that age. No Mormon scripture supports this age for deacons.

Did Jesus Christ atone for our sins in the garden or on the cross?

In the Garden of Gethsemane Jesus Christ atoned for our sins.

In the Garden of Gethsemane, Christ atoned for the sins of all mankind. . . . Even his crucifixion would not surpass the bitter anguish that he suffered in Gethsemane. (*Gospel Principles,* 1978, 1979, 1981, 1985, 1986, p. 58, item #7; also see p. 61.)

In the Garden of Gethsemane, when he took upon himself the sins of the world, he sweat "great drops of blood" (Luke 22:44), and his suffering caused him "to bleed at every pore." (D&C 19:118; *Doctrinal New Testament Commentary,* [Apostle] Bruce R. McConkie, Vol. 3, p. 223)

According to Luke 22:43–44, Jesus' anguish was so deep that "his sweat was as it were great drops of blood falling down to the ground," an observation that harmonizes with the view that **Jesus suffered most in Gethsemane** during his Atonement. . . . Modern LDS leaders have emphasized that Jesus' **most challenging experience came in Gethsemane.** Speaking in a general conference of the Church in 1982, Marion G. Romney, a member of the First Presidency, observed that Jesus suffered "the pains of all men, which he did, **principally, in Gethsemane, the scene of his great agony**" (*Ensign* 12:6 [May 1982]). Church President Ezra Taft Benson wrote that "**it was in Gethsemane that Jesus took on Himself the sins of the world, in Gethsemane** that His pain was equivalent to the cumulative burden of all men, **in Gethsemane** that He descended below all things so that all could repent and come to Him" (Benson, p. 7). (*Encyclopedia of Mormonism,* Vol. 2, under "Gethsemane")

This thinking is evidenced in the fact that no LDS church or temple uses the cross as a symbol.

On the cross Jesus Christ atoned for our sins.

It, therefore, became necessary for the Father to send his Only Begotten Son, who was free from sin, to atone for our sins as well as for Adam's transgression, which justice demanded should be done. He accordingly offered himself a sacrifice for sins, and **through his death upon the cross took upon himself both Adam's transgression and our individual sins,** thereby redeeming us from the fall, and from our sins, on condition of repentance. (*Doctrines of Salvation,* Joseph Fielding Smith Jr., 1:126)

With all my heart and the fervency of my soul, I lift up my voice in testimony today as a special witness and declare that God does live. Jesus is his Son the Only Begotten of the Father in the flesh. He is our Redeemer; he is our Mediator with the Father. He it was **who died on the cross to atone for our sins.** ([Apostle] Thomas S. Monson, *Conference Report,* April 1966, p. 63)

At the commencement of what we term the Christian dispensation, the Lord had a most stupendous work to perform; therefore Christ came into the world, and **died the ignominious death of the cross, to atone for the sins of the world**, established his kingdom, and chose many disciples. (Author not identified, probably by the editor, Apostle John Taylor, *Times and Seasons* 5:504 [April 15, 1844])

Even the Book of Mormon says the Lord's **death** was for all men.

. . . for it behooveth the great Creator that he suffereth himself to become subject unto man in the flesh, and **die for all men**, that all men might become subject unto him. (2 Nephi 9:5)

And I, Nephi, saw that he was lifted up **upon the cross and slain for the sins of the world**. (1 Nephi 11:33)

And my Father sent me **that I might be lifted up upon the cross; and after that I had been lifted up upon the cross**, that I might draw all men unto me, that as I have been lifted up by men even so should men be lifted up by the Father, to stand before me, to be judged of their works, whether they be good or whether they be evil. (3 Nephi 27:14)

The Book of Mormon does not mention the Garden of Gethsemane.

The Bible is clear that the Lord's suffering was part of his atonement.

Forasmuch then as **Christ hath suffered for us** in the flesh, arm yourselves likewise with the same mind: for he that hath suffered in the flesh hath ceased from sin. (1 Peter 4:1)

It is also clear that the Lord's death **on the cross** and his resurrection were significantly more important than his suffering in Gethsemane. This is also consistent with the offering the people of Israel performed in their Jerusalem temple. The death of the animal and the shedding of its blood were critical in the ceremony, not the prior suffering of the animal.

If his offering be a burnt sacrifice of the herd, let him offer a male without blemish: he shall offer it of his own voluntary will at the door of the tabernacle of the congregation before the Lord. And he shall put his hand upon the head of the burnt offering; and it shall be accepted for him to make **atonement for him**. And he **shall kill the bullock** before the LORD: and the priests, Aaron's sons, shall bring the blood, and sprinkle the blood round about upon the altar that is by the door of the tabernacle of the congregation. (Leviticus 1:3-5)

And Aaron shall bring the bullock of the sin offering, which is for himself, and shall make an atonement for himself, and for his house, and **shall kill the bullock** of the sin offering which is for himself. (Leviticus 16:11)

The suffering of the animal is not mentioned once.

How Might Mormons Respond?

As we cautioned earlier, some Mormons may reject all of the above examples, saying: "Anything said by any of the top Mormon leaders can be ignored if it is not in the *standard works*. Anything that is not in the *standard works* is just someone's opinion, no matter what the source, so all you are doing is comparing personal opinions." If a Mormon responds to you in this way, point out that this position is *his* or *her* opinion, as such an idea is not found in the *standard works* either. Then ask: "Whose opinion is more important relative to Church teachings—yours or that of the Prophet of the Church?" (The answer is clearly, "the opinion of the Prophet.") It may also prove helpful to review the statements of the top Mormon leaders given at the start of this chapter. In addition, point out that the past practice of the Mormon Church has *clearly* shown that a teaching need not be found in the *standard works* to be taught to the membership and practiced by the top leadership and members.

The chief example to mention is the practice of polygamy from the early 1830s to 1890. It was not in scripture until 1876 and not voted on by Mormon Church membership until 1880. In fact, existing Mormon scripture (see Jacob 1:15; 2:24; Mosiah 11:2; Ether 10:35; 1835 D&C 101:4, p. 251, which was in place from 1830 to 1876) *rejected* polygamy. It was called a wicked practice and an abomination in God's sight.

It is clear that the excuse "Mormon leaders were just expressing their own opinions" cannot be used to cancel out the evidence presented in this chapter or to diminish its significance.

At this point, ask the Mormon whether he or she feels it is wise to follow the teachings of the top Mormon leaders. Will their teachings lead him or her to God's true gospel message?

CHANGES IN THE BOOK OF MORMON

The Book of Mormon is one of the four canonized scriptures used by the Mormon Church.[1] First note what top Mormon leaders have said about the reliability of this book.

The Reliability of the Book of Mormon

The Book of Mormon is the most correct book.

President Joseph Smith on Sunday, November 28, 1841, said:

> I told the brethren that the Book of Mormon was the **most correct** of any book on earth, and the **keystone** of our religion, and a man would get nearer to God by abiding by its precepts, than **any other book**. (*History of the Church* 4:461)

The Book of Mormon is not corrupted by religionists.

Unlike the Bible,[2] which passed through generations of copyists, translators, and **corrupt religionists who tampered with the text**, the Book of Mormon came from writer to reader in just one inspired step of translation. (President Ezra Taft Benson, *Ensign*, January 1992, p. 5)

More will be saved by the Book of Mormon than by the Bible.

Then Apostle and later President Ezra Taft Benson quotes Apostle Bruce R. McConkie as follows:

> "Men can get nearer to the Lord, can have more of the spirit of conversion and conformity in their hearts, can gain a better understanding of the doctrines of salvation **through the Book of Mormon than they can through the Bible**. . . . there will be more people saved in the kingdom of God—ten thousand times over—because of the Book of Mormon than there will be because of the Bible." *(Ensign,* November 1984, p. 7)

The Book of Mormon has practically all religious truths.

> Practically all of the religious truths taught and practiced in **any Gospel dispensation** are given in a clear and forceful way in the *Book of Mormon.* In fact, many of the principles are presented more clearly in that record than in any of the other ancient scriptures. (*The Gospel Through the Ages*, Milton R. Hunter of the First Council of the Seventy, 1945, p. 86)

The printer was not friendly, no original thought was changed, all changes were in harmony with the original text.

Apostle Joseph Fielding Smith said in answer to a question about changes to the Book of Mormon:

> In the case of the Book of Mormon, your attention is called to the fact that the publisher of it was unfriendly to the Church. It required the utmost care on that account. Being unfriendly, it would have been a natural thing for him to permit some errors to appear. A careful check of the list of changes submitted by these critics shows there is **not one change** or **addition** that is not in **full harmony** with the original text. Changes have been made in punctuation and a few other minor matters that needed correction, **but never has any alteration or addition changed a single original thought**. As it appears to us, the **changes mentioned are**

such that make the text clearer and indicate that they were omit-ted. I am sure that the mistakes or omissions in the first edition were in large measure the fault of the compositor of the printer. (*Answers to Gospel Questions* 2:200)

The printer was unfriendly, few changes were made, most of them typographical.

In a talk at the October 1961 General Conference, Apostle Joseph Fielding Smith said:

> During the past week or two I have received a number of letters from different parts of the United States written by people, some of whom at least are a little concerned because they have been approached by enemies of the Church and enemies of the Book of Mormon, who had made the statement that there have been one or two or more thousand changes in the Book of Mormon since the first edition was published. Well, of course, THERE IS **NO TRUTH** IN THAT STATEMENT.
>
> It is true that when the Book of Mormon was printed, the printer was a man who was unfriendly. The publication of the book was done under adverse circumstances, and **there were a few errors**, most typographical—conditions that arise in most any book that is being published—but there was **not one** thing in the Book of Mormon or in the second edition or any other edi-tion since that **in any way** contradicts the first edition, and such CHANGES as were made were made BY THE PROPHET JOSEPH SMITH because under those adverse conditions, the Book of Mormon was published. But there was **no change of doctrine**.
>
> Now, those SONS OF BELIAL who circulate these reports ev-idently know better. I will not use THE WORD that is in my mind. (*Improvement Era*, December 1961, pp. 924–25)

A comparison of a first edition (1830) of the Book of Mor-mon with the present edition will show that many of the changes were indeed relatively minor, as Mr. Smith said, but many were not. A detailed analysis will show that almost 4,000 changes were made, and a number of them were significant. The original thought *was* changed, and the changes were *not* in full harmony with the original text. A full analysis has already been completed in the book *3,913 Changes in the Book of Mormon* by Jerald and Sandra Tanner. They photocopied every page in the first edition of the Book of Mormon and clearly marked the differences between it and the 1964 edition. Some of the changes are illustrated below. The Tanners' book, on page 17 of their text and page 26 of the photocopy of the Book of Mormon, discusses the change made to what is now 1 Nephi 11:32 (chapter 3, p. 26 of the original Book of Mormon). Using a photocopy of the original handwritten manuscript, they clearly demonstrate that the original manuscript and the first edition agreed. The printer of the first edition did not introduce changes that needed correction. It was the changes introduced *later* by the LDS Church that were significantly different from the original handwritten manuscript.

Many of the changes made to the original edition of the Book of Mormon were corrections in spelling, grammar, and arranging the book into chapter and verse. None of these types of changes will be included in the few examples given here. But if several of the witnesses to the events leading to the publishing of the Book of Mormon are correct, then one has to wonder why even these changes were needed.

How Was the Book of Mormon Translated?

David Whitmer, one of the three witnesses whose statement is found in the Introduction of the Book of Mormon, had this to say concerning how the Book of Mormon was translated from the gold plates:

> I will now give you a description of the manner in which the Book of Mormon was translated. Joseph Smith would put the seer stone into a hat, and put his face in the hat, drawing it closely around his face to exclude the light; and in the darkness the spir-

itual light would shine. A piece of something resembling parchment would appear, and on that appeared the writing. One character at a time would appear, and under it was the interpretation in English. Brother Joseph would read off the English to Oliver Cowdery, who was his principal scribe, and when it was written down and repeated to Brother Joseph to see if it was correct, then it would disappear, and another character with the interpretation would appear. Thus the Book of Mormon was translated by the gift and power of God, and not by any power of man. (*An Address to All Believers in Christ,* David Whitmer, Richmond, Mo., 1887, p. 12)

This same quote is used and accepted by Elder Russell M. Nelson of the Quorum of the Twelve Apostles in his article "A Treasured Testament" in the July 1993 *Ensign,* page 62.

Deward [*sic* Edward?] Stevenson had this to say:

He [Martin Harris] also stated that the Prophet translated a portion of the Book of Mormon with a seerstone in his possession. The stone was placed in a hat that was used for that purpose, and with the aid of this seerstone the Prophet would read sentence by sentence as Martin wrote, and if he made any mistake the sentence would remain before the Prophet until corrected, when another sentence would appear. When they became weary, as it was confining work to translate from the plates of gold, they would go down to the river and throw stones into the water for exercise. Martin on one occasion picked up a stone resembling the one with which they were translating, and on resuming their work, Martin placed the false stone in the hat. He said that the Prophet looked quietly for a long time, when he raised his head and said: "Martin, what on earth is the matter, all is dark as Egypt." Martin smiled and the seer discovered that the wrong stone was placed in the hat. When he asked Martin why he had done so he replied, to stop the mouths of fools who had declared that the Prophet knew by heart all that he told him to write, and did not see by the seerstone; when the true stone was placed in the hat, the translation was resumed, as usual. ("Witnesses," *Selections from Autobiography of Deward* [*sic,* Edward?] *Stevenson,*

1820–1897, Edward Stevenson, MS 48, 1886, pp. 389–90; Joseph Grant Stevenson, ed., Provo: Stevenson's Genealogical Center, 1986; from the *LDS Historical Library,* Infobase, Inc., 1992, 1st edition, 3/92)

Emma Smith, the wife of Joseph Smith, had a similar observation to share with her son Joseph Smith III when she said: "In writing for your father I frequently wrote day after day, often sitting at the table close by him, he sitting with his face buried in his hat, with the stone in it . . ." (*Saints' Herald,* 1 October 1879, pp. 289–90; also in *History of the Re-organized Church of Jesus Christ of Latter Day Saints,* Independence, Mo.: Herald House, 1952, p. 356, as quoted in "The Translation of the Book of Mormon," *The Word of God,* James E. Lancaster, Signature Books, 1990, pp. 98–99)

"The Translation of the Book of Mormon" also reports on page 103 that Oliver Cowdery's widow, Elizabeth (David Whitmer's sister), along with Michael Morse (Emma Smith's brother-in-law), also supported the reports of Emma Smith and David Whitmer. This same article, on page 105, arrives at the conclusion that only the first 116 pages of the translation, the ones lost by Martin Harris,[3] were translated by the use of the Urim and Thummim,[4] and that the rest were done by means of the seer stone, as described above.

If the Book of Mormon were truly the product of such divinely guided translation work, it would seem reasonable to expect that no changes at all should be found in subsequent editions. With this in mind, consider the changes documented in the next few pages.

Some Changes

The examples of changes in Mormon scriptures given below are just a sample of the many that could be given.

Original 1830 edition

And he said unto me: Behold, the virgin whom thou seest is the mother of God, after the manner of the flesh. (1 Nephi, chapter 3, p. 25)

Present edition

And he said unto me: Behold, the virgin whom thou seest is the mother of **the Son of** God, after the manner of the flesh. (1 Nephi 11:18)

Original 1830 edition

And the angel said unto me: Behold the Lamb of God, yea, even the Eternal Father! Knowest thou the meaning of the tree which thy father saw? (1 Nephi, chapter 3, p. 25)

Present edition

And the angel said unto me: Behold the Lamb of God, yea, even **the Son of** the Eternal Father! Knowest thou the meaning of the tree which thy father saw? (1 Nephi 11:21)

Original 1830 edition

And it came to pass that the angel spake unto me again, saying: Look! And I looked and beheld the Lamb of God, that he was taken by the people; yea, the everlasting God was judged of the world; and I saw and bear record. (1 Nephi, chapter 3, p. 26)

Present edition

And it came to pass that the angel spake unto me again, saying: Look! And I looked and beheld the Lamb of God, that he was taken by the people; yea, **the Son of** the everlasting God was judged of the world; and I saw and bear record. (1 Nephi 11:32)

Original 1830 edition

> And the angel spake unto me, saying: These last records, which thou hast seen among the Gentiles, shall establish the truth of the first, which are of the twelve apostles of the Lamb, and shall make known the plain and precious things which have been taken away from them; and shall make known to all kindred, tongues, and people, that the Lamb of God is the Eternal Father, and the Savior of the world; and that all men must come unto him, or they cannot be saved. (1 Nephi, chapter 3, p. 32)

Present edition

> And the angel spake unto me, saying: These last records, which thou hast seen among the Gentiles, shall establish the truth of the first, which are of the twelve apostles of the Lamb, and shall make known the plain and precious things which have been taken away from them; and shall make known to all kindred, tongues, and people, that the Lamb of God is **the Son of** the Eternal Father,[5] and the Savior of the world; and that all men must come unto him, or they cannot be saved. (1 Nephi 13:40)

Note that in the verses just quoted the addition of the words "the Son of" in later editions significantly changes the meaning. Within present-day Mormon doctrine the Father, the Son, and the Holy Ghost are each distinct and separate beings (*Teachings of the Prophet Joseph Smith*, p. 370). The Father has a body of flesh and bones, and the Son has a body of flesh and bones. The Father is not the Son and the Son is not the Father in present-day Mormon doctrine. Apostle Bruce R. McConkie in his book *Mormon Doctrine*, page 317, says: "By definition, God (generally meaning the Father) is the one supreme and absolute Being; the ultimate source of the universe. . . ." On page 278 he says: "God the Eternal Father, our Father in Heaven, is an exalted, perfected, and glorified Personage. . . . All men, Christ included, were born as his children in pre-existence." The Mormon temple endowment ceremony agrees. In the creation scenes, the Father gives direction to the Son. The Father is clearly in charge and above the Son. The Son is not the Father. The phrase "the Son of" had to be inserted into the verses to make them consistent with the new Mormon doctrine Joseph Smith started teaching in the late 1830s and early 1840s.

Original 1830 edition

> And then shall they rejoice; for they shall know that it is a blessing unto them from the hand of God; and their scales of darkness shall begin to fall from their eyes; and many generations shall not pass away among them, save they shall be a white and delightsome people. (2 Nephi, chapter 12, p. 117)

Present edition

> And then shall they rejoice; for they shall know that it is a blessing unto them from the hand of God; and their scales of darkness shall begin to fall from their eyes; and many generations shall not pass away among them, save they shall be a **pure** and delightsome people. (2 Nephi 30:6)

Note that "white" has been changed to "pure." This changes the meaning of the verse. Something can be pure and not be white, or can be white and not be pure. While white is a color that is sometimes used to indicate purity, as in a wedding dress, the context does not indicate that usage here, but refers to skin color.

Original 1830 edition

> And now Limhi was again filled with joy in learning from the mouth of Ammon that king Benjamin had a gift from God, whereby he could interpret such engravings; yea, and Ammon also did rejoice. (Mosiah, chapter 9, p. 200)

Present edition

And now Limhi was again filled with joy in learning from the mouth of Ammon that king **Mosiah** had a gift from God, whereby he could interpret such engravings; yea, and Ammon also did rejoice. (Mosiah 21:28)

Original 1830 edition

And the Lord commanded the brother of Jared to go down out of the mount from the presence of the Lord, and write the things which he had seen; and they were forbidden to come unto the children of men until after that he should be lifted up upon the cross; and for this cause did king Benjamin keep them, that they should not come unto the world until after Christ should show himself unto his people. (Ether, chapter 1, p. 546)

Present edition

And the Lord commanded the brother of Jared to go down out of the mount from the presence of the Lord, and write the things which he had seen; and they were forbidden to come unto the children of men until after that he should be lifted up upon the cross; and for this cause did king **Mosiah** keep them, that they should not come unto the world until after Christ should show himself unto his people. (Ether 4:1)

King Mosiah is a totally different person than king Benjamin, so these alterations change the meaning of the verse.

Original 1830 edition

And now, I will speak unto you concerning those twenty-four plates, that ye keep them, that the mysteries and the works of darkness, and their secret works, or the secret works of those people who have been destroyed, may be made manifest unto this people; yea, all their murders, and robbings, and their plunderings, and all their wickedness and abominations, may be made manifest unto this people; yea, and that ye preserve these directors. (Alma, chapter 17, p. 328)

Present edition

And now, I will speak unto you concerning those twenty-four plates, that ye keep them, that the mysteries and the works of darkness, and their secret works, or the secret works of those people who have been destroyed, may be made manifest unto this people; yea, all their murders, and robbings, and their plunderings, and all their wickedness and abominations, may be made manifest unto this people; yea, and that ye preserve these **interpreters**. (Alma 37:21)

Elsewhere the Book of Mormon uses the expression "interpreters" (also called Urim and Thummim) to denote a device enabling one to read an unknown language; the "directors" (also called Liahona) are a compass-like device, according to Ether 4:5; Mosiah 8:13; and D&C 17:1 with 1 Nephi 16:10. So the alteration at Alma 37:21 changes the meaning of the verse.

It might prove beneficial at this point for you to review what top Mormon leaders said about Book of Mormon changes. Were the leaders correct?

DOCTRINE AND COVENANTS COMPARED TO THE *BOOK OF COMMANDMENTS*

The Doctrine and Covenants is one of the four canonized scriptures of the Mormon Church. The first authorized collection of the revelations God allegedly gave Joseph Smith was published in 1833 under the title *Book of Commandments*. The first update of this book was published in 1835 as the Doctrine and Covenants, the name now used. Be sure to see Appendix 1 for more information on both of these. In the comparisons below note that each section is introduced by a brief historical heading. Note the date of each revelation, the people involved, the subject, and the place where the revelation was received. But first let us see what LDS leaders and scriptures have said.

Claims by Leaders and Scriptures

There is no need for eliminating, changing, or adjusting any part.

Inspiration is discovered in the fact that each part, as it was revealed, dovetailed perfectly with what had come before. **There was no need for eliminating, changing, or adjusting any part to make it fit**; but each new revelation on doctrine and priesthood fitted in its place perfectly to complete the whole structure, as it had been prepared by the Master Builder. (*Doctrines of Salvation,* [Apostle] Joseph Fielding Smith, 1:170)

The Lord played a role in the revelations Joseph Smith received; they are true and faithful.

> . . . for verily the voice of the Lord is unto all men. . . . for I the Lord have commanded them. Behold, this is mine authority, and the authority of my servants, and **my Preface** unto the Book of my Commandments, **which I have given them** to publish unto you, O inhabitants of the earth. . . . Behold I am God and have spoken it: **these commandments are of me**, and were given unto my servants in their weakness, after the manner of their language. . . . [that they] might have power to lay the foundation of this church, and to bring it forth out of obscurity, and out of darkness, the only true and living church upon the face of the whole earth. . . . **Search these commandments for they are true and faithful**. . . . (*Book of Commandments,* chapter 1, verses 1, 2, 5, and 7. This also can be found in the present-day D&C 1:2, 5, 6, 30, and 37.)

Notice the claims that the revelations in the Doctrine and Covenants are "true and faithful" and from the Lord, from God.

President Ezra Taft Benson said:

> The Author of the Doctrine and Covenants is the Lord Jesus Christ, through the instrumentality of the Prophet Joseph Smith. . . . The introduction of the preface includes an invitation to all mankind, especially members of his Church, to heed the revelations, for the "voice of warning" shall be unto all people. (v. 4 [D&C 1:4]) (*Ensign,* January 1993, p. 2)

The Book of Commandments *is considered true.*

> In the second day's proceedings of the conference [November 2, 1831] it is recorded; "The revelation of last evening read by the moderator (this was Oliver Cowdery). The brethren then arose in turn and bore witness to the **truth of the Book of Commandments**, after which Brother **Joseph Smith, Jun.**, arose and expressed his feelings and gratitude concerning the commandments

and preface received yesterday." (Far West Record, p. 16) (*History of the Church* 1:222, footnote)

With this kind of testimony and with the previous declaration that Jesus Christ is allegedly the author of the *Book of Commandments,* it seems reasonable to expect that there would be no need for corrections or revisions in a later edition. Is that the case? In answering this question while reading the comparisons below, also keep in mind the discussions in the preface and chapter 2 of this book.

Some Changes

1833 B of C

> *A Revelation given to Joseph and Oliver, in Harmony, Pennsylvania, April, 1829, when they desired to know whether John, the beloved disciple, tarried on earth. Translated from parchment written and hid up by himself.*
>
> 1 And the Lord said unto me: John, my beloved, what desirest thou? and I said Lord, give unto me power that I may bring souls unto thee.–And the Lord said unto me: Verily, verily, I say unto thee, because thou desirest this thou shalt tarry until I come in my glory:
>
> 2 And for this cause the Lord said unto Peter: If I will that he tarry till I come, what is that to thee? For he desired of me that he might bring souls unto me, but thou desirest that thou mightest speedily come unto me in my kingdom: I say unto thee, Peter, this was a good desire; but my beloved has undertaken a greater work.
>
> 3 Verily I say unto you, ye shall both have according to your desires, for ye both joy in that which ye have desired. (chapter 6, p. 18)

Present edition D&C

> *Revelation given to Joseph Smith the Prophet and Oliver Cowdery, at Harmony, Pennsylvania, April 1829, when they inquired through*

the Urim and Thummim as to whether John, the beloved disciple, tarried in the flesh or had died. The revelation is a translated version of the record made on parchment by John and hidden up by himself, HC 1:35–36.

1 AND the Lord said unto me: John, my beloved, what desirest thou? **For if you shall ask what you will, it shall be granted unto you.**

2 **And I said unto him: Lord, give unto me power over death,** that I may live and bring souls unto thee.

3 And the Lord said unto me: Verily, verily, I say unto thee, because thou desirest this thou shalt tarry until I come in my glory, **and shalt prophesy before nations, kindred, tongues and people.**

4 And for this cause the Lord said unto Peter: If I will that he tarry till I come, what is that to thee? For he desired of me that he might bring souls unto me, but thou desirest that thou mightest speedily come unto me in my kingdom.

5 I say unto thee, Peter, this was a good desire; but my beloved has **desired that he might do more, or a greater work yet among men than what he has before done.**

6 **Yea, he has** undertaken a greater work; **therefore I will make him as flaming fire and a ministering angel; he shall minister for those who shall be heirs of salvation who dwell on the earth.**

7 **And I will make thee to minister for him and for thy brother James; and unto you three I will give this power and the keys of this ministry until I come.**[1]

8 Verily I say unto you, ye shall both have according to your desires, for ye both joy in that which ye have desired. (D&C 7:1–8. This is the same as section 33 in the 1835 D&C, but note that the verse numbering is different.)

Note that in the historical statements each version claims to be a translation from a parchment hidden by the Apostle John (the New Testament John). The full revelation is given in both cases, so one has to wonder how the earlier "translation" published in 1833 in the *Book of Commandments* could leave so much out when translating the same parchment. If, on the other hand, the additional material is from a new revelation to Joseph Smith, why is there not a new date and a comment to that effect?

1833 B of C

A Revelation given to Joseph and Martin, in Harmony, Pennsylvania, March, 1829, when Martin desired of the Lord to know whether Joseph had, in his possession, the record of the Nephites.

2 And now, behold, this you shall say unto him:—I the Lord am God, and I have given these things unto my servant Joseph, and I have commanded him that he should stand as a witness of these things, nevertheless I have caused him that he should enter into a covenant with me, that he should not show them except I commanded him, and he has no power over them except I grant it unto him; and he has a **gift to translate the book**, and I have commanded him **that he shall pretend to no other gift**, for I will grant him **no other gift**. (chapter 4, p. 10)

Present edition D&C

Revelation given through Joseph Smith the Prophet, at Harmony, Pennsylvania, March 1829, at the request of Martin Harris, HC 1:28–31.

2 And now, behold, this shall you say unto him—**he who spake unto you, said unto you**: I, the Lord, am God, and have given these things unto you, my servant Joseph **Smith, Jun.**, and have commanded you that you should stand as a witness of these things;

3 And I have caused you that you should enter into a covenant with me, that you should not show them except to those persons to whom I commanded you; and you have no power over them except I grant it unto you.

4 **And you** have a gift to translate the plates; **and this is the first gift that I bestowed upon you**; and I have commanded that **you should** pretend to no other gift **until my purpose is fulfilled in this**; for I will grant unto you no other gift **until it is finished**. (D&C 5:2–4. This is part of section 32:1 in the 1835 D&C.)

(Photostats reproduced at the end of this chapter show more clearly the changes made.)

Note that the 1833 version says Joseph Smith has a gift, and he shall pretend to no other gift, and no other gift *will be granted.* Period! (The context does not change the meaning at all.) Two years later the 1835 D&C (and the present edition of the D&C) says that translating the plates is the *first gift,* and that no other gift will be given *until* the Lord's purpose is fulfilled, *until* the translation is finished. This is a significantly different message!

Code Names in the Early Mormon Scriptures

Code names were used in some early Mormon scripture verses in place of actual names of people and places. Even Jesus Christ had other names. Except for the Lord's name, only the code names were used in certain sections of the 1835 D&C. Sometime later, newer editions of the D&C used the code names and real names together. Finally, in the 1981 edition the code names were dropped entirely.[2] By whose authority were code names used? By men, according to Apostle Orson Pratt. He reported that the code names were *not* in the original manuscript revelations but were added before printing because of "persecution" in Kirtland[3] and regions nearby (*Journal of Discourses* 16:156). Jesus Christ is allegedly the source of the D&C (see D&C 1:2–6). Couldn't he in 1832 to 1834, when the revelations were allegedly given, anticipate that in 1835 code names would have to be used due to "persecution"? (It then took over 145 years to return the wording back to the original revelation.)

The present edition of the D&C 1:2 and the 1835 D&C 1:1 both say, "the voice of the Lord is unto **all men**." In Luke 8:17 the Lord said, "Nothing is secret . . . neither any thing hid." How could the 1835 D&C be unto *all* men if codes were used to hide information?

Some examples of these code names are in the following:

> . . . I have commanded you, saith your Redeemer, even the Son Ahman. . . . (1835 D&C 75:4, p. 205. The same wording is in 78:20 in the 1968 D&C.)

> . . . saith Son Ahman; or, in other words, Alphus; or, in other words, Omegus; even Jesus Christ your Lord. . . . (1835 D&C 95:3, p. 234. The same wording is in 1968 D&C 95:17.)

> . . . write speedily unto Cainhannoch. . . . (1835 D&C 98:13, p. 245)

From 104:81 in the 1968 edition we learn that Cainhannoch is New York. It says:

> . . . write speedily unto Cainhannoch (New York). . . .

> . . . let my servant Pelagoram have . . . and the lot of Tahhanes . . . my servant Mahemson . . . my servant Zombre . . . my servant Gazelam . . . my servant Shederlaomach . . . my servant Olihah . . . have the Lane-shine-house. . . . (1835 D&C 98:3–5, pp. 241–42)

From 104:20–29 in the 1968 edition we learn that Pelagoram is Sidney Rigdon; Tahhanes is the tannery; Mahemson is Martin Harris; Zombre is John Johnson; Gazelam is Joseph Smith, Jr.; Shederlaomach is Frederick G. Williams; Olihah is Oliver Cowdery; Lane-shine-house is the printing office.

There are many more instances that could be mentioned. This subject is covered in *History of the Church* 1:256, 268, 352, 363; 2:56, 57, 60 and *Journal of Discourses* 16:156.

Changes and the Mormon Priesthood

One of the unique aspects of the Mormon Church is the claimed restoration of the Aaronic and Melchizedek Priesthoods, one or the other of which is held by most male members twelve years and older. They are taught and believe that this is their authority to act in the name of God.[4] The historical foundation for the bestowal of the priesthoods is on shaky ground. As noted below, the prefaces of the same revelation in the various editions (D&C) contradict each other, and the verses pertaining to priesthood ordination were added later.

1833 B of C

A Commandment to the church of Christ, given in Harmony, Pennsylvania, September 4, 1830,
LISTEN to the voice of Jesus Christ, your Lord, your God, and your Redeemer, whose word is quick and powerful.

2 For, behold, I say unto you, that it mattereth not what ye shall eat or what ye shall drink when ye partake of the sacrament, if it so be that ye do it with an eye single to my glory;

3 Remembering unto the Father my body which was laid down for you, and my blood which was shed for the remission of your sins:

4 Wherefore, a commandment I give unto you, that you shall not purchase wine, neither strong drink of your enemies:

5 Wherefore, you shall partake of none, except it is made new among you, yea, in this my Father's kingdom which shall be built up on the earth.

6 Behold this is wisdom in me, wherefore, marvel not, for the hour cometh that I will drink of the fruit of the vine with you, on the earth, and with all those whom my Father hath given me out of the world:

7 Wherefore, lift up your hearts and rejoice, and gird up your loins, and be faithful until I come—even so. Amen. (chapter 28:1–7, p. 60)

1835 D&C

Revelation given September, 1830.
1 Listen to the voice of Jesus Christ, your Lord, your God, and your Redeemer, whose word is quick and powerful. For, behold,

I say unto you, that it mattereth not what ye shall eat or what ye shall drink when ye partake of the sacrament, if it so be that ye do it with an eye single to my glory—remembering unto the Father my body which was laid down for you, and my blood which was shed for the remission of your sins. Wherefore, a commandment I give unto you, that you shall not purchase wine neither strong drink of your enemies; Wherefore, you shall partake of none except it is made new among you; yea, in this my Father's kingdom which shall be built up on the earth.

2 Behold, this is wisdom in me; wherefore, marvel not, for the hour cometh that I will drink of the fruit of the vine with you on the earth, and with **Moroni, whom I have sent unto you to reveal the Book of Mormon, containing the fulness of my everlasting gospel, to whom I have committed the keys of the record of the stick of Ephraim; And also with Elias, to whom I have committed the keys of bringing to pass the restoration of all things spoken by the mouth of all the holy prophets since the world began, concerning the last days; And also John the son of Zacharias, which Zacharias he (Elias) visited and gave promise that he should have a son, and his name should be John, and he should be filled with the spirit of Elias; Which John I have sent unto you, my servants, Joseph Smith, Jun., and Oliver Cowdery, to ordain you unto the first priesthood which you have received, that you might be called and ordained even as Aaron; And also Elijah, unto whom I have committed the keys of the power of turning the hearts of the fathers to the children, and the hearts of the children to the fathers, that the whole earth may not be smitten with a curse; And also with Joseph and Jacob, and Isaac, and Abraham, your fathers, by whom the promises remain; And also with Michael, or Adam, the father of all, the prince of all, the ancient of days:**

3 **And also with Peter, and James, and John, whom I have sent unto you, by whom I have ordained you and confirmed you to be apostles, and especial witnesses of my name, and bear the keys of your ministry and of the same things which I revealed unto them; Unto whom I have committed the keys of my kingdom, and a dispensation of the gospel for the last times; and for the fulness of times, in the which I will gather together in one all things, both which are in heaven, and which are on**

earth; And also with all those whom my Father hath given me out of the world. Wherefore, lift up your hearts and rejoice, and gird up your loins, **and take upon you my whole armor, that ye may be able to withstand the evil day, having done all, that ye may be able to stand. Stand, therefore, having your loins girt about with truth, having on the breastplate of righteousness, and your feet shod with the preparation of the gospel of peace, which I have sent mine angels to commit unto you; Taking the shield of faith wherewith ye shall be able to quench all the fiery darts of the wicked; And take the helmet of salvation, and the sword of my Spirit, which I will pour out upon you, and my word which I reveal unto you, and be agreed as touching all things whatsoever ye ask of me,** and be faithful until I come, **and ye shall be caught up, that where I am ye shall be also.**[5] Amen. (1835 D&C 50:1–3; the present 1986 edition of the Doctrine and Covenants 27:1–18 reads the same except for the heading, verse numbering, and some punctuation.)

Newer D&C editions used the following three headings for this same revelation. While the heading is different for the three, the revelation reads the same as the above 1835 D&C 50:1–3 except for the summary of verses given, verse numbering, and some punctuation.

Heading from the 1891 D&C

The first four verses of the following Revelation, were given through Joseph, the Seer, in Harmony, Penn., **August 1830,** *and the remainder in Fayette, New York,* **September, 1830.** *(D&C 27)*

Heading from the 1977 D&C

REVELATION given to Joseph Smith the Prophet, at Harmony, Pennsylvania, **August 1830.** *HC 1:106–8. In preparation for a religious service at which the sacrament of bread and wine was to be administered, Joseph set out to procure wine for the occasion. He was met by a heavenly messenger and received this revelation,* **the first four** *paragraphs of which were written at the time, and the remainder in the September following.* . . . *The prior ordination of Joseph Smith, Jun., and Oliver Cowdery to the Apostleship avowed.* . . . *(D&C 27)*

Heading from the present edition D&C

Revelation given to Joseph Smith the Prophet, at Harmony, Pennsylvania, **August 1830**. *HC 1:106–8. In preparation for a religious service at which the sacrament of bread and wine was to be administered, Joseph set out to procure wine for the occasion. He was met by a heavenly messenger and received this revelation, a portion of which was written at the time, and the* **remainder in the September following**. *Water is now used instead of wine in the sacramental services of the Church. (D&C 27)*

Some Mormons may point to other references to support the restoration of the Mormon priesthood.

Present edition D&C

Ordination of Joseph Smith and Oliver Cowdery to the Aaronic Priesthood along the bank of the Susquehanna River, near Harmony, Pennsylvania, May 15, 1829. HC 1:39–42. The ordination was done by the hands of an angel, who announced himself as John, the same that is called John the Baptist in the New Testament. The angel explained that he was acting under the direction of Peter, James, and John, the ancient apostles, who held the keys of the higher priesthood, which was called the Priesthood of Melchizedek. The promise was given to Joseph and Oliver that in due time the Priesthood of Melchizedek would be conferred upon them. See also Section 27:7, 8, 12.

UPON you my fellow servants, in the name of Messiah I confer the Priesthood of Aaron, which holds the keys of the ministering of angels, and of the gospel of repentance, and of baptism by immersion for the remission of sins; and this shall never be taken again from the earth, until the sons of Levi do offer again an offering unto the Lord in righteousness. (D&C 13 heading and 13:1)

This revelation was not part of the Mormon scriptures until the 1876 edition, which was not accepted "by common consent" until 1880. The same idea is also in the Pearl of Great Price, *Joseph Smith—History*, verses 68–69, which was also not accepted as scripture until 1880.

The Reorganized Church of Jesus Christ of Latter Day Saints, which claims to be the true continuation of the church Joseph Smith founded, denies that Peter, James, and John "restored" the Melchizedek Priesthood. The following statement by Joseph Fielding Smith from *Doctrines of Salvation* 3:95 explains their position:

"REORGANITES" DENY RESTORATION OF MELCHIZEDEK PRIESTHOOD. Was the Melchizedek Priesthood conferred upon Joseph Smith and Oliver Cowdery by Peter, James, and John?

In the *History of the Church,* no account is given of the date when the Melchizedek Priesthood was restored. For this reason certain parties not of the Church, who profess to believe in the divine mission of the martyred Seer, in order to bolster up their weak position, have made the claim that this priesthood was not restored by those heavenly messengers, but that it grew out of the Aaronic Priesthood, which was restored by John the Baptist on the 15th day of May, 1829. According to this claim, the Prophet and Oliver Cowdery, having received the Aaronic Priesthood, did, by virtue of that priesthood, on the 6th day of April, 1830, ordain each other elders, and that this eldership ordained high priests and apostles.

The actual statement, as officially published by the so-called "Reorganized" Church, is: "In justification of the course taken, and the principles involved on 'the question of authority,' we have ever courted, and still do, investigation of the rigid character of the facts in the first organization. Here they are: Joseph Smith and Oliver Cowdery were ordained to the lesser priesthood by an angel; then, by this authority and a commandment they, on the 6th day of April, ordained each other elders, and this eldership ordained high priests and apostles, and this high priesthood ordained, by commandment, the President of the High Priesthood—the highest office in the church; so that the alleged lesser ordained *[sic]* the greater, is common to both the first organization and the Reorganization alike. The same class of facts justify both or condemn both."

David Whitmer, one of the three witnesses of the Book of Mormon, also denies that the priesthood was in the early Mormon Church in the beginning. Excerpts from his booklet, *An Address to All Believers in Christ,* are as follows:

Now Brethren, seeing they had no High Priests in the church of Christ of old, and none in the church of Christ in these last days until almost two years after its beginning—when the leaders began to drift into error; remembering the fact of the revelation being changed two years after it was given to include High Priests. . . .

In no place in the word of God does it say that an Elder is after the order of Melchisedec,[6] or after the order of the Melchisedec Priesthood. . . . This matter of "priesthood," since the days of Sydney *[sic]* Rigdon, has been the great hobby and stumbling–block of the Latter Day Saints. . . . This matter of the two orders of priesthood . . . all originated in the mind of Sydney *[sic]* Rigdon. He explained these things to Brother Joseph in his way, out of the old Scriptures, and got Brother Joseph to inquire, etc. He would inquire and as mouthpiece speak out the revelations just as they had it fixed up in their hearts. . . . How easily a man can receive some other spirit, appearing as an Angel of Light, believing at the time that he is giving the revealed will of God. . . . (pp. 64–65)

These examples of Doctrine and Covenants changes are just a few of the dozens that could be shown. *Mormonism—Shadow or Reality?* by Jerald and Sandra Tanner, starting on page 18, shows fourteen pages out of the 1833 *Book of Commandments* that average over one dozen significant changes *on each page.* On these pages, as in the examples shown here, the historical statement at the heading of each revelation is unchanged in its key elements identifying persons, places, dates, and so on. No explanation is offered to the effect that God had changed his mind or that Joseph Smith or someone else had made a mistake or changed his mind. Simple honesty and the supposed sacred nature of the subject and source certainly should have required some explanation for revising these alleged revelations.

If, as the 1833 *Book of Commandments* says in 1:7, "these commandments . . . are **true and faithful**," then why were any changes needed? Or, if the present edition of the Doctrine and Covenants is "true and faithful" (1:37) after the changes, does this mean the 1833 *Book of Commandments* was not?

First Corinthians 14:33 says: "God is not the author of confusion, but of peace, as in all churches of the saints." (Also see D&C 132:8.) The changes shown here in Mormon scriptures constitute sufficient confusion to cast doubt on divine authorship. Add to this the disagreements between Mormon scriptures and the disagreements between top Mormon leaders and Mormon factions (RLDS), as shown above, and it becomes clear that there is much confusion in Mormonism that should not be there if it is of God. The changes cited here are not isolated examples, and the disagreements demonstrate conflict within the very heart of Mormonism—its scriptures and its top leaders. Again recall the standards that Mormon scriptures and leaders themselves set for judging their own validity. (See the preface, chapter 2, and the beginning of chapter 4.) These standards leave little or no room for errors and disagreements of the type demonstrated here.

unto me, Knowest thou the condescention of God? And I said unto him, I know that he loveth his children; nevertheless, I do not know the meaning of all things. And he said unto me, Behold, the virgin which thou seest, is the mother of God, after the manner of the flesh.

And it came to pass that I beheld that she was carried away in the spirit; and after that she had been carried away in the spirit for the space of a time, the angel spake unto me, saying, look! And I looked and beheld the virgin again, bearing a chid in her arms. And the angel said unto me, behold the Lamb of God, yea, even the Eternal Father! Knowest thou the meaning of the tree which thy father saw? And I answered him, saying: Yea, it is the love of God, which sheddeth itself abroad in the hearts of the children of men; wherefore, it is the most desirable above all things. And he spake unto me, saying, Yea, and the most ioyous to the soul. And after that he had

First Book of Nephi, chapter 3, page 25, Book of Mormon, 1830 (First edition)

1 NEPHI 11:9–25   **20**

looked and beheld a tree; and it was like unto the *tree which my father had seen; and the *beauty thereof was far beyond, yea, exceeding of all beauty; and the 'whiteness thereof did exceed the whiteness of the driven snow.

9 And it came to pass after I had seen the tree, I said unto the Spirit: I behold thou hast shown unto me the tree which is *precious above all.

10 And he said unto me: What desirest thou?

11 And I said unto him: To know the *interpretation thereof—for I spake unto him as a man speaketh; for I beheld that he was in the *form of a man; yet nevertheless, I knew that it was the Spirit of the Lord; and he spake unto me as a man speaketh with another.

12 And it came to pass that he said

17 And I said unto him: I know that he loveth his children; nevertheless, I do not know the meaning of all things.

18 And he said unto me: Behold, the *virgin whom thou seest is the *mother of the Son of God, after the manner of the flesh.

19 And it came to pass that I beheld that she was carried away in the Spirit; and after she had been carried away in the *Spirit for the space of a time the angel spake unto me, saying: Look!

20 And I looked and beheld the virgin again, bearing a *child in her arms.

21 And the angel said unto me: Behold the *Lamb of God, yea, even the *Son of the Eternal *Father! Knowest thou the meaning of the *tree which thy father saw?

1 Nephi 11:18-21, Book of Mormon, 1981

1 Nephi 11:18–25 in Book of Mormon, 1981 edition, and chapter 3, page 25 in original 1830 first edition. Copyright © 1981 Corporation of the President of The Church of Jesus Christ of Latter-day Saints.

CHAPTER VI.

1 *A Revelation given to Joseph and Oliver, in Harmony, Pennsylvania, April, 1829, when they desired to know whether John, the beloved disciple, tarried on earth. Translated from parchment, written and hid up by himself.*

AND the Lord said unto me, John my beloved, what desirest thou? ~~and I said Lord, give unto me power that I may bring souls unto thee.~~ And the Lord said unto me: Verily, verily I say unto thee, because thou desiredst this, thou shalt tarry till I come in my glory:

2 And for this cause, the Lord said unto Peter:— If I will that he tarry till I come, what is that to thee? for he desiredst of me that he might bring souls unto me: but thou desiredst that thou might speedily come unto me in thy kingdom: I say unto thee, Peter, this was a good desire, but my beloved has undertaken a greater work.

3 Verily I say unto you, ye shall both have according to your desires, for ye both joy in that which ye have desired.

Book of Commandments, Chapter VI, Page 18, as first published in 1833.

1–3, John the Beloved shall live until the Lord comes; 4–8, Peter, James, and John hold gospel keys.

AND the Lord said unto me: John, my *beloved, what *desirest thou? For if you shall ask what you will, it shall be granted unto you.

2 And I said unto him: Lord, give unto me *power over *death, that I may live and bring souls unto thee.

3 And the Lord said unto me: Verily, verily, I say unto thee, because thou desirest this thou shalt *tarry until I come in my *glory, and shalt *prophesy before nations, kindreds, tongues and people.

4 And for this cause the Lord said unto Peter: If I will that he tarry till I come, what is that to thee? For he desired of me that he might bring *souls unto me, but thou de-sirest that thou mightest speedily come unto me in my *kingdom.

5 I say unto thee, Peter, this was a good desire; but my beloved has desired that he might do more, or a greater *work yet among men than what he has before done.

6 Yea, he has undertaken a greater work; therefore I will make him as flaming fire and a *ministering angel; he shall minister for those who shall be *heirs of salvation who dwell on the earth.

7 And I will make thee to minister for him and for thy brother James; and unto you three I will *give this power and the *keys of this ministry until I come.

8 Verily I say unto you, ye shall both have according to your desires, for ye both *joy in that which ye have desired.

Doctrine & Covenants, Section 7, 1981 Edition.

Doctrine and Covenants, 1981 edition, section 7, contrasted with *Book of Commandments,* chapter VI, page 18, published in 1833. Copyright © 1981 Corporation of the President of The Church of Jesus Christ of Latter-day Saints.

2 And now, behold, this shall you say unto him: —I the Lord am God, and I have given these things unto my servant Joseph, and I have commanded him that he should stand as a witness of these things, nevertheless I have caused him that he should enter into a covenant with me, that he should not show them except I command him, and he has no power over them except I grant it unto him; and he has a gift to translate the book, and I have commanded him that he shall pretend to no other gift, for I will grant him no other gift. 3 And verily I say unto you, that wo shall come unto the inhabitants of the earth, if they will not hearken unto my words, for, behold, if they will not believe my words, they would not believe my servant Joseph, if it were possible that he could show

Book of Commandments 4:2, printed in 1833, Independence, Missouri.

2 And now, behold, this shall you say unto him—he who spake unto you, said unto you: I, the Lord, am God, and have given these things unto you, my servant Joseph Smith, Jun., and have commanded you that you should stand as a *witness of these things;

3 And I have caused you that you should enter into a *covenant with me, that you should not *show them except to those *persons to whom I commanded you; and you have no *power over them except I grant it unto you.

4 And you have a gift to *translate the plates; and this is the first gift that I bestowed upon you; and I have commanded that you should pretend to no other gift until my purpose is fulfilled in this; for I will grant unto you no other gift until it is finished.

5 Verily, I say unto you, that *woe shall come unto the inhabitants of the earth if they will not *hearken unto my words;

6 For hereafter you shall be *ordained and go forth and deliver my *words unto the children of men.

7 Behold, if they will not *believe my words, they would not believe you, my servant Joseph, if it were possible that you should show them all these things which I have committed unto you.

8 Oh, this *unbelieving and *stiff-necked generation—mine *anger is kindled against them.

9 Behold, verily I say unto you, I have *reserved those things which I have entrusted unto you, my

| 5 1a D&C 5: 23 (23–24); JS-H 1: 61. | 4a D&C 3: 12; 6: 25 (25, 28). | b Morm. 8: 33. TG Haughtiness; |

Doctrine & Covenants 5:4, 1989 (Columns shifted to save space).

Doctrine and Covenants, 1989 edition, 5:4, 6, contrasted with *Book of Commandments,* chapter 4:2, published in 1833. Copyright © 1981 Corporation of the President of The Church of Jesus Christ of Latter-day Saints.

ABSURDITIES IN MORMONISM

When an organization claims to be the one true Church led by prophets of God, and at the same time has God the Son, in one of its unique scriptures, saying about other churches that "they were all wrong . . . their creeds were an abomination . . . those professors were all corrupt" (*Joseph Smith—History* 1:19), then that organization should be prepared to have *all* the teachings of its own top leaders and scriptures examined. With that in mind let us now look at some of the absurd ideas and stories that have come out of Mormonism. Note that *all* the key references are from the LDS Church or by top Mormon leaders, so Mormons should have no question about their reliability.

Were the bones of Zelph the white Lamanite found?

On the top of the mound were stones which presented the appearance of three altars having been erected one above the other, according to the ancient order; and the remains of bones were strewn over the surface of the ground. The brethren procured a shovel and a hoe, and removing the earth to the depth of about one foot, discovered the skeleton of a man, almost entire, and between his ribs the stone point of a Lamanitish arrow, which evidently produced his death. Elder Burr Riggs retained the arrow. The contemplation of the scenery around us produced peculiar sensations in our bosoms: and subsequently the visions of the past being opened to my [Joseph Smith's] understanding by the Spirit of the Almighty, I discovered that the person whose skeleton was before us was **a white Lamanite**, a large, thick-set man, and a **man of God**. His name was Zelph. He was a warrior and chieftain under the great prophet Onandagus, who was known from the Hill Cumorah, or eastern sea to the Rocky mountains. The curse was taken from Zelph, or, at least, in part—one of his thigh bones was broken by a stone flung from a sling, while in battle, years before his death. He was killed in battle by the arrow found among his ribs, during the last great struggle of the Lamanites and Nephites. (June 3, 1834, *History of the Church* 2:79–80)

According to Elder Kimball's journal, the facts concerning the person whose bones had been found in the ground were not revealed to the Prophet Joseph until the camp had departed from the mound. He says: "While on our way we felt anxious to know who the person was who had been killed by the arrow. It was made known to Joseph that he had been an officer who fell in battle in the last destruction among the Lamanites, and his name was Zelph. This caused us to rejoice much, to think that God was so mindful of us as to show these things to His servant. Brother Joseph had inquired of the Lord, and it was made known in a vision." (June 3, 1834, *History of the Church* 2:80, footnote. An account of this affair was also written up in the Church newspaper, *Times and Seasons* 6:788.)

To understand why Zelph was called "a white Lamanite," you need to read some verses from the Book of Mormon. The Book of Mormon people, Lehi's group as found in 1 Nephi, which supposedly came to the New World in 600 B.C., split into two groups. The righteous branch called Nephites stayed white. The unrighteous branch called Lamanites received dark skins. Zelph was apparently born a dark-skinned Lamanite, but became white because he became a man of God. The following Book of Mormon verses provide background information helpful in understanding this.

The Lamanites are given a "skin of blackness."

The Nephites separate themselves from the Lamanites, keep the law of Moses, and build a temple—Because of their unbelief, the Laman-

*ites are cursed, **receive a skin of blackness**, and become a scourge unto the Nephites. (2 Nephi chapter 5 heading)*

And he had caused the cursing to come upon them, yea, even a sore cursing, because of their iniquity. For behold, they had hardened their hearts against him, that they had become like unto a flint; wherefore, as **they were white, and exceedingly fair and delightsome**, that they might not be enticing unto my people the Lord God **did cause a skin of blackness** to come upon them. (2 Nephi 5:21)

And the skins of the Lamanites were **dark**, according to the mark which was set upon their fathers, which was a curse upon them because of their transgression and their rebellion against their brethren [the righteous branch, called Nephites]. . . . (Alma 3:6)

And also that the seed of this people may more fully believe his gospel, which shall go forth unto them from the Gentiles; for this people shall be scattered, and shall become **a dark, a filthy, and a loathsome people**, beyond the description of that which ever hath been amongst us, yea, even that which hath been among the Lamanites, and this because of their unbelief and idolatry. (Mormon 5:15)

They become white like the Nephites.

And it came to pass that those Lamanites who had united with the Nephites were numbered among the Nephites; **And their curse was taken from them**, and their **skin became white** like unto the Nephites; And their young men and their daughters **became exceedingly fair**, and they were numbered among the Nephites, and were called Nephites. . . . (3 Nephi 2:14–16)

Where was Zelph killed? The "last great struggle of the Lamanites and Nephites" allegedly occurred in A.D. 385 (see Mormon 6:1–15) at Hill Cumorah near Palmyra, New York, over 700 miles away, as the crow flies, from where Zelph was found. According to *History of the Church* (pp. 78–79), Zelph was found buried in a high mound (above the tops of the trees) on the banks of the

Illinois River in the State of Illinois, not far from present-day Florence, Illinois, which is about 75–100 miles north of St. Louis, near where I36 crosses the Illinois River. The mound that Joseph Smith dug into on June 2, 1834, is still there and is one of about thirty-five bluff-top mounds covering about a mile along the river. Archaeologists estimate that it dates from between 50 B.C. and A.D. 50, based upon the style of the artifacts found in it and the age of nearby mounds that have been radiocarbon-dated from 50 B.C. to A.D. 250.[1]

How likely is it that a man who got an arrow between his ribs at Hill Cumorah in New York would then travel over 700 miles to die? No, the man Joseph Smith dug up must have been killed near where Smith found him. It does not seem likely that Zelph's friends or comrades carried him to the banks of the Illinois River. They would be looking out for their own lives. Moreover, according to Mormon 6:15 and 8:2, the Nephites as they escaped went southward, not west to the banks of the Illinois River over 700 miles away.

Did Shiz, with his head cut off, raise up on his hands?

And it came to pass that when they had all fallen by the sword, save it were Coriantumr and Shiz, behold Shiz had fainted with the loss of blood. And it came to pass that when Coriantumr had leaned upon his sword, that he rested a little, he smote off the head of Shiz. And it came to pass that after he had smitten off the head of Shiz, that Shiz **raised up on his hands** and fell; and after that he had struggled for breath, he died. (Ether 15:29–31)[2]

The absurdity here is the thought that a headless man could raise himself up and struggle for breath. Both actions are impossible without connection to a brain or brain stem.[3]

Did flocks and herds leave no trail?

And it came to pass that they could find no way to deliver themselves [the Nephites] out of bondage, except it were to take **their**

women and children, and their flocks, and their herds, and their tents, and depart into the wilderness; for the Lamanites being so numerous, it was impossible for the people of Limhi to contend with them, thinking to deliver themselves out of bondage by the sword. . . . And king Limhi caused that his people should gather their flocks together; and he sent the tribute of wine to the Lamanites; and he also sent more wine, as a present unto them; and they did drink freely of the wine which king Limhi did send unto them. . . . And it came to pass that the people of king Limhi did depart by night into the wilderness with their **flocks** and their **herds**, and they went round about the land of Shilom in the wilderness, and bent their course towards the land of Zarahemla, being led by Ammon and his brethren. . . . And they had taken all their **gold, and silver**, and their **precious things**, which they could carry, and **also their provisions** with them, into the wilderness; and they pursued their journey. . . . And after they [the Lamanites] had pursued them two days, they could **no longer follow their tracks**; therefore they were lost in the wilderness. (Mosiah 22:2, 10–12, 16)

Notice that King Limhi's people had flocks and herds with them and they carried gold, silver, precious things, and their provisions. No numbers are given, but all the people are referred to in the plural, and flocks and herds are plural. Within a flock and a herd there are many animals and there are at least two flocks and two herds. These animals, coupled with the burdens—the gold, silver, precious things, and provisions—carried by the people or by pack animals, would have left evidence. It seems reasonable from the wording to assume that this was not a small group. Could it really be that no grass was eaten, no plants or tree limbs were broken, no human footprints and no tracks or droppings from the animals were left? Even if they were on rock the human and animal droppings should have been evident.

Could hundreds of thousands die at and near Hill Cumorah and leave no artifacts behind as evidence?

He saw that there had been slain by the sword already nearly **two millions** of his people, and he began to sorrow in his heart; yea, there had been slain **two millions** of mighty men, and also their **wives and their children.** . . . And it came to pass that the army of Coriantumr did pitch their tents by the hill Ramah; and it was that same hill [Hill Cumorah] where my father Mormon did hide up the records unto the Lord, which were sacred. (Ether 15:2, 11; also see verses 15–30)

These are the pre-Nephite people (Jaredites) that were just coming to their end with the arrival of the main Book of Mormon people, Lehi and his family, as they arrived from Jerusalem in 600 B.C. The final battle allegedly took place on the same Hill Cumorah as the following extermination battle between the Nephites and the Lamanites in A.D. 385.

And when they had gone through and hewn down all my people **save it were twenty and four of us,** (among whom was my son Moroni) and we having survived the dead of our people, did behold on the morrow, when the Lamanites had returned unto their camps, from the top of the hill Cumorah, the **ten thousand** of my people who were hewn down, being led in the front by me. And we also beheld the **ten thousand** of my people who were led by my son Moroni. And behold, the **ten thousand** of Gidgiddonah had fallen, and he also in the midst. And Lamah had fallen with his **ten thousand**; and Gilgal had fallen with his **ten thousand**; and Limhah had fallen with his **ten thousand**; and Jeneum had fallen with his **ten thousand**; and Cumenihah, and Moronihah, and Antionum, and Shiblom, and Shem, and Josh, had fallen **with their ten thousand each.** And it came to pass that there were **ten more who did fall by the sword, with their ten thousand each**; yea, even all my people, save it were those twenty and four who were with me, and also a **few** who had escaped into the **south countries**, and a few who had deserted over unto the Lamanites, had fallen; and their flesh, and bones, and blood lay upon the face of the earth, being left by the hands of those who slew them to molder upon the land, and to crumble and to return to their mother earth. (Mormon 6:11–15)

And now it came to pass that after the great and tremendous battle at Cumorah, behold, the Nephites who had escaped into the
country **southward** were hunted by the Lamanites, **until they
were all destroyed.** And my father also was killed by them, and
I even remain alone to write the sad tale of the destruction of my
people. But behold, they are gone, and I fulfil the commandment
of my father. And whether they will slay me, I know not. (Mormon 8:2–3)

This is the extermination battle on Hill Cumorah that allegedly
killed 240,000 Nephite warriors[4] and probably the same number of Lamanites. Zelph was among those who died in the battle. The Book of Ether in the Book of Mormon also relates that
another great battle took place here (see Ether 15, part of which
is above). It seems reasonable to expect that items that would not
decay easily, such as arrowheads, stone axe heads, copper, silver,
and gold jewelry, gold and silver coins (see Alma chapter 11 heading and 11:4–19), would be found in the farming of the land and
in excavations at the site. Also iron and steel (yes, the Book of
Mormon people had iron and steel, so it says)[5] would leave their
oxides, that is the rust, as they decayed. Also note that in 1843
Joseph Smith claimed to have found Zelph's bones still visible.
So at the very least some bones should also be found. But the reality is that no unusual artifacts have ever been found at or around
Hill Cumorah.

Is the Book of Mormon the most correct book?

Sunday, 28.—I [Joseph Smith] spent the day in the council with
the Twelve Apostles at the house of President Young, convers-
ing with them upon a variety of subjects. Brother Joseph Fielding was present, having been absent four years on a mission to
England. I told the brethren that the **Book of Mormon was** *the
most correct of any book on earth*, and the **keystone** of our religion, and a man would get **nearer to God** by abiding by its precepts, than by any other book. (November 28, 1841, *History of
the Church* 4:461)[6]

7. It is to be expected that when the angel restores the gospel it will be **restored in fullness** and in the **most perfect simplicity and plainness** so that **every point** of the doctrine of Christ shall be **clearly revealed** and expressed in such language that no two persons **could understand it differently**. . . . Nothing short of such a revelation can ever redeem mankind from their errors of doctrine; nothing else can be an **infallible standard** of the Christian religion; nothing else can reclaim them from divisions and strifes; nothing else will give certainty and stability so necessary to the happiness and salvation of man; and nothing else could be expected in the revelation of the gospel by an angel. *Such a revelation is the Book of Mormon;* the most infallible certainty characterizes every ordinance and every doctrinal point revealed in that book. In it **there is no ambiguity—no room for controversy—no doctrine so imperfectly expressed** that two persons would draw **two different conclusions** there from. Such a revelation was greatly needed and **such a revelation the angel has revealed**. (*Divine Authenticity of the Book of Mormon*, [Apostle] Orson Pratt, 1851, No. 6, p. 83; also in *Orson Pratt's Works,* Important Works in Mormon History, Vol. 2, [Apostle] Orson Pratt, Grandin Book Co., 1990)

Practically all of the religious truths taught and practiced in any Gospel dispensation are given **in a clear and forceful way** in the *Book of Mormon.* In fact, many of the principles are presented more clearly in that record than in any of the other ancient scriptures. (*Gospel Through the Ages*, Milton R. Hunter of the First Council of the Seventy, 1945, p. 86)

The Third cornerstone[7]—the Book of Mormon. . . . The evidence for its truth and validity lies within the covers of the book itself. The test of truth lies in reading it.[8] (President Gordon B. Hinckley, second counselor in the First Presidency, at General Conference, Sunday Morning Session, October 7, 1984; *Ensign*, November 1984, p. 52)

From this we learn that the evaluation of the Book of Mormon's validity and truth should be based upon its contents, and not on anything external to it. This is the approach we have taken in this book.

The changes that were made in the Book of Mormon, as shown in the previous chapter, conflict with Joseph Smith's and Orson Pratt's statements. Now using President Hinckley's suggestion (reading the Book of Mormon), let us test Elder Milton R. Hunter's statement. It is easy to do as, contrary to Elder Hunter's ideas, there is much Mormon doctrine *not* found in the Book of Mormon. So how could it be the "most correct book"? Examples of Mormon doctrine *not* found in the Book of Mormon are:

1. That God the Father has a body of flesh and bones. In truth the Book of Mormon teaches that God is a spirit (Mosiah 15:1–5; Alma 18:26–29; 19:25–27; 22:8–11; 31:15–38). Note in Alma 31 that the speaker who says God is a spirit is not corrected by the alleged prophet involved.
2. That the Father, Son, and Holy Ghost are separate and distinct Gods.
3. That they are one God in that they are one in purpose.
4. That God the Father was once a man like us and progressed until he became God. In reality the Book of Mormon says God has always been God from eternity to eternity (Mosiah 3:5; 2 Nephi 27:23; 29:9; Moroni 7:22; 8:18; Mormon 9:9, 19).
5. That there are three levels in heaven.
6. That we can progress and become Gods with "all the power, glory, dominion, and knowledge" the Father and Son have.
7. The elaborate priesthoods and organization in present-day Mormonism.
8. That our spirits and the spirit of Jesus Christ were born in the pre-existence (a pre-mortal life).
9. The "new and everlasting covenant," the practice of polygamy, as taught in D&C 132. In fact, polygamy is condemned in the Book of Mormon (Jacob 2:24, 27; Mosiah 11:2; Ether 10:5).

10. That matter is eternal and all Jesus Christ did in his cre-
    ation was to organize and form it.
11. Vicarious work for the dead as now done in Mormon tem-
    ples. In reality the Book of Mormon rules out such a prac-
    tice (2 Nephi 26:11; Alma 5:28; 34:31–35; Mosiah 16:5, 11;
    26:25–27).
12. That God is married and there is a mother in heaven.
13. That the sacred (to the Mormons) temple endowment cer-
    emonies are needed to pass through the veil to spend eter-
    nity with God.
14. That Jesus Christ atoned for our sins in the Garden of Geth-
    semane. In fact the Book of Mormon does not even men-
    tion the Garden of Gethsemane. It says Jesus Christ died
    for all men on the cross (see 2 Nephi 9:5; 1 Nephi 11:33;
    3 Nephi 27:14).

Many of the above are needed, according to LDS teachings,[9]
to allow a person who accepts and lives them, to reach exaltation[10] (becoming a God) in the celestial kingdom of God. In addition, the many offshoot sects (over 100)[11] of Joseph Smith's
Mormonism, most or all of which use the Book of Mormon, and
have significantly different teachings, show that the book does
allow for different conclusions and for controversy.

Do the planet earth and the animals living on it have spirits similar to man's?

ANIMALS HAVE SOULS. The idea prevails in general, I believe,
in the religious world where the gospel truth is misunderstood,
that man is the only being on the earth that has what is called a
soul or a spirit. We know this is not the case, for the Lord has said
that not only has man a spirit, and is thereby a living soul, but
**likewise the beasts of the field, the fowl of the air, and the fish
of the sea have spirits, and hence are living souls**. . . .

FORM OF ANIMAL SPIRITS. The fish, the fowl, the beasts
of the field, lived before they were placed naturally in this earth,

and so did the plants that are upon the face of the earth. The spirits that possess the bodies of the animals are in the similitude of their bodies. In other words, the bodies of animals conform to the spirits which possess them, and which existed before they were placed on the earth; "that which is spiritual being in the likeness of that which is temporal; and that which is temporal in the likeness of that which is spiritual; the spirit of man in the likeness of his person, as also the spirit of the beast, and every other creature which God has created." (*Doctrines of Salvation*, [Apostle] Joseph Fielding Smith, 1:63–64)

Some say the earth exists without spirit; I do not believe any such thing; **it has a spirit as much as any body has a spirit**. How can anything live, except it has a living spirit? How can the earth produce vegetation, fruits, trees, and every kind of production, if there is no life in it? It could not, any more than a woman could produce children when she is dead: she must be alive to produce life, to manifest it, and show it to the world. (Heber C. Kimball, counselor to Brigham Young, August 23, 1857, *Journal of Discourses* 5:172)

... the earth itself is subject to certain laws of progression and salvation because of which it eventually will become a fit abode for exalted beings. **This earth was created as a living thing**, and the Lord ordained that it should live a celestial law. It was baptized in water and will receive the baptism of fire; it will die, be resurrected and attain unto a state of celestial exaltation. In the course of its eternal existence, it is destined to pass through certain stages of existence. (*Doctrines of Salvation*, vol. 1, pp. 72–89; Parley P. Pratt, *Voice of Warning*, ch. 5.) (*Mormon Doctrine*, [Apostle] Bruce R. McConkie, p. 210)

... as is the case with man, the **earth itself is passing through a plan of salvation**. It was created (the equivalent of birth); it fell to its present mortal or telestial state; **it was baptized** by immersion, when the universal flood swept over its entire surface (Ether 13:2–11); it will be baptized by fire (the equivalent of baptism of the Spirit) in the day when it is renewed and receives its paradisiacal glory; it will die; and finally it will be

quickened (or resurrected) and become a celestial sphere. Evolutionary theories take no account of any of this. (*Mormon Doctrine*, p. 251)

Mormon leaders today teach that the spirits of the earth and animals were created by God, unlike ours, which were procreated by God the Father and our Mother in heaven, each of whom have bodies of flesh and bones. The Bible says nothing about the earth or animals having a created spirit. In fact, the Mormon leaders have it backwards; man's spirit was created, as shown in the following biblical verses.

Every living creature brings forth after its kind.

And the earth brought forth grass, and herb yielding seed **after his kind**, and the tree yielding fruit, whose seed was in itself, **after his kind**: and God saw that it was good. . . . And God created great whales, and every living creature that moveth, which the waters brought forth abundantly, **after their kind**, and every winged fowl **after his kind**: and God saw that it was good. (Genesis 1:12, 21)

Flesh bears flesh; spirit bears spirit.

That which is born of the flesh is flesh; and that which is born of the Spirit is spirit. (John 3:6)

Can the fig tree bear olives?

Doth a fountain send forth at the same place sweet water and bitter? Can the fig tree, my brethren, bear olive berries? either a vine, figs? so can no fountain both yield salt water and fresh. (James 3:11–12)

These three references refute the Mormon teaching that God the Father and Mother in heaven, who each have bodies of flesh and bones, procreated spirit children. These verses make it clear that like begets like.

Our spirit is given by the Lord.

Then shall the dust return to the earth as it was: and the **spirit shall return unto God who gave it**. (Ecclesiastes 12:7)

The Lord gives us our spirit.

Thus saith God the Lord, he that created the heavens, . . . he that **giveth breath** unto the people upon it, **and spirit** to them that walk therein . . . (Isaiah 42:5)

We are the work of his hands.

But now, O Lord, thou art our father; we are the clay, and thou our potter; and **we all are the work of thy hand**. (Isaiah 64:8)

The Lord forms our spirit within us.

The burden of the word of the Lord for Israel, saith the Lord, which stretcheth forth the heavens, and layeth the foundation of the earth, and **formeth the spirit of man within him**. (Zechariah 12:1)

God created us.

Have we not all one father? hath not one **God created us**? . . . (Malachi 2:10)

These five verses make it clear that the spirits of people were created by God.

Do you check your brains at the door?

We have our marching orders.

President Ezra Taft Benson has said, "Therefore, the most important reading we can do is any of the words of the Prophet contained each week in the Church Section of the *Deseret News* and any words of the Prophet contained each month in our Church magazines. Our **marching orders** for each six months are found in the general conference addresses which are printed in the *En-*

sign magazine" ("Fourteen Fundamentals in Following the Prophets," 1980 *Devotional Speeches of the Year*, [Provo, Utah: Brigham Young University Press, 1981], p. 27). (*Search These Commandments*, Melchizedek Priesthood Personal Study Guide, a teaching manual for men, published and copyrighted [1984] by the Mormon Church, p. 273)

The thinking has been done for us.

When our leaders speak the thinking has been done. When they propose a plan—it is God's plan. When they point the way, there is no other which is safe. When they give direction, it should mark the end of controversy. (*The Improvement Era*, under "Ward Teacher's Message for June 1945," p. 354; also in *Deseret News,* Church Section, May 26, 1945, p. 5)

Learn to do as you are told, even if it is wrong.

In regard to our situation and circumstances in these valleys, brethren, WAKE UP! WAKE UP, YE ELDERS OF ISRAEL, AND LIVE TO GOD and none else; and **learn to do as you are told, both old and young: learn to do as you are told** for the future. And when you are taking a position, if you do not know that you are right, do not take it—I mean independently. But if you are told by your leader to do a thing, do it. **None of your business whether it is right or wrong.** You will get water, if you dig away. That is rather presumptuous doctrine with some people; but with me it is not. (Heber C. Kimball, November 8, 1857, *Journal of Discourses* 6:32)

We cannot make up our own minds on the Word of God; we must receive the Prophet's words as if from God.

How is it about this? **Have we not a right to make up our minds in relation to the things recorded in the word of God,** and speak about them, whether the living oracles believe our views or not? **We have not the right.** Why? Because the mind of man is weak: one man may make up his mind in this way, and another man may make up his mind in another way, and a third individual may have his views; and thus every man is left to be his own authority, and is governed by his own judgment, which he takes as his standard.

God placed Joseph Smith at the head of this Church; God has likewise placed Brigham Young at the head of this Church; and he has required you and me, male and female, to sustain those authorities thus placed over us in their position; and **that authority is binding on all Quorums and individuals of Quorums**. He has never released you nor me from those obligations. **We are commanded to give heed to their words in all things, and receive their words as from the mouth of God**, in all patience and faith. When we do not this, we get into darkness. (Orson Pratt, January 29, 1860, *Journal of Discourses* 7:374)

In Deuteronomy 13:1–5 and 18:20–22 are enumerated ways to test a prophet. Another test is in 1 Thessalonians 5:21, which says to "prove all things." And 1 John 4:1 tells us to "try the spirits whether they are of God." How do we do this? We compare what is being said to what God has already said (the Bible). We have the Holy Spirit to guide us in this comparison (John 10:4–5; 14:26; 16:13; 1 Corinthians 2:5, 12; 12:4–11). Matthew 22:37 tells us to use our minds in loving the Lord our God. Nowhere does the Bible say, "Check your brains at the door and follow blindly."

Is the Nauvoo House a resting place for Joseph Smith and his house forever and ever, generation to generation?

Doctrine and Covenants 124 is allegedly a revelation from God to Joseph Smith given January 1841 in Nauvoo, Illinois. In verses 56 through about 82 Joseph is commanded to build what amounts to a hotel to be named the "Nauvoo House," and at the same time he is given the details for funding it. Parts of the revelation read as follows:

56 And now I say unto you, as pertaining to my boarding house which I have commanded you to build for the boarding of strangers, let it be built unto my name, and **let my name be named**

upon it,[12] and **let my servant Joseph and his house have place therein, from generation to generation.**

59 Therefore, let my servant Joseph and his seed after him **have place in that house, from generation to generation, forever and ever, saith the Lord.**

60 And let the **name of that house be called Nauvoo House;** and let it be a delightful habitation for man, and a resting-place for the weary traveler, that he may contemplate the glory of Zion, and the glory of this, the corner-stone thereof;

62 Behold, verily I say unto you, let my servant George Miller, and my servant Lyman Wight, and my servant John Snider, and my servant Peter Haws, organize themselves, and appoint one of them to be a president over their quorum for the purpose of building that house.

63 And they shall form a constitution, whereby they may receive stock for the building of that house.

64 And they shall not receive less than fifty dollars for a share of stock in that house, and they shall be permitted to receive fifteen thousand dollars from any one man for stock in that house.

65 But they shall not be permitted to receive over fifteen thousand dollars stock from any one man.

66 And they shall not be permitted to receive under fifty dollars for a share of stock from any one man in that house.

67 And they shall not be permitted to receive any man, as a stockholder in this house, except the same shall pay his stock into their hands at the time he receives stock.

68 And in proportion to the amount of stock he pays into their hands he shall receive stock in that house; but if he pays nothing into their hands he shall not receive any stock in that house.

69 And if any pay stock into their hands it shall be stock in that house, for himself, and for his generation after him, from generation to generation, so long as he and his heirs shall hold that stock, and do not sell and convey the stock away out of their hands by their own free will and act, if you will do my will, saith the Lord your God.

72 Verily I say unto you, let my servant Joseph pay stock into their hands for the building of that house, as seemeth him good, but my servant Joseph cannot pay over fifteen thousand dollars

stock in that house, nor under fifty dollars; neither can any other man, saith the Lord.

74 Therefore, I say unto you concerning my servant Vincent Knight, if he will do my will let him put stock into that house for himself, and for his generation after him, from generation to generation.

77 Verily I say unto you, let my servant Hyrum [Joseph's brother] put stock into that house as seemeth him good, for himself and his generation after him, from generation to generation.

78 Let my servant Isaac Galland put stock into that house; for I, the Lord, love him for the work he hath done, and will forgive all his sins; therefore, let him be remembered for an interest in that house from generation to generation.

82 Let my servant William Law pay stock into that house, for himself and his seed after him, from generation to generation.

83 If he will do my will let him not take his family unto the eastern lands, even unto Kirtland; nevertheless, I, the Lord, will build up Kirtland, but I, the Lord, have a scourge prepared for the inhabitants thereof.

85 Let no man go from this place who has come here essaying to keep my commandments. (D&C 124:56, 59–60, 62–69, 72, 74, 77–78, 82–83, 85)

The amount of detail is incredible in light of D&C 58:26, which has:

For behold, it is not meet that I should command in all things; for he that is compelled in all things, the same is a slothful and not a wise servant; wherefore he receiveth no reward.

Does the commandment to build the Nauvoo House seem like instruction to further the sanctification of the believers, or a business speculation?

On Wednesday, February 21, 1843, in a public address Joseph Smith had the following to say about the Nauvoo House:

The building of the Nauvoo House is just as sacred in my view as the Temple [the Nauvoo temple was then under construction].

> I want the Nauvoo House built. It *must* be built. Our salvation
> [as a city][13] depends on it. (*History of the Church* 5:285)

The construction work on this hotel was started October 2,
1841, with the laying of the cornerstone, but it appears that the
stone foundation was not complete until sometime before August 1845, for (Apostle) John Taylor reported in his journal that
the brick work started August 18, 1845. This building was to be
in an "L" shape, with two wings, each 120 feet long, 40 feet deep,
three stories high. It was estimated the cost would be about
$150,000. It was never completed to these dimensions, and what
was eventually built was finished well after Joseph Smith's death.
He and his brother Hyrum never lived in the completed structure, but they were buried in the cellar for a short period of
time. With the death of Joseph, title to the Nauvoo House passed
to his wife Emma. Her new husband, Lewis Bidamon, completed only a small portion of the original plans. It was then
called the Riverside Mansion.[14] The building is now owned by
the RLDS, who use it as a residence and hostel. None of the
Smith family lives there now. The main body of LDS Mormons
abandoned Nauvoo in 1846 when they left for what is now Salt
Lake City.

Was Joseph Smith a true prophet of God?

Yes, LDS leaders think Joseph Smith was a true prophet of God.

. . . the New Testament is true, that Jesus is the Christ, that the
holy Prophets are true, that the Book of Mormon is true, and **that
Joseph Smith was a Prophet and Revelator.** (Brigham Young,
February 18, 1855, *Journal of Discourses* 2:189)

I teach the people that **Joseph Smith was greater than any
other Prophet that ever lived,** except Jesus Christ. (President
B. Young: "That is true. How can it be otherwise?") It can't;
and I tell you that he is just as active to-day as ever he was, and

he can do more for this people and for the cause of Zion than he could when here. (John Young, April 8, 1857, *Journal of Discourses* 6:231–32)

My message to the young people of the Church is this:
Joseph Smith was and is a prophet of the true and the living God. Joseph Smith was the instrument in the hands of God of establishing upon the earth the true gospel of the Lord Jesus Christ. . . .—Era, 24:869. (*Gospel Standards,* President Heber J. Grant, 1943, p. 180)

Joseph Smith is a true prophet of the living God and his successors likewise. The mantle of authority and prophecy and revelation and power lies in his choice servant who now leads us, and he is God's prophet not only to Latter-day Saints, but to every living soul in all the world. This is my testimony. (*Faith Precedes the Miracle,* President Spencer W. Kimball, 1975, p. 328)

The Prophet Joseph Smith was the instrument in God's hands in restoring the gospel and establishing the true Church of Christ again upon the earth. (*Teachings of Ezra Taft Benson,* President Ezra Taft Benson, 1988, p. 111)

LDS leaders to the present time think Joseph Smith was a true prophet of God. These are just a sample of the many testimonies that could be given. But what does the record show?

Joseph Smith's prophetic record

The following was recorded at an official Mormon Church meeting which took place on February 14 and 15, 1835:

President Smith then stated that **the meeting had been called, because God had commanded it.** . . . and it was the will of God that those who went to Zion, with a determination to lay down their lives, if necessary, should be ordained to the ministry, and go forth to prune the vineyard for the last time, or **the coming of the Lord, which was nigh—even fifty-six years should wind up the scene.** (*History of the Church* 2:182)

In other words, the Lord should arrive by February 16, 1891.

At this same meeting on February 14, 1835, twelve apostles (D&C 18:27) were named (*History of the Church* 2:180–86) and nine men[15] were ordained and given blessings (*History of the Church* 2:187, 189 and *Comprehensive History of the Church* 1:374–75). Heber C. Kimball, one of the nine men ordained by Oliver Cowdery, David Whitmer, and Martin Harris (three of the witnesses that allegedly saw the gold plates), relates how those ordained then had hands laid upon them by Joseph Smith, Sidney Rigdon, and Frederick Williams (the First Presidency) to confirm the blessings[16] and ordinations they had previously received (*Comprehensive History of the Church* 1:375; *Times and Seasons* 6:868). Three of these blessings were:

> The blessing of Lyman E. Johnson was, in the name of Jesus Christ, . . . and that no power of the enemy shall prevent him from going forth and doing the work of the Lord; and that **he shall live until the gathering is accomplished**, according to the holy prophets; and he shall be like unto Enoch; and his faith shall be like unto his; and he shall be called great among all the living; and Satan shall tremble before him; **and he shall see the Savior come and stand upon the earth with power and great glory.** (*History of the Church* 2:188)

Lyman E. Johnson was excommunicated from the Mormon Church on April 13, 1838, and he died in December 1856 at Prairie du Chien, Wisconsin, at age 45.

> John F. Boynton's Blessing: . . . Thou shalt lead the elect triumphantly to the places of refuge; thou shalt be like the brethren who have been blessed before thee. **Thou shalt stand in that day of calamity when the wicked shall be consumed, and present unto the Father, spotless, the fruits of thy labor.** Thou shalt overcome all the evils that are in the world; thou shalt have wisdom to put to silence all the wisdom of the wise; and **thou shalt see the face of thy Redeemer in the flesh.** These blessings are pro-

nounced and sealed upon thee. Even so. Amen. (*History of the Church* 2:191)

John F. Boynton was excommunicated in 1837 and died in 1890 at the age of 79 at Syracuse, New York.

> William Smith's [the Prophet Joseph Smith's brother] Blessing: ... He shall be mighty in the hands of God, in bringing about the restoration of Israel. The nations shall rejoice at the greatness of the gifts which God has bestowed upon him: that his tongue shall be loosed; he shall have power to do great things in the name of Jesus. **He shall be preserved and remain on the earth, until Christ shall come to take vengeance on the wicked.** (*History of the Church* 2:191)

William Smith became involved with some of the off-shoots of Mormonism after his brother was killed and was excommunicated on October 19, 1845. He died in 1893 at the age of 82 at Osterdock, Iowa.

At the April 1843 General Conference Joseph Smith said:

> Were I going to prophesy, I would say the end (of the world) would not come in 1844, 5, or 6, or in forty years. **There are those of the rising generation who shall not taste death till Christ comes.... I prophesy in the name of the Lord God, and let it be written—the Son of Man will not come in the clouds of heaven till I am eighty-five years old.** (*History of the Church* 5:336)

Joseph Smith was born on December 23, 1805, which means the Lord would come after December 23, 1890.

Some Mormons might say the above items by Joseph Smith were recorded incorrectly, are not understood, or were isolated incidents, but members also heard Joseph Smith teach the same thing at other meetings. Two members recorded the following in their journals:

> At the April conference, 1840, the Prophet Joseph, while speaking of some of the elders on this matter said they were mistaken;

the Lord would not come in ten years; no, nor in twenty years; no, nor in thirty years; no, nor in forty years, and **it will be almost fifty years before the Lord will come**. ("Luman Shurtliff Autobiography, 1807–1847," typescript, Brigham Young University, Special Collections Library, p. 44; *LDS Historical Library*, Infobase, Inc., copyright 1992)

. . . also concerning the Millerites.[17] They were preparing a place for the Savior to come and meet with them, on a certain day, in that month in Illinois. They were making great preparations by cleaning a certain piece of ground and spreading carpets, etc. Brother Joseph was speaking on the "Resurrection" and the "Second Coming of the Son of God." "You can go and tell Brother Miller he won't come on that day nor the next, nor the next year. **In the name of Jesus Christ I prophesy he won't come in forty years.**" . . . He was enquiring of the Lord concerning his second coming; the answer was, **"If you live to be (I think it was eighty) years old you will see the face of the Son of God."** (Martha Thomas Autobiography, in Daniel Thomas Family History, 1927, pp. 32–33; *LDS Historical Library*, Infobase, Inc., copyright 1992)

There is no evidence that any of the people above ever saw the face of the Lord, and obviously the Lord did not return. The Bible warns us about people who would set dates for the Lord's Second Coming (Matthew 25:13).

Joseph Smith prophesied concerning a war that would involve all nations:

Verily, thus saith the Lord concerning the wars that will shortly come to pass, beginning at the rebellion of South Carolina, which will eventually terminate in the death and misery of many souls; And the time will come that war will be poured out upon all nations, beginning at this place. For behold, the Southern States shall be divided against the Northern States, and the Southern States will call on other nations, even the nation of Great Britain, as it is called, and they shall also call upon other nations, in order to defend themselves against other nations; and then **war shall**

be poured out upon all nations. And it shall come to pass, after many days, slaves shall rise up against their masters, who shall be marshaled and disciplined for war. And it shall come to pass also that the remnants who are left of the land will marshal themselves, and shall become exceedingly angry, and shall vex the Gentiles with a sore vexation. And thus, with the sword and by bloodshed the inhabitants of the earth shall mourn; and with famine, and plague, and earthquake, and the thunder of heaven, and the fierce and vivid lightning also, shall the inhabitants of the earth be made to feel the wrath, and indignation, and chastening hand of an Almighty God, until the consumption decreed **hath made a full end of all nations**. (December 25, 1832, D&C 87:1–6)

The potential of a civil war was general knowledge at the time this revelation was allegedly given. The State of South Carolina passed a tariff nullification ordinance on November 24, 1832. This action and northern anti-slavery agitation led to talk of armed conflict at this time.[18] Newspapers quickly carried this information all over the country. Even a January 1833 Mormon newspaper covered the subject.[19] Note that Smith's prophecy says that "war shall be poured out upon all nations." This did not happen in the Civil War nor in any of the wars that followed for more than the next one hundred years. There also has not been "a full end of all nations."

It is interesting to note that this revelation, which is dated December 25, 1832, was not made scripture until after the Civil War. It was not in the *Book of Commandments* (1833) or in the 1835 and 1844 editions of the Doctrine and Covenants. It was included in the 1876 edition. It was also included in the first publication of the Pearl of Great Price, by F. D. Richards in England in 1851. However, the Pearl of Great Price and the 1876 D&C were not canonized until 1880.

On another occasion Joseph Smith said:

Verily thus saith the Lord: It is wisdom in my servant David W. Patten, that he settle up all his business as soon as he possibly can, and make a disposition of his merchandise, **that he may perform a mission unto me next spring [spring 1839], in company with others, even twelve including himself, to testify of my name and bear glad tidings unto all the world**. (April 17, 1838, D&C 114:1)

David W. Patten was killed on October 25, 1838, at the age of 38 at the Battle of Crooked River, Missouri. Obviously he never went on his mission "next spring." (Some Mormons would say he went on his mission in the "spirit world." But note that the alleged revelation says "next spring, in company with others, . . . to bear glad tidings **unto all the world**." This must be the world we live in, not the "spirit world," where he would be alone on his mission.)

Joseph Smith also prophesied as follows:

A revelation of Jesus Christ unto his servant Joseph Smith, Jun., and six elders, as they united their hearts and lifted their voices on high. **Yea, the word of the Lord concerning his church, established in the last days for the restoration of his people**, as he has spoken by the mouth of his prophets, and for the gathering of his saints to stand upon Mount Zion, which shall be the city of New Jerusalem. Which city shall be built, beginning at the temple lot,[20] which is appointed by the finger of the Lord, in the western boundaries of the State of Missouri, and dedicated by the hand of Joseph Smith, Jun., and others with whom the Lord was well pleased. Verily this is the word of the Lord, that the city New Jerusalem shall be built by the gathering of the saints, beginning at this place, even the place of the temple, **which temple shall be reared in this generation. For verily this generation shall not all pass away until an house shall be built unto the Lord**, and a cloud shall rest upon it, which cloud shall be even the glory of the Lord, which shall fill the house. (September 1832, D&C 84:1–5)

This temple has not been built even to this day, and the land is not owned by the Mormon Church (of Salt Lake City) or the RLDS Church. Historical evidence shows that Mormons of Joseph

Smith's day, and after his death, expected the temple to be built in their lifetime.[21]

Some would say in his defense that Joseph Smith used "in this generation" as in Matthew 24:34: "Verily I say unto you, This generation shall not pass, till all these things be fulfilled." They say that, because the Lord has not come, "this generation" must have another meaning in the Bible and in Smith's usage. But Joseph Smith's translation of this verse in *Joseph Smith—Matthew* 1:34 (which some Bible scholars agree with),[22] in Pearl of Great Price, page 45, reads: "Verily, I say unto you, **this generation, in which these things shall be shown forth, shall not pass away** until all I have told you shall be fulfilled." Jesus was speaking, not about his contemporary generation, but about "this" future generation whose situation he was describing. Smith, on the other hand, was speaking about his own generation, as his contemporaries testified. That generation passed away without the temple's being built.

The Bible warns us about false prophets (Matthew 24:11; 7:15–20) and tells us how to judge them:

> But the prophet, which shall presume to speak a word in my name, which I have not commanded him to speak, or that shall speak in the name of other gods, even that prophet shall die. And if thou say in thine heart, How shall we know the word which the LORD hath not spoken? When a prophet speaketh in the name of the LORD, if the thing **follow not, nor come to pass**, that is the thing which the LORD hath not spoken, **but the prophet hath spoken it presumptuously: thou shalt not be afraid of him**. (Deuteronomy 18:20–22)

Should we be afraid of Joseph Smith? Now let us see what a Mormon apostle said on this subject:

> False prophets—the curse and scourge of the world! How awful and awesome and evil it is when one pretends and professes to speak for God in leading men to salvation, but in fact has a message that is false, a doctrine that is not true, and **a prophecy that**

will not come to pass. (*The Mortal Messiah*, [Apostle] Bruce R. McConkie, 2:168–69)

This LDS leader has the right idea: it is evil for a person to profess to speak for God and not have the prophecy come to pass. It is sad that Mormons do not apply this to Joseph Smith.

Will animal sacrifices be restored?

Mormon leaders' teachings show that they expect animal sacrifices to be reinstituted as part of the restoration of all things.

> RESTORATION OF BLOOD SACRIFICES. We are living in the dispensation of the fulness of times into which all things are to be gathered, and all things are to be restored since the beginning. Even this earth is to be restored to the condition which prevailed before Adam's transgression. Now in the nature of things, **the law of sacrifice will have to be restored, or all things which were decreed by the Lord would not be restored. It will be necessary, therefore, for the sons of Levi,**[23] **who offered the blood sacrifices anciently in Israel, to offer such a sacrifice again to round out and complete this ordinance in this dispensation.** Sacrifice by the shedding of blood was instituted in the days of Adam and of necessity will have to be restored.
>
> **The sacrifice of animals will be done to complete the restoration when the temple spoken of is built; at the beginning of the millennium, or in the restoration, blood sacrifices will be performed long enough to complete the fulness of the restoration in this dispensation.** Afterwards sacrifice will be of some other charactor [*sic*]. (*Doctrines of Salvation*, Joseph Fielding Smith, 3:94)

Malachi foretold that such offerings would be attended to again in the day of the Second Coming of Christ. (Mal. 3:1–4) Joseph Smith, commenting upon Malachi's prophecy explained how this could be: "It is generally supposed that sacrifice was entirely done away when the great sacrifice, the sacrifice of the Lord Jesus was offered up and that there will be no necessity for the ordinance of sacrifice in (the) future; but those who assert this are certainly not acquainted with the duties, privileges and authority of the priesthood, or with the prophets.

"**The offering of sacrifice** has ever been connected and forms a part of the duties of the priesthood. It began with the priesthood, and **will be continued until after the coming of Christ**, from generation to generation. We frequently have mention made of the offering of sacrifice by the servants of the Most High in ancient days, prior to the law of Moses; which ordinances will be continued when the priesthood is restored with all its authority, power and blessings. . . .

"**These sacrifices**, as well as every ordinance belonging to the priesthood, will, when the Temple of the Lord shall be built, and **the sons of Levi be purified, be fully restored and attended to in all their powers, ramifications, and blessings**. This ever did and ever will exist when the powers of the Melchizedek Priesthood are sufficiently manifest; else how can the restitution of all things spoken of by the holy prophets be brought to pass. It is not to be understood that the law of Moses will be established again with all its rites and variety of ceremonies; this has never been spoken of by the prophets; **but those things which existed prior to Moses' day, namely sacrifice, will be continued**." (Teachings, pp. 172–73; *Doctrines of Salvation*, vol. 3, p. 94) (*Mormon Doctrine*, [Apostle] Bruce R. McConkie, p. 666, under "Sacrifices")

According to Apostle Bruce R. McConkie, the restoration is to precede the Second Coming of Christ.

In speaking of the restoration of all things, as promised by all the holy prophets since the world began, and after quoting Malachi's promise that the Lord, at his Second Coming, would purify the sons of Levi so that once again they could and **would offer anew unto him their ancient sacrifices**, the Prophet Joseph Smith said: "It is generally supposed that sacrifice was entirely done away when the Great Sacrifice (i.e.,) the sacrifice of the Lord Jesus was offered up, and that there will be no necessity for the ordinance of sacrifice in (the) future; but those who assert this are certainly not acquainted with the duties, privileges and authority of the Priesthood, or with the Prophets." (*The Mortal Messiah*, [Apostle] Bruce R. McConkie, 1:156–57, in footnote 1)

The Bible says Jesus was the final sacrifice; we need no other. This teaching of restoring blood sacrifices makes a mockery of the sacrifice of Jesus for our sins. The following are just a few of the Scriptures that refute this Mormon teaching:

Neither by the blood of goats and calves, but **by his own blood** he entered in **once** into the holy place, having obtained **eternal redemption** for us. For if the blood of bulls and of goats, and the ashes of an heifer sprinkling the unclean, sanctifieth to the purifying of the flesh: How much more shall the **blood of Christ**, who through the eternal Spirit offered himself without spot to God, purge your conscience from dead works to serve the living God? (Hebrews 9:12–14)

For the law having a shadow of good things to come, and not the very image of the things, can never with those sacrifices which they offered year by year continually make the comers thereunto perfect. . . . For it is not possible that the blood of bulls and of goats should take away sins. . . . By the which will [of God] we are sanctified through the offering of the body of Jesus Christ once for all. **And every priest standeth daily ministering and offering oftentimes the same sacrifices, which can never take away sins: But this man, after he had offered one sacrifice for sins for ever, sat down on the right hand of God. . . . For by one offering he hath perfected *for ever* them that are sanctified.** (Hebrews 10:1, 4, 10–12, 14)

Christ also hath **once suffered for sins**, the just for the unjust, that he might bring us to God, being put to death in the flesh, but quickened by the Spirit. . . . (1 Peter 3:18)

Even the Book of Mormon says Jesus was the last sacrifice:

And ye shall offer up unto me **no more the shedding of blood; yea, your sacrifices and your burnt offerings shall be done away, for I will accept none of your sacrifices and your burnt offerings**. And ye shall offer for a sacrifice unto me a broken heart and a contrite spirit. (3 Nephi 9:19–20)

For it is expedient that there should be a **great and last sacrifice**; yea, not a sacrifice of man, neither of beast, neither of any manner of fowl; for it shall not be a human sacrifice; but it must be an **infinite and eternal sacrifice**. . . . Therefore, it is expedient that there should be a **great and *last* sacrifice**; and then shall there be, or it is expedient there should be, a stop to the shedding of blood; then shall the law of Moses be fulfilled; yea, it shall be all fulfilled, every jot and tittle, and none shall have passed away. And behold, this is the whole meaning of the law, every whit pointing to that **great and last sacrifice; and that great and last sacrifice will be the Son of God, yea, infinite and eternal**. (Alma 34:10,13–14)

Yes, that "great and last sacrifice" was the Son of God himself. It is absurd and unbiblical to believe that animal sacrifices will be reinstituted.

Does it make sense?

Notice that all of the above examples, with the possible exception of the items on animal spirits and Joseph Smith's prophecies, are mundane and do not include miraculous events done by the power of God. All are part of the routine of human activity. There is no hint of a miracle, so each item may be judged by its own reasonableness. If there were two or three of these, perhaps they could be ignored, "swept under the rug," so to speak, but the sheer volume makes that impossible. There are just too many absurdities to be ignored and explained away as human error, or the work of men (the printers?) out to damage the Church.

IN CONCLUSION

We have fairly presented the statements of the Mormon Church, its presidents, scriptures, and publications regarding their claim to be the one true Church, the only true Church of Jesus Christ on earth. We have also presented the statements claiming that the Doctrine and Covenants are from Jesus Christ and are "true and faithful," as well as the assertions that the Book of Mormon is from God.

To test these claims, we have compared Mormon scriptures to Mormon scriptures on various subjects, compared Mormon president to Mormon president on specific teachings, looked at changes in Mormon scriptures, and looked at absurd statements by Mormon leaders and in Mormon scriptures. Except for the absurdities, in evaluating and judging the comparisons, we have used the standards given by Mormon presidents and Mormon scriptures. (We have not used our own standards, as they would not be accepted by Mormons—and this is understandable.) In looking at the absurdities, we have used logic and common sense as the standard.

In each case Mormonism has flunked the test. And it has flunked in not just a few instances, but in over seventy-five items it has missed the mark. With this level of confusion, can this really be God's "only true Church," as Presidents John Taylor and Spencer W. Kimball said, and the "only true message," as President Ezra Taft Benson said?

IS THERE SOMETHING BETTER?

Why Is the Bible Reliable?

One of the dangers of Mormonism is the teaching that makes adherents hostile to the genuine Christian churches and leaves them in confusion about the reliability of the Bible. One of the first things I (John Farkas) did after I realized Mormonism was false was to examine the reliability of the Bible by studying books on its history and how we received it. Covering this subject could be a book in itself, so I will just summarize my findings. The following are reasons why I now consider that the Bible is from God and should be used as a rule for faith, salvation, and action:

1. It is logical that God would give us something written.
2. It is inspirational and intrinsically correct and good, and if followed leads to a quality life.
3. There is good evidence that it was transmitted and handed down to us with only very minor errors, none of which are important.[1] Mormonism's position that significant parts are missing and that it has been translated incorrectly conflicts with the Bible's own statements. The Bible assures me: "Heaven and earth shall pass away: but **my words shall not pass away**" (Mark 13:31). "Being born again, not of corruptible seed, but of incorruptible, **by the word of God, which liveth and abideth for ever**" (1 Peter 1:23). "Neither pray I for these [the apostles] alone, but for them [us]

also which shall believe on me **through their word** . . ."
(John 17:20).

4. Many parts of it are historically verifiable.
5. It is a record of prophecy (Old Testament) and its fulfillment (New Testament).
6. The personal witness and testimony of some of its writers,
   along with what Jesus' followers did after he died, rose from
   the grave, and ascended to heaven, speak clearly of its divine source.

Read the Bible every day (start with the Gospel of John), while
considering and studying in depth all the above (and more you
might add). Then pray regularly, asking God to witness the truth
of the Bible to you. I prayed to the one true God of all creation,
the God of the Old Testament prophets, the God of Abraham,
Isaac, Jacob, and Moses. I said I didn't want any counterfeits. If
you do your part, you can expect the Holy Spirit to give you a
personal testimony. Remember James 1:5: "If any of you lack
wisdom, let him ask of God . . ."; and 1 Thessalonians 5:21: "Prove
all things. . . ." Note that wisdom is the proper use of knowledge,
and we must first do our part in gathering that knowledge before we ask God for wisdom.

Note in item 3 above that Mark 13:31 consists of Jesus' words.
If Mormonism is correct in saying that parts are missing from
the Bible and it is mistranslated and there was a complete apostasy, then Jesus lied to us, and I reject that idea! In 1 Peter 1:23
the Apostle Peter tells us that the word of God lives and is with
us forever! Did he lie? Mormonism seems to say he did. The Mormon Church teaches that shortly after Jesus died many of his important teachings were lost, but were restored through Joseph
Smith starting in 1830.[2] In John 17:20 Jesus in his great inter-
cessory prayer asks the Father to bless those in the future who
believe in him through the word of the apostles. It is illogical to
believe that the Lord's special prayer for the future faithful was
honored for a short period and then was ignored for about 1800
years. We would also have to believe that the Holy Spirit (John

14:26; 16:13; Acts 1:8) was a failure and that the apostles the Lord appointed, and then their disciples, and so on were all complete and dismal failures. These ideas are also illogical!

There Is Something Better!

Frequently Christians will hear: "Do you have something better to offer? What else is there?" As an ex-Mormon I (John Farkas) can give a strong and firm Yes to this question. There is something better! When I left the LDS Church on March 15, 1984, I was left essentially with the beliefs that I held in 1974 before I joined this Church. I believed in a Supreme Being, a God, but I did not accept the Bible as the Word of God and I did not accept Jesus Christ as his Son.

Rather than try to write to a broad spectrum of beliefs ex-Mormons may hold, I will just cover what I experienced. I had a very strong desire to know of these things, and I can only consider that desire a gift from God. Because of this gift I did the following:

- I studied books about the Bible. Was it historically and archaeologically correct; was it correct factually? My conclusions are as outlined above. Books on this subject are listed separately in the Recommended Reading section of this book.
- Through all of this I associated with Christians as much as possible. I also went to church services *every* Sunday. For many weeks I went to a different church each Sunday.
- Once I established *in my mind* the reliability of the Bible (as described above) and that it is the Word of God, and is Scripture, I then examined some key doctrinal items. My prime concerns were the divinity of Jesus Christ and the doctrine of the Trinity.
- When I established *in my mind* that the Lord Jesus Christ was God, the real One according to the Scriptures (see

1 Corinthians 15:3–4), and I accepted the concept of the
Trinity, I was then ready for more.

• With help from others I went through the following steps,
not necessarily in this order:

I learned that feelings were *not* important. I didn't need a "religious experience," a burning in the bosom, a "tingling."
The promise of the real Almighty God was enough, the
promise in John 3:16! "God so loved the world that he gave
his only begotten Son, that **whosoever** believeth in him
should not perish, but have everlasting life." The promise
was the important thing, not feelings, and it applied to me!

I admitted that I was a sinner, repented of my sins, and confessed my sins to God (see Luke 13:3; Acts 2:38; 17:30–31;
1 John 1:9–10; and Proverbs 28:13).

I believed in the real God of the Bible, and his Son, the real
Lord Jesus Christ (see John 3:16–18; Acts 16:31; Ephesians
2:8–9).

I confessed my faith to men (see Romans 10:9–10). On Sunday, July 29, 1984, I answered an altar call at a local Christian church. It was a church God had chosen. My wife and
son had been attending there for nine years. The congregation had been praying for me all that time. After that I
wanted to tell people about my Lord and Savior, Jesus Christ.

Yes, there is something better! The real Jesus Christ, a Bible
you can have complete faith in (not just "as far as it is translated
correctly"), a local Bible-believing and teaching church, and good
Christian friends. My conversion was an answer to the prayers
of my family, Christian friends, and a congregation. For years
my wife claimed for me, "Ye shall know the truth, and the truth
shall make you free" (John 8:32). We have heard of many others set free by the promise of this powerful verse.

WITNESSING TO MORMONS

We are frequently asked to provide ideas and assistance to people in witnessing to their friends, relatives, and acquaintances. The usual plea is: "Tell me what to say; give me some ideas." The most frustrating of all is: "The Mormon missionaries are coming tonight. What can I say to them?" Witnessing to people trapped in counterfeit Christianity is not a casual activity, even for us who have been doing it for years. It takes concern, preparation, study, and prayer. In this respect Mormonism is no different from other sects. In fact it may require more study and time than many of the others before a Christian is ready to deal effectively with Mormons.

Who Can Witness?

Can mature Christians[1] who know little or nothing about Mormonism witness *effectively* to Mormons? We don't believe it is possible. They will misunderstand what the Mormons are saying or will not be able to pick out their mistakes or their attempts to present only the more palatable aspects of Mormon doctrine or even to misrepresent it.[2] Many times we have heard Christians, who have spoken to Mormon missionaries, tell us, "They believe the same as we do."

But if Christians do a little bit of homework, then the answer is: Yes, an effective witness is possible. And their effectiveness can be multiplied tenfold if they also know the weak spots of Mormonism and have a well-thought-out approach. This book covers an approach that is usable with longtime Mormons, with "investigators" (potential converts), and with those interested. Our book *Mormons Answered Verse by Verse* provides biblical answers for Mormons, and *How to Rescue Your Loved One from Mormonism* features techniques for witnessing to loved ones along with documentation from Mormon publications to show many of their unique doctrines.

We strongly recommend that a baby Christian by himself or herself *not* witness to Mormons. It should be done with a mature Christian. We recommend that two Christians always work together, or with another Christian within earshot at the very least, particularly when witnessing at Mormon events or Mormon locations. Hostile situations can arise too easily under these circumstances, and in some cases false accusations have been made against Christians. When two people are witnessing together, it is vital that one person lead the activity. This should be determined beforehand. The second person has only one job: to help the person leading the activity. The one helping should not change the subject, should not interrupt the discussion, and should search out references for the leader. This takes a great deal of self-control for most of us, but it must be done; otherwise the effectiveness of the witnessing will be seriously reduced.[3]

What Does the Bible Say?

Prior to undertaking the responsibility of witnessing to a Mormon, or someone interested in Mormonism, it is important to understand the direction we receive from the Bible on this subject. The Lord wants us to witness and he tells us how we are to witness. Some examples are:

Warn the wicked.

When I say unto the wicked, Thou shalt surely die; and thou givest him not warning, nor speakest to warn the wicked from his wicked way, to save his life; the same wicked man shall die in his iniquity; but his blood will **I require at thine hand**. Yet **if thou warn the wicked**, and he turn not from his wickedness, nor from his wicked way, he shall die in his iniquity; but thou hast delivered thy soul. (Ezekiel 3:18–19)

Teach all nations.

Go ye therefore, and **teach all nations**, baptizing them in the name of the Father, and of the Son, and of the Holy Ghost. (Matthew 28:19)

Be ready to give an answer in meekness.

But sanctify the Lord God in your hearts: and **be ready always to give an answer** to every man that asketh you a reason of the hope that is in you **with meekness and fear**. (1 Peter 3:15)

Preach, reprove, rebuke, exhort with longsuffering and doctrine.

Preach the word; be instant in season, out of season; **reprove, rebuke, exhort** with all **longsuffering and doctrine**. (2 Timothy 4:2)

Discern good and evil.

But strong meat belongeth to them that are of full age, even those who by reason of use have their senses exercised to **discern both good and evil**. (Hebrews 5:14)

Contend for the faith.

Beloved, when I gave all diligence to write unto you of the common salvation, it was needful for me to write unto you, and exhort you that ye should **earnestly contend for the faith** which was once delivered unto the saints. (Jude 3)

Go to the market and synagogue to reason and dispute.

Now when they had passed through Amphipolis and Apollonia, they came to Thessalonica, where was a synagogue of the Jews: And Paul, as his manner was, **went in** unto them, and three sabbath days **reasoned with them** out of the scriptures. . . . Therefore **disputed** he in the synagogue with the Jews, and with the devout persons, and **in the market daily** with them that met with him. (Acts 17:1–2, 17)

And he **reasoned** in the synagogue every sabbath, and **persuaded** the Jews and the Greeks. (Acts 18:4)

And he went into the synagogue, and **spake boldly** for the space of three months, **disputing** and **persuading** the things concerning the kingdom of God. But when divers were hardened, and believed not, but spake evil of that way before the multitude, he departed from them, and separated the disciples, **disputing daily in the school of one Tyrannus**. (Acts 19:8–9)

Be gentle, patient, meek while instructing.

And the servant of the Lord must not strive; but **be gentle unto all men**, apt to teach, **patient**, in **meekness instructing** those that oppose themselves; if God peradventure will give them repentance to the acknowledging of the truth; and that they may recover themselves out of the snare of the devil, who are taken captive by him at his will. (2 Timothy 2:24–26)

Be Prepared!

Try to remember two very essential ingredients before, during, and after witnessing:

1. Pray for the person and for your witnessing.
2. Show Christian love and friendship for the person.

When you pray about your witnessing, ask for wisdom (James 1:5) and guidance. (Keep in mind that wisdom is the proper use of knowledge, so you have to do your part.) If you feel it appropriate, pray with the person you are witnessing to at the start and end of your witnessing. But you should be the one doing the praying, and you should use it to teach gospel principles. (Be aware that most Mormons do not pray to the God of the Bible, although they think they do; or at least they have many misconceptions about him.)

If you have a friendship with a Mormon, you should seriously consider giving a prayerful, gentle, and loving witness even if you risk losing your friend. But it should be a well-thought-out risk, taken with prayer and preparation. Then do your witnessing at the right time and location, and with the right people present. If you think you may get only one try, that single witness needs to be planned carefully. Keep in mind that, while you should have an overall strategy, you need have only the first two hours or so planned in detail. There is more on this below.

Be prepared for your first attempts at witnessing to be significantly less than perfect. You will get better with experience. Even those highly experienced, in a review of a witnessing activity, can think of better ways to have handled it. Most of us have 20-20 hindsight, but critically reviewing our witnessing attempts will make us better at it. Also, you should not be the one to break up a friendship if your witnessing attempt is rejected. Other opportunities may present themselves in the future.

As part of your preparation you should be versed in the material presented in the preface and chapter 1. You should also be familiar with the Mormon viewpoint on the topic you plan to cover. For example, if you are going to cover "Mormon Presidents Compared" then prepare by studying "Mormon Standards for Following the Words of the Top Mormon Leaders." Don't forget to use the material in chapter 9 ("Is There Something Better?").

Before you get into the comparisons, you should set the stage by reading together the statements of top Mormon leaders and Mormon scriptures quoted in the preface and chapter 2 ("The Basis for Evaluating Scripture Comparisons"). The purpose of this is to establish the authoritative importance Mormons attach to the references. This is a very important step and it should not be ignored.

Some Mormons may challenge the accuracy or reliability of the quotes. If you have good reason to believe this will happen, then see if you can borrow some of the materials referred to, or at least get full-page copies of a few of them before your discussion starts. Most of the references, with the exception of *The Seer*, *Journal of Discourses*, and maybe *History of the Church* should be found in a local Mormon ward library or in personal collections of Mormons in the congregation.[4] You may also be able to borrow them or obtain copies of pages through the inter–library loan network.

Some Mormons may not have the patience for this preparatory review. If you see signs of impatience, then skip it for now. But immediately go back to it with the first dismissal of the comparisons. Obviously someone just getting interested or involved in Mormonism will not be familiar with any of the references. If this is the case, select a few from Appendix 1 and read them. This may help the newcomer see the contrast sooner. It is important to keep the quotes in mind during your witnessing.

As you go through the comparisons, the Latter–day Saint will likely offer defenses based on the excuse "This was one man, not the Church" or "This was just an opinion." Go back to the authority of the references, as appropriate, to counter such defenses. Keep going back to them and keep stressing that these are Mormon standards. While in the comparisons, if you hear something like "Well, it doesn't mean that," then ask what it does mean. Read it again. If you have the reference or a copy of the page, then read it from your copy. Keep working the topic; *do not* let the Mormon change the subject. Put off subject changes politely and firmly by taking a written note of the proposed new subject and then saying something like "We can talk about that later, but now we are on this subject."

Be prepared for the Mormon to say that everything in this book is lies and distortions or half-truths and the rantings and ravings of anti-Mormons. This can result from just one look at the material or from finding one item that is perceived to be wrong (therefore all of it is wrong!) or just from looking at the cover. You cannot stop this kind of thinking, but you do not have to accept it or leave it unchallenged. Ask the Mormon to be specific as to what is wrong. Insist on specific details, and do not let him or her get away with broad generalities. If the Mormon thinks one item is wrong, ask what specifically is wrong about it. If it appears that the Mormon does not understand the comparison, then try reviewing it. Remember that he or she owes you just as much evidence as to why an item of comparison is wrong as you do in presenting it. If a person will not engage in such a constructive review and discussion, then give serious thought to dropping any additional discussion with that person until he or she is ready to do so.

Keep Your Discussions Short

It is wise to keep your discussions to less than three hours. After this, fatigue takes over with most people, and the mind slows down too much. It is better to have several sessions than one very long one. But there may be no alternative if you are concerned about the possibility of having another session. The old adage "A bird in the hand is worth two in the bush" may apply here. In other words, if you have a reasonable doubt about getting another chance, then get in as much material as you can the first time.

Throughout your discussion, do not lose sight of your ultimate goal, which is to help the person to accept Jesus Christ as Lord and Savior. It is just your short-term strategy to undermine confidence and faith in the Mormon Church. Until you do this, stay away from trying to refute Mormon doctrine with the Bible. Because Mormons discount the Bible so much, and because they place so much confidence in Mormon Church teachings, biblical discussions early on are usually fruitless and end up something like playing a game of Ping-Pong. The scriptures are shot back and forth, but no progress is made. In other words, hold off attempting to refute and teach doctrine until the person becomes teachable. You cannot *make* this happen, so don't become frustrated. It may be that your job is just to plant the seed or water someone else's seed (1 Corinthians 3:6; John 4:35–38). Just as some wildflower seeds with "hard" seed coats need years of environmental "softening" before they will germinate, many Mormons don't show any "softening" for years. Don't be discouraged by the lack of immediate results. It took me (John Farkas) over eight years.

"We Don't Attack You, Why Are You Attacking Us?"

Some Mormons and Christians admonish us for attacking the Mormon Church because it is negative. They say to us, "We should only say good things about each other." Others maintain that we should use our resources instead to care for the poor. While we believe in and practice charitable works, we also agree with Jesus when he said, "Man shall not live by bread alone" (Matthew 4:4). While *only* saying and doing good things about and for each other sounds good on the surface, in reality it is not biblical. (Nor is it a practice followed by the Mormon Church from its beginning to the present day.) The usual Mormon comment is: "We don't attack you, so why are you attacking us?" The following should help you answer this question.

Based upon personal experience we (and others) have to say that the best answer to this question is: "I'm just defending my beliefs and my church from the attacks of the Mormon Church and taking up the challenge of past Mormon Church leaders" (see the preface). Most Mormons will deny that they or their Church attacks other churches, so you may need to use the following Mormon scriptures to show that these attacks exist.

> And he said unto me: Behold there are save two churches only; the one is the church of the Lamb of God, and the **other** is the **church of the devil**; wherefore, whoso belongeth **not** to the church of the Lamb of God belongeth to that great church, which is the mother of abominations; and she is the whore of all the earth.... which is the great and abominable church of all the earth, **whose founder is the devil**.... (1 Nephi 14:10, 17)

As was shown in the preface, the Mormon Church through its publications and top leaders claims to be the one true church restored by Jesus Christ. It claims to be the church of the Lamb of God. Then where does that leave us and our church, seeing that we don't believe this was said by God? We should be offended by the implication that we are part of the "great and abominable church" founded by the devil. This passage is in every Book of Mormon, which the missionaries give away by the millions (4.6 million in 1993).

In another Mormon scripture we read:

> ... I asked the Personages who stood above me in the light, which of all the sects was right (for at this time it had never entered into my heart that all were wrong)—and which I should join. I was answered that I must join none of them, for they were **all wrong**; and the Personage who addressed me said that all their **creeds were an abomination** in his sight; that those **professors were all**

corrupt; that: "they draw near to me with their lips, but their hearts are far from me, they teach for doctrines the commandments of men, having a form of godliness, but they deny the power thereof." . . . I have learned for myself that Presbyterianism is not true. (*Joseph Smith—History* 1:18–20)

These verses are found in every set of Mormon scriptures sold and are just a sample of what has been said through the years. Some Mormons might say that 1:18–20 applied only to the 1820 period. But it can be shown that the creeds in place in 1820 are essentially the same ones now in place. The "professors" are not college teachers but are, as shown in the 1828 *Webster's Dictionary*, the people who accept the creeds and profess them as their beliefs. The churches (Methodists, Baptists,[5] and Presbyterians) that are referred to in verses 5, 8, and 9 (not shown) are still in existence. So if they were all wrong in 1820 and still have the same creeds and beliefs, then they must also be wrong now. Christians were probably upset with this accusation when it was made available to the general public with the publication in 1851 of the Pearl of Great Price, and many are upset with it now. When Christians write or speak against Mormonism, they do so in self-defense.

Some Mormons might say that Joseph Smith was merely quoting God. You then need to state that you do not believe that God said these things. Ask the Mormon to at least look at it from your viewpoint, even if he or she doesn't agree. This kind of request in many cases defuses the Mormon hostility and allows you to proceed with your witnessing mission.

We have a right to defend our churches and beliefs from such attacks. The biblical references under "What Does the Bible Say?" above clearly support this. In addition, we have the example of the Apostle Paul, who went to the marketplaces and the synagogues reasoning, persuading, and disputing (Acts 17:1, 2, 17; 18:4; and 19:8–9). According to Ephesians 5:3 and Hebrews 5:14 we are to "discern both good and evil." Jude 3 tells us to "contend for the faith." So there is suitable scriptural support for pointing out errors if it is done in love and concern, to help win souls for Christ and not just to win an argument.

Should You Pray about the Book of Mormon?

Frequently Mormons will ask: "Have you read the Book of Mormon and prayed about it?" Or "Will you read the Book of Mormon and pray about it?" Sometimes they will quote from Moroni 10:4:

> And when ye shall receive these things, I would exhort you that ye would ask God, the Eternal Father, in the name of Christ, if these things **are not true**; and if ye shall ask with a sincere heart, with real intent, having faith in Christ, he will manifest the truth of it unto you, by the power of the Holy Ghost.

Many non-Mormons do not know how to answer this challenge to pray about the Book of Mormon. There are at least three ways to respond to it:

1. If you know enough about the changes made in the Mormon scriptures (see "Some Changes" in chapter 5), then ask: "Which Book of Mormon do you want me to read and pray about? Do you want me to pray about the 1830 edition of the Book of Mormon or the present edition?" This question usually results in a quizzical look and a question or comment like "What do you mean?" or "I don't understand you." You then have the opportunity to take control of the conversation in order to undermine the Mormon's confidence in the Book of Mormon. You may start to cover the key changes not only in the Book of Mormon but also in the Doctrine and Covenants (chapter 6).

2. Another approach is to ask the question: "Are there some things we should not pray about?" Most people don't know how to answer this one. After a hesitation, answer your own question by asking another question: "If I needed money, would it be proper for me to ask God, while kneeling in prayer, 'Should I go

into town and rob the bank?'" Most will agree that this is not a proper prayer. There are some things we should not pray about, and they are the items that God has already given us commands on. Then quote 1 Thessalonians 5:21, which tells us to "Prove all things; hold fast that which is good." It doesn't say, as Moroni 10:4 does, to assume it is true and then prove it wrong, but to prove it and then hold onto it if it is good. How do we prove the Book of Mormon? By comparing it to what God has already spoken, the Bible. If you know the Book of Mormon and the Bible fairly well, launch into such a comparison. Or, if you prefer, ask the Mormon why he or she is presenting the Book of Mormon when so much Mormon doctrine is not in it (see "Is the Book of Mormon the most correct book?" in chapter 7).

3. Another way to respond is to ask: "Before we consider praying about the Book of Mormon, could you please point out for me the key added truths in it that are not in the Bible?" The mature (well-versed) student of Mormonism and the Book of Mormon may ask what appears to be a simple question: "The Introduction of the Book of Mormon, in the first paragraph, says it 'contains, as does the Bible, the fulness of the everlasting gospel.' What does this mean and where can it be found in the Book of Mormon?"[6] This could lead to a detailed discussion that could encompass the first two approaches, and others not covered.

Some worldly examples show how dishonest it is to present the Book of Mormon as if it represented Mormonism, when it really doesn't. The practice of realtors in many areas is to require the seller of a house to tell the buyer about any hidden defects. There is a federal law that requires a lender of money to tell the borrower up front about the true cost of borrowing the money. If such candor is required even for worldly things, should it not be more so for spiritual things? Why do Mormon missionaries keep secret from their prospective converts the facts found in this book? Probably for the same reason that Jehovah's Witnesses don't tell their prospective members about the shunning that will occur if they and their family become Jehovah's Witnesses and then one of them changes his or her mind later on. They would not make many converts if such information were known.

It is beyond the scope of this book to cover more of the many tools and materials helpful in witnessing. For more witnessing helps we recommend our books *Mormons Answered Verse by Verse* and *How to Rescue Your Loved One from Mormonism.*

AUTHORS' TESTIMONIES

John R. Farkas

It is an early morning late in February 1984. As usual I am reading the scriptures while eating breakfast. I am in the Book of Mormon, 1 Nephi 18:25. This verse mentions the cow, ox, ass, horse, goat, and wild goat. This morning is a little unusual, though, in that I find myself questioning how some of these animals could have been in the New World. Didn't the experts (historians, paleozoologists) say that full-size horses were not in the New World until the European explorers and settlers arrived? This thought had occurred to me at least once before, I think while I was investigating the Church of Jesus Christ of Latter-day Saints. But this time the question stayed with me, and I found myself thinking about other questions that I apparently had suppressed in the past. I now had become teachable and open, a necessary prerequisite to receiving productive witnessing.

Starting with the late February period when I questioned the presence of certain animals in the New World, and continuing for about two months, I seldom had a complete night's sleep. Almost every night I woke up to study for one or two hours, in addition to using all of my free time for the same thing. By the end of February I had shared my doubts with my resident Mormon expert, my born-again Christian wife, Phyllis. In 1975, when I had joined the LDS Church, she became a Christian and started her studies of Mormonism. I had gone on to become the elders quorum president of the Fairport Ward (1981–1984), and in early 1984 of the newly reorganized Rochester 1st Ward, both in the Rochester, New York Stake, while Phyllis became an expert in Mormon studies and acquired a very extensive library. When I asked her for certain information, I almost always had it within minutes.

By March 15th I had made up my mind to leave the Mormon Church. I knew it when I woke up that night and removed my temple garments.[1] I felt free! My drive to study and learn continued, this time to grow in depth and breadth in Mormon studies and about the Bible and Jesus Christ (see chapter 9, "Is There Something Better?").

On March 20, 1984, I sent Stake President Dale Dallon my letter of resignation. The reasons I noted in my letter were: changes in the *Book of Commandments* versus Doctrine and Covenants; changes in the Book of Mormon; conflicts between early and present-day teachings; and the translation of the *Book of Abraham*. I said that "Joseph Smith was a fraud and has pulled off one of the greatest hoaxes ever!!!" My name was formally taken off the Church rolls at a Church court on May 10, 1984.

How did I get involved with the Mormon Church in the first place? It was my wife's fault—I now say that partially in jest. In 1974, when I became concerned about the food supply chain and saw a need to have a long-term supply of food at home, Phyllis said, "The Mormons do that sort of thing. I'll send them a letter in Salt Lake City." Well, she did, and the LDS missionaries brought the answer to us. We both took the missionary lessons. As a result I joined in July 1975; Phyllis became a Christian. (Growing up amidst the tug-of-war between Christian and Mormon parents was hard on our son, Alan. Children suffer in such conflicts.)

During that time I asked a very significant question without realizing how significant it was. I said to Phyllis, "If we are both praying to the same God, how come we are getting different answers?" Now I realize that the Mormon gods are not of the Bible. Mormonism is not biblical Christianity.

When I left the Mormon Church on March 15, 1984, I was left essentially with the beliefs that I had held in 1974 before I joined the Church. I was still a spiritual infant. I believed in a supreme being, a God, but I did not accept the Bible as the Word of God and I did not accept Jesus Christ as his Son and my Savior. I had a desire to know, so I studied the Bible and books about the Bible, associated with Christians, and attended Christian Sunday services and Sunday school. Through this I came to know that the Bible is the Word of God, and I came to know the real Lord Jesus Christ. But even at this point I didn't know I was "saved."

Only after prayerful reading of John 3:16 with my friend Ross Amico—the founder of a group that was to become Berean Christian Ministries, an organization dedicated to exposing cults—did I fully realize the truth of John 3:16 and that I was the "whosoever" mentioned in this verse. The promise that I could claim was the important thing. Ironically, I accepted Jesus in the Palmyra, New York, Christian church that is adjacent to the Mormon chapel where I had been baptized nine years earlier *to the very week.* These are both thirty-five miles from my home; therefore I believe it was God's wisdom for it to happen there. On Sunday, July 19, 1984, I answered an altar call at a Webster, New York, Christian church and made public my faith in the real Lord Jesus Christ. Now I know of the simplicity and beauty of his gospel.

I also had a drive to share my newfound knowledge and faith with others, both Mormons and non-Mormons. It is interesting that I had never had anything like this drive to share Mormonism with others. I had not been a good member missionary. In fact, in my last four to six months of Church membership my feeling against missionary work surfaced. This became evident to me as my bishop attempted to increase missionary activity in our ward, and I gave him only passive support; but I didn't understand it then.

The Mormon people are a great people. They and their church have many characteristics that I found appealing. They are hardworking, conservative, successful, well-organized, and they give great socials. They are good people in a worldly sense and should have the real Jesus Christ of the Bible. Using the Bible, they present some convincing arguments that appear to support their doctrine. It is important for Christians to know the Bible and to know the real Lord Jesus Christ. A weak Christian is no match against the Mormon story; it is very appealing. It is easier to keep people from joining the Mormon Church than to get members out.

Groups like Berean Christian Ministries perform a multi-function service in combating the false non-Christian teachings of the Mormon Church and similar groups. They help to educate Christians, Mormons, and others; they organize activities that individuals could not handle; they provide support for those trying to get out from under the control of Mormonism and similar organizations.

For over seven years I have coordinated the Berean Christian Ministries outreach at the Mormon Hill Cumorah Pageant held annually in July near Palmyra, New York. It is the largest outdoor pageant in America, and up to 100,000 people attend each year. Over 13,000 pieces of Christian literature have been distributed each year.

I am a graduate of the University of Connecticut with a B.S. degree in mechanical engineering, and I am a licensed New York State professional engineer. From 1962 to 1991 I worked at Xerox Corporation as a project engineer and a project engineering manager. My wife, Phyllis, is editor of *The Berean Report.*

One of the reasons I share the items in this last paragraph with you is to illustrate that worldly accomplishment and intellectual capability are different from spiritual capability. I have often been asked how an intelligent person could believe Mormon doctrine, and I can understand why the question is asked. But when the Mormon missionaries came to our house, I was a spiritual baby, and they taught only the milk of the Mormon "gospel." The meat comes later. As Hebrews 5:14 says, I was not "of full age": "Strong meat belongeth to them that are of full age, even those who by reason of use have their senses exercised to discern both good and evil." I was not able to discern the real gospel of Jesus Christ from the "gospel" the Mormon missionaries had.

Through the prayers of concerned Christians, including my wife, who persevered through a rough situation, I became teachable and then "of full age." I hope and pray that the biblical Jesus Christ is your Lord and Savior as he is mine.

David A. Reed

My early religious training was in a big, white Unitarian church in rural New England south of Boston, where, at age fourteen, I concluded that religion was "the opium of the people." Later I went on to Harvard University and found that such atheism was perfectly acceptable there. By the time I was twenty-two, however, I came to realize that godless evolution offered me only a pointless existence in a meaningless universe, followed by a "dead" end. I began to think about God again.

At that time a Jehovah's Witness was assigned to work alongside me at my job, so I began asking him questions about his beliefs. His answers amazed me. It was the first time that I had ever heard religious thoughts presented in a tight-knit, logical framework. In no time I became a very zealous Witness myself, and remained in the Watchtower organization for thirteen years, serving as a fulltime minister and a congregation elder.

I married Penni Scaggs, who was raised in the organization and was also a zealous Witness. Between the two of us we conducted home Bible studies with dozens of people and brought well over twenty of them into the sect as baptized Jehovah's Witnesses. What interrupted this life of full dedication to the Watchtower Society? In one word, *Jesus*. Let me explain.

When Penni and I were at a large Witness convention, we saw a handful of opposers picketing outside. One of them carried a sign that read, "Read the Bible, Not the Watchtower." We had no sympathy for the picketers, but we did feel convicted by this sign, because we knew that we had been reading Watchtower publications to the exclusion of reading the Bible. Later on we actually counted up all of the material that the organization expected JWs to read. The books, magazines, lessons, etc., added up to over three thousand pages each year—compared with less than two hundred pages of Bible reading assigned—and most of that was in the Old Testament. The majority of Witnesses were so bogged down by the three thousand pages of the organization's literature that they seldom got around to the Bible reading.

After seeing the picket sign, Penni turned to me and said, "We should be reading the Bible *and* the Watchtower material." I agreed, so we began doing regular personal Bible reading with the aim of becoming better Jehovah's Witnesses.

But as we read the New Testament, we became impressed with Jesus as a person: what he said and did, how he treated people. We wanted to be his followers. Especially we were struck with how Jesus responded to the hypocritical religious leaders of the day, the scribes and Pharisees. I remember reading over and over again the accounts relating how the Pharisees objected to Jesus' healing on the Sabbath, his disciples' eating with unwashed hands, and other details of behavior that violated their traditions. How I loved Jesus' response: "You hypocrites, Isaiah aptly prophesied about you, when he said, 'This people honors me with their lips, yet their heart is far removed from me. It is in vain that they keep worshiping me, because they teach commands of men as doctrines'" (Matthew 15:7–9, Watchtower's *New World Translation*).

Commands of men as doctrines! That thought stuck in my mind, and I began to realize that, in fulfilling my role as an elder, I was acting more like a Pharisee than a follower of Jesus. For example, the elders were the enforcers of all sorts of petty rules about dress and grooming, and this reminded me of the Pharisees who condemned Jesus' disciples for eating with unwashed hands.

Grooming was not the real issue, however. For me it was a question of whose disciple I was. Was I a follower of Jesus, or an obedient servant to a human hierarchy? The elders who eventually put me on trial knew that that was the real issue, too. They kept asking, "Do you believe that the Watchtower Society is God's organization? Do you believe that the Society speaks as Jehovah's mouthpiece?"

With the new perspective that I was gaining from Bible reading, it upset me to see the organization elevate itself above Scripture, as it did when the December 1, 1981, *Watchtower* said: "Jehovah God has also provided his visible organization. . . . Unless we are in touch with this channel of communication that God is using, we will not progress along the road to life, no matter how much Bible reading we do" (p. 27). It really disturbed me to see those men elevate themselves above God's Word. I voiced criticisms at the meetings, but was then blocked from speaking, so I decided to try writing. That's when I started publishing the newsletter *Comments from the Friends*.

The elders wanted to put me on trial for publishing it, but my wife and I simply stopped going to the Kingdom Hall. By that time most of our former friends there had become quite hostile toward us. One young man called on the phone and threatened to "come over and take care of" me if he got another newsletter. And another Witness actually left a couple of death threats on our answering machine.

It was a great relief to be out from under the oppressive yoke of that organization. But we now had to face the challenge of where to go and what to believe. It takes some time to rethink your entire religious outlook on life. And we had not yet come into fellowship with Christians outside the JW organization.

All Penni and I knew was that we wanted to follow Jesus and that the Bible contained all the information we would need. We were amazed at what we found in prayerfully reading the New Testament over and over again—things that we had never appreciated before, like the closeness that the early disciples enjoyed with the risen Lord, the activity of the Holy Spirit in the early church, and Jesus' words about being born again.

All those years we were Jehovah's Witnesses, the Watchtower had taken us on a guided tour through the Bible. We gained a lot of knowledge about the Old Testament, and we could quote a lot of Scripture, but we never heard the gospel of salvation in Christ.

We never learned to depend on Jesus for our salvation and to look to him personally as our Lord. Everything centered around the Watchtower's works program, and people were expected to come to Jehovah God through the organization.

When I realized from reading Romans 8 and John 3 that I needed to be born of the Spirit, I was afraid at first. Jehovah's Witnesses believe that born-again people who claim to have the Holy Spirit are actually possessed by demons. And so I feared that if I prayed out loud to turn my life over to Jesus Christ, some demon might be listening, and the demon might jump in and possess me, pretending to be the Holy Spirit. (Many Jehovah's Witnesses live in constant fear of the demons. Some of our friends would even throw out second-hand furniture and clothing, fearing that the demons could enter their homes through those articles.) But then I read Jesus' words in Luke 11:9–13 (NKJV). In a context where he was teaching about prayer and casting out unclean spirits, Jesus said: "I say to you, ask, and it will be given to you; seek, and you will find; knock, and it will be opened to you. For everyone who asks receives, and he who seeks finds, and to him who knocks it will be opened. If a son asks for bread from any of you who is a father, will he give him a stone? Or if he asks for a fish, will he give him a serpent instead of a fish? Or if he asks for an egg, will he offer him a scorpion? If you then, being evil, know how to give good gifts to your children, how much more will your heavenly Father give the Holy Spirit to those who ask Him!"

I knew, after reading those words, that I could safely ask for Christ's Spirit (Romans 8:9), without fearing that I would receive a demon. So, in the early morning privacy of our kitchen, I proceeded to confess my need for salvation and to commit my life to Christ.

Penni teaches fifth grade now in a Christian school that has students from about seventeen different churches. She really enjoys it, because she can tie the Scriptures in to all sort of subjects. And I publish *Comments from the Friends* as a quarterly aimed at reaching Jehovah's Witnesses with the gospel and helping Christians who are talking to JWs.

Although the thrust of my outreach ministry is toward Jehovah's Witnesses, I also take advantage of opportunities to share the gospel with Mormons and have had numerous conversations with them—on the street when they were canvassing for potential converts, and in my home when I have accepted their offer of a free copy of the Book of Mormon, which they personally deliver as a way to start weekly discussions. My research on Mormonism started out as preparation for such visits by the missionaries.

The most important lesson Penni and I have learned since leaving the Jehovah's Witnesses is that Jesus is not just a historical figure that we read about. He is alive and is actively involved with Christians today, just as he was back in the first century. He personally saves us, teaches us, and leads us. This personal relationship with God through his Son Jesus Christ is wonderful! The individual who knows Jesus and follows him will not even think about following anyone else: "A stranger will they not follow, but will flee from him: for they know not the voice of strangers. . . . My sheep hear my voice, and I know them, and they follow me: And I give unto them eternal life; and they shall never perish, neither shall any man pluck them out of my hand" (John 10:5, 27, 28).

Appendix 1

REFERENCES

The following very brief description of most of the references used in this book is provided to help the reader understand the importance of each document. This listing is alphabetical by title.

See Appendix 2 for a brief description of the authors and others named in the references.

Books and Manuals

Achieving a Celestial Marriage, Student Manual for "Preparing for a Celestial Marriage" and "Building a Celestial Marriage," prepared by the Church Educational System, Salt Lake City: The Church of Jesus Christ of Latter-day Saints, 1976, copyrighted "1976 Corporation of the President of The Church of Jesus Christ of Latter-day Saints."[1] Pages 129–32 are a summary of many of the Church's unique teachings.

An Address to All Believers in Christ, David Whitmer, 1805–1888, Richmond, Mo., 1887. This book covers some of the changes in Mormon scripture.

Answers to Gospel Questions, (Apostle)[2] Joseph Fielding Smith, compiled and edited by Joseph Fielding Smith Jr., 5 volumes, Salt Lake City: Deseret Book Co., 1957, 1974 printing.

Articles of Faith (the book), James E. Talmage, One of the Twelve Apostles of the Church, Salt Lake City: The Church of Jesus Christ of Latter-day Saints, 1899, 1976 printing, 52nd edition, "Copyright 1974 By [President] Spencer W. Kimball, Trustee-in-Trust for the

Church of Jesus Christ of Latter-day Saints." This is a detailed analysis of the thirteen Articles of Faith; or, as the title page of the 1976 edition says, "Being a consideration of the principal Doctrines of The Church of Jesus Christ of Latter-day Saints."

Comprehensive History of the Church of Jesus Christ of Latter-day Saints, (President of the First Council of Seventy) B. (Brigham)[3] H. (Henry) Roberts, 6 volumes plus an index, Provo, Utah: Published by The Church, Brigham Young University Press, 1965, reprinted 1976, "Copyright 1957 by Corporation of the President of the Church of Jesus Christ of Latter-day Saints." It was first published between 1909 and 1915 as a series of magazine articles. It was revised by the author and brought up to the date April 6, 1930, with input from a committee (according to page viii of the preface, all were members of the Council of the Twelve Apostles) appointed by the First Presidency of the Church.

Discourses of Brigham Young, President Brigham Young, selected and arranged by (Apostle) John A. Widtsoe, Salt Lake City: Deseret Book Co., about 1925, 1977 edition, "Copyright 1954 by [President] David O. McKay, Successor in Trust for the Church of Jesus Christ of Latter-day Saints."

Doctrines of Salvation, sermons and writings of (Apostle) Joseph Fielding Smith, compiled by (Apostle) Bruce R. McConkie, 3 volumes, Salt Lake City: Bookcraft, 1954–1956.

Doctrines of the Gospel, Student Manual, Religion 231 and 232, prepared by the Church Educational System, Salt Lake City: The Church of Jesus Christ of Latter-day Saints, 1992, "Copyright 1976, 1992 by Corporation of the President of The Church of Jesus Christ of Latter-day Saints." The Introduction says: "Doctrines of the Gospel, Religion 231 and 232, is a course designed to help you systematically study the principles and doctrines of the gospel of Jesus Christ from the four standard works of the Church."

Encyclopedia of Mormonism, 4 volumes, New York: Macmillan Publishing Co., a division of Macmillan, Inc., copyright 1992. The Editor in Chief was Daniel H. Ludlow, Brigham Young University. Apostles Neal A. Maxwell and Dallin H. Oaks were advisers (*Church News,* December 7, 1991, p. 7). Also on CD-ROM disk, Orem, Utah: Infobase, Inc., copyright 1990–1992.

Evidence and Reconciliations, (Apostle) John A. Widtsoe, 1 volume, Salt Lake City: Bookcraft, 1943, 1960.

Evolution of the Mormon Temple Ceremony: 1842–1990, Jerald and Sandra Tanner, Salt Lake City: Utah Lighthouse Ministry, 1990, 182 pages. It shows in great detail the changes made to the Mormon temple endowment ceremony since 1842 and contains the complete typescript of the present ceremony (as of April 1990) as recorded on audiotape by a temple patron.

Family Home Evening, Personal Commitment, Salt Lake City: The Church of Jesus Christ of Latter-day Saints. The title page has: "Published By The First Presidency Of The Church of Jesus Christ of Latter-day Saints; Copyright 1972, Corporation of the President of The Church of Jesus Christ of Latter-day Saints." This book was published for use as an aid and teaching manual for Mormon families when holding family home evenings.[4] Pages 125–26 describe how Jesus Christ was conceived in Mary in the same way we were by our parents.

Gospel Doctrine, (President) Joseph F. Smith, selections from his sermons and writings, Salt Lake City: Deseret Book Co., 1963 edition, "Copyright 1919 by Heber J. Grant, Trustee-in-Trust for the Church of Jesus Christ of Latter-day Saints," and 1939 by Deseret Book Co., Inc.

Gospel Infobase Library, CD-ROM disk, Orem, Utah: Infobase, Inc., copyright 1992, 2nd edition, 6/92. It contains the *standard works* and thirty-five publications by twenty-one past and present top leaders in the Mormon Church.

Gospel Kingdom, (President) John Taylor, selections from his writings, edited by G. Homer Durham, Salt Lake City: Bookcraft, 1987.

Gospel Principles, Salt Lake City: Deseret Book Co., 1978, "Copyright 1986, Corporation of the President of The Church of Jesus Christ of Latter-day Saints." 1986 or older editions are best as in newer editions some items have been changed or removed. As said in the Introduction: "This manual has been prepared for new members of the Church. Through studying it, you can learn the basic principles of the gospel and become better prepared to live them." The following pages show the unique teachings: 5, 9, 15, 17, 289–91, 326, 353.

Gospel Standards, President Heber J. Grant, selections from his sermons and writings, compiled by Dr. G. Homer Durham under the direction of (Apostle) John A. Widtsoe and (Apostle) Richard L. Evans, Salt Lake City: The Improvement Era (a Mormon Church internal organization) 7th edition, 1943.

Gospel Through the Ages, The, Milton R. Hunter of the First Council of the Seventy, 1945. This book, as stated on the title page, was "written and published under the direction of the General Priesthood Committee of the Council of the Twelve of the Church of Jesus Christ of Latter-day Saints." This was a priesthood study manual for Mormon men.

History of the Church, edited by B. H. Roberts, 7 volumes with index, Salt Lake City: The Deseret Book Co., 1902–1932, 2nd edition, 1978. This work is also called *A History of Joseph Smith, the Prophet, By Himself* and is sometimes referred to as *Documentary History of the Church.* It covers Mormon history into 1848.

Jesus the Christ, James E. Talmage, One of the Twelve Apostles of The Church of Jesus Christ of Latter-day Saints, Salt Lake City: Deseret Book Co., 1915, 1973 printing, 33rd edition, "Copyright October 1973 by [President] Harold B. Lee, Trustee-in-Trust for The Church of Jesus Christ of Latter–day Saints." The preface says: "The author of this volume entered upon his welcome service under request and appointment from the presiding authorities of the Church; and the completed work has been read to and is approved by the First Presidency and the Council of the Twelve."

Joseph Smith's First Vision, Milton V. Backman, Jr., Salt Lake City: Bookcraft, Inc., 1971, 2nd edition, 1980. It provides a history of the various versions of the First Vision.

Joseph Smith Translation (of the Bible), Joseph Smith, 1833. The JST is not published in its entirety by the LDS Church, but only as excerpts in the footnotes and Appendix of the Mormon Church's edition of the King James Bible, demonstrating Smith's variation from the King James Version. The Reorganized Church of Jesus Christ of Latter Day Saints calls it *Joseph Smith's New Translation* or the *Inspired Version.* The RLDS published (Herald, 1970) a side-by-side comparison of the New Translation with the King James Version. Joseph started this translation of the Bible allegedly at the commandment of the Lord and on January 10, 1832, he was commanded to continue the work until it was finished (D&C 73:3–4). On February 2, 1833, he said the New Testament was completed, and on July 2, 1833, he said the translation of the scriptures had been completed (*History of the Church* 1:324, 368–69). Some scholars say he left it unfinished. Seeing he said he was commanded by the Lord to complete it and said he finished the New Testament and, later, the Bible, we will take him at his word that he completed it. This was a translation done by "inspiration," Smith claimed, and not by consulting Greek manuscripts, as most others are.

Journal of Discourses, talks by top Mormon leaders between 1844 and 1886, photolithographic reprints of the original edition of 1855–1886, 1974 reprint (the name of the publisher is not given), 26 volumes, plus an index (the index was compiled and edited at Brigham Young University Library, 1959). From Volume 1, page v, we learn that these books were authorized by the First Presidency, Brigham Young, Heber C. Kimball, and Willard Richards. In a letter of June 1, 1853, they said:

> . . . Elder George D. Watt, by our counsel, spent much time . . . to acquire the art of reporting in Phonography, which he has faithfully and fully accomplished. . . . You will perceive at once that this will be work of mutual benefit, and we cheerfully and warmly request your co–operation in the purchase and sale. . . .

The prefaces to Volumes 4 and 8 include similar comments from "The Publisher." Volume 4 says:

> It would be altogether gratuitous and uncalled–for, on our part, to write a commendatory preface to the discourses of the First Presidency and Twelve Apostles of this Church. To the Saints **their words are as the words of God**, their teachings fraught with heavenly wisdom, and their directions leading to salvation and eternal lives.

The preface of Volume 8 says:

> The *Journal of Discourses* deservedly ranks as one of **the standard works** of the Church, and every rightminded Saint will certainly welcome with joy every Number as it comes forth from the press as an additional reflector of "light that shines from Zion hill."

LDS Historical Library, CD-ROM disk, Orem, Utah: Infobase, Inc., copyright 1992, 1st edition, 3/92. It contains *Journal of Discourses,*

History of the Church, Comprehensive History of the Church and *Writings of Early Church Members.*

"LDS Church Authority and New Plural Marriages, 1890–1904," in *Dialogue,* D. Michael Quinn, Vol. 18, No. 1, Spring 1985, pages 9–105, Salt Lake City: Dialogue Foundation. Mr. Quinn was professor of American History at Brigham Young University when this was written.

Mormon Doctrine, (Apostle) Bruce R. McConkie, Salt Lake City: Bookcraft, 1958, 1966 edition, 1979 printing, 856 pages. This is a one-volume encyclopedia about Mormon doctrine. The authority of this book is validated by frequent reference to it in Mormon Church manuals.

Mormonism—Shadow or Reality? Jerald and Sandra Tanner, Salt Lake City: Utah Lighthouse Ministry, 5th edition, 1987. This is the single best book for a comprehensive, detailed study of the errors of Mormonism. It uses many copies from old LDS publications. The authors can be reached at P.O. Box 1884, Salt Lake City, UT 84110.

Mormon Polygamy—A History, Richard S. Van Wagoner, Salt Lake City: Signature Books, 1986. It is an excellent coverage of the history of Mormon polygamy, from its start in the 1830s to the present.

Mortal Messiah, The, part of the 6-volume Messiah Series, (Apostle) Bruce R. McConkie, Salt Lake City: Deseret Book Co., 1979–1981.

1993–1994 Church Almanac, Salt Lake City: Deseret News, 1992, 416 pages. The *Almanac* contains information on the General Authorities, past and present officers, scope of the Mormon Church throughout the world, mission locations, temples, detailed historical chronology, and statistics.

Orson Pratt's Works, Important Works in Mormon History, Vol. 2, Orson Pratt, Orem, Utah: Grandin Book Co., 1990.

Personal Writings of Joseph Smith, The, compiled and edited by Dean C. Jessee, Salt Lake City: Deseret Book Co., 1984.

Search These Commandments, Melchizedek Priesthood Personal Study Guide, Salt Lake City: The Church of Jesus Christ of Latter-day Saints, 1984, "Copyright 1984 by Corporation of the President of The Church of Jesus Christ of Latter-day Saints." It is a teaching manual for Mormon men.

Sharing the Gospel with Others, (President) George Albert Smith, Salt Lake City: Deseret Book Co., 1948.

Stand Ye in Holy Places, (President) Harold B. Lee, Salt Lake City: Deseret Book Co., 1874.

Teachings of Ezra Taft Benson, (President) Ezra Taft Benson, from his sermons, talks, and books, Salt Lake City: Bookcraft, 1988.

Teachings of the Prophet Joseph Smith, "selected and arranged by the Historian [and Apostle] Joseph Fielding Smith, and his Assistants in the Historian's Office of the Church of Jesus Christ of Latter-day Saints," Salt Lake City: Deseret Book Co., 1976.

Teachings of Spencer W. Kimball, The, (President) Spencer W. Kimball, Salt Lake City: Bookcraft, 1982.

3,913 Changes in the Book of Mormon, Jerald and Sandra Tanner, Salt Lake City: Utah Lighthouse Ministry, no date. This is a photo reprint of the original 1830 edition of the Book of Mormon with all the changes marked to show different readings in the 1964 edition. The authors can be reached at P.O. Box 1884, Salt Lake City, UT 84110.

Truth Restored: A Short History of the Church of Jesus Christ of Latter-day Saints, Gordon B. Hinckley of the First Presidency of The Church of Jesus Christ of Latter-day Saints, Salt Lake City: The Church of Jesus Christ of Latter-day Saints, 1979, "Copyright 1979 by Corporation of the President of The Church of Jesus Christ of Latter-day Saints."

Words of Joseph Smith, compiled and edited by Andrew F. Ehat and Lyndon W. Cook, Provo, Utah: Religious Studies Center, Brigham Young University, 1980.

Periodicals

The Mormon Church almost from its beginning published a variety of newspapers and later published magazines also. Those referenced in this book are:

Deseret News. This newspaper was first published in Salt Lake City in June 1850. It continues to the present day and is now a daily paper.

Ensign. This magazine, fully titled *The Ensign of the Church of Jesus Christ of Latter-day Saints,* is for English-speaking adults and has been published since 1971. It replaced the *Improvement Era*, the *In-*

structor, and the *Relief Society Magazine*, all for adults; its circulation in 1990 was 615,000.

Improvement Era. Starting in 1897, this was at first a magazine for young men, published by the Young Men's Mutual Improvement Association of the Church of Jesus Christ of Latter-day Saints. It later became an adult magazine, still within the Mormon Church. It was succeeded by the *Ensign* in 1971.

Millennial Star. Officially called *The Latter-day Saints' Millennial Star*, it was published from 1840–1970 in England.

Saints' Herald. This periodical, started circa 1860, is published by the Reorganized Church of Jesus Christ of Latter Day Saints, now in Independence, Missouri.

The Seer. (Apostle) Orson Pratt published this periodical primarily in Washington, D.C., 1853–1854. Its purpose was "illucidating [*sic*] the doctrines of the Church of Jesus Christ of Latter Day Saints," according to Mr. Pratt. On page 2 is a letter of appointment from the First Presidency, Brigham Young, Heber C. Kimball, and Willard Richards. This letter is dated September 13, 1852, and says: "This certifies that Professor Orson Pratt of the University of Deseret. . . . is appointed by us, with the sanction of the special Conference . . . to preside over the affairs of the Church throughout the United States . . . and to write and publish Periodicals, Pamphlets, Books &c., illustrative of the principles and doctrines of the Church. . . ."

Times and Seasons. This newspaper was published by the Church of Jesus Christ of Latter-day Saints in Nauvoo, Illinois, from November 1839 to February 1846.

Scriptures

The LDS Church has four official canonized scriptures. They are called the *standard works* and are the Holy Bible, Book of Mormon, Doctrine and Covenants, and Pearl of Great Price.

Holy Bible, Authorized King James Version with Explanatory Notes and Cross References to the *standard works* of the Church of Jesus Christ of Latter-day Saints, Salt Lake City: The Church of Jesus Christ of Latter-Day Saints, 1979.

Book of Mormon, Salt Lake City: The Church of Jesus Christ of Latter-day Saints, 1981 edition, 1986 printing. Like the Bible, the Book of Mormon is composed of books, fifteen in total. They are: First Book of Nephi (1 Nephi), Second Book of Nephi (2 Nephi), Book of Jacob, Book of Enos, Book of Jarom, Book of Omni, The Words of Mormon, Book of Mosiah, Book of Alma, Book of Helaman, Third Nephi (3 Nephi), Fourth Nephi (4 Nephi), Book of Mormon, Book of Ether, Book of Moroni. The Book of Mormon was allegedly translated by Joseph Smith from gold plates the angel Moroni gave him at Hill Cumorah. The first edition was published in 1830.

Doctrine and Covenants, Salt Lake City: The Church of Jesus Christ of Latter-day Saints, 1981 edition, 1986 printing. It is a collection of revelations (138) and declarations (2), attributed primarily to God the Son, allegedly revealed mainly to Joseph Smith but also some to the other top leaders. D&C 1:6, 30 says:

> Behold, this is mine [Jesus Christ's] authority, and the authority of my servants, and **my preface** unto the book of my commandments, **which I have given them** to publish unto you, O inhabitants of the earth. . . . **the only true and living church** upon the face of the whole earth, with which I, the Lord, am well pleased. . . . (Also see 1:1.)

This book did not spring forth in its present form. An evolutionary process resulted in the book now used and described above. The following is a description of the first and second editions (the key ones referred to in this book).

Book of Commandments (the full title is *A Book of Commandments, For the Government of the Church of Christ, organized according to law, on the 6th of April, 1830*), 1833. This was the first collection of revelations God the Son allegedly gave to Joseph Smith the prophet (chapter 1, verses 1–2, 5). Only sixty-five of the seventy-one given up to that time ended up in the book because the printing press and building were destroyed and the galley sheets and type scattered before it could be completed.[5] The galleys printed were salvaged and distributed to Church members.

Doctrine and Covenants of the Church of the Latter Day Saints, 1835 edition. This book is an expansion of the *Book of Commandments*. It consists of two parts. The first part, called "On the Doctrine of the Church of the Latter Day Saints," contains seven "Lectures on Faith," theology lectures, originally given to a School for the Elders (1834–1835) in Kirtland, Ohio. These lectures were the doctrine portion of the 1835 and following editions of the Doctrine and Covenants, but were quietly removed beginning with the 1921 edition.

The second part is called the "Covenants and Commandments of the Lord to His Servants in the Church of the Latter Day Saints." It is the collection of supposed revelations (102) received by Joseph Smith the prophet up to the publication of this edition. It also includes major changes to many revelations that were first published in the *Book of Commandments* in 1833.

Changes in the name of the Mormon Church account for the different name on each book. The names have been: Church of Christ (1830–1834); Church of Latter Day Saints (1834–1838); The Church of Jesus Christ of Latter-day Saints (1838 to the present).

Pearl of Great Price, Salt Lake City: The Church of Jesus Christ of Latter-day Saints, 1981 edition, 1986 printing. This volume was first published in 1851 and became scripture by action of the First Presidency at the General Conference on October 10, 1880 (Introductory Note, in the front of Pearl of Great Price). It is made up of five writings:

Book of Moses. It is called "An extract from the translation of the Bible as revealed to Joseph Smith, June 1830–February 1831."

Book of Abraham. The heading declares: "TRANSLATED FROM THE PAPYRUS, BY JOSEPH SMITH A translation of some ancient Records, that have fallen into our hands from the catacombs of Egypt.—The writings of Abraham while he was in Egypt, called the Book of Abraham, **Written by his own hand,** upon papyrus. See *History of the Church, vol. 2,* pp. 235, 236, 348, 351."

Joseph Smith—Matthew. It is called "An extract from the translation of the Bible as revealed to Joseph Smith the Prophet in 1831: Matthew 23:39 and chapter 24."

Joseph Smith—History. The heading says: "EXTRACTS FROM THE HISTORY OF JOSEPH SMITH, THE PROPHET; History of the Church, Vol. 1, Chapters 1–5."

Articles of Faith. The official name is *The Articles of Faith of the Church of Jesus Christ of Latter-day Saints,* with the subheading *History of the Church, Vol. 4, pp. 535–41.* It consists of thirteen items, on two pages, that are claimed to summarize Mormon Church beliefs, but actually omit much of the Church's unique doctrine.

Appendix 2

MORMON WRITERS AND PERSONALITIES

Backman, Milton V., Jr., Ph.D.: Professor of Church History and Doctrine at Brigham Young University. He has written several books and articles on Mormonism. He is an active member of the Mormon Church and lives in Provo, Utah.

Bennett, John Cook: Special assistant to President Joseph Smith (April 1841–May 25, 1842). He left (or was thrown out of?) the Mormon Church in 1842 and provided the first real public exposure of the practice of polygamy in Nauvoo.

Benson, Ezra Taft (1899–1994): Apostle (1943–1985), thirteenth President (1985–1994). He wrote *The Teachings of Ezra Taft Benson*. He also served under U.S. President Dwight D. Eisenhower as Secretary of Agriculture.

Cannon, George Quayle (1827–1901): Apostle (1860), assistant counselor to President Brigham Young (May 1874), and a first counselor to President Wilford Woodruff and President Lorenzo Snow.

Cowdery, Oliver (1806–1850): First Assistant President (1834). He was the main scribe for Joseph Smith in writing the Book of Mormon as it was allegedly translated by Joseph Smith from the gold plates; he was Joseph's right-hand man during the first seven years of the Mormon Church. He was called the "second elder." From October 1834 to May 1835 he was the editor of the *Messenger & Advocate*, the Mormon Church's paper published in Kirtland, Ohio (near present-day Cleveland). In 1838 he probably let it out that Joseph Smith had committed adultery (an early polygamist marriage) and was soon excommunicated.[1] He supposedly rejoined in November 1848 shortly before his death (March 1850).

Grant, Heber Jeddy: Apostle (1882–1918), seventh President (1918–1945). He wrote *Gospel Standards.*

Jessee, Dean C.: Research historian at the Joseph Fielding Smith Institute for Church History at Brigham Young University. He compiled and edited *The Personal Writings of Joseph Smith* and has written several books on Mormon history. He lives in Salt Lake City, Utah.

Kimball, Spencer Woolley: Apostle (1943–1973), twelfth President (1973–1985). He wrote *The Teachings of Spencer W. Kimball;* he denied that Brigham Young taught Adam-God. He allegedly received a revelation in 1978 that all men (thus including black men) could receive the priesthood.

Law, William: Second counselor to President Joseph Smith (1841–April 18, 1844). He was one of the principals behind the *Nauvoo Expositor,* the newspaper that exposed the practice of plural marriages and the teaching of plural Gods in Nauvoo. The destruction of this paper and the press by men under the command of the Nauvoo City Council and Mayor Joseph Smith led to Smith's arrest and killing in the Carthage Jail on June 27, 1844.

Lee, Harold B. (1899–1973): Apostle (1941–1972), President (1972–1973). He wrote *Stand Ye in Holy Places.*

McConkie, Bruce R.: Apostle (1972–1985). He wrote *Mormon Doctrine, New Witness for the Articles of Faith,* and the Messiah Series.

Pratt, Orson: Early member, Apostle (1835–1842, 1843–1881). He was the author of *The Seer.* He was excommunicated August 20, 1842, because of problems he had with polygamy.[2] On January 20, 1843, he was rebaptized and reinstated as an Apostle. He would have been the third Prophet and President if this had not happened.

Roberts, Brigham Henry (1857–1933): Ordained a Seventy in March 1877 and sustained as one of the First Seven Presidents (the leadership of what was then the Quorum of Seventy) in October 1888 at age 31. An apologist for the Church, he compiled *History of the Church* and *Comprehensive History of the Church of Jesus Christ of Latter-day Saints.* In the 1920s he started to question the authenticity of the Book of Mormon (see *Studies of the Book of Mormon,* by B. H. Roberts, edited by Brigham D. Madsen, University of Illinois Press, 1985).

Smith, Emma (Joseph's first wife): She had to know of some of Joseph's polygamous wives but was openly hostile to the idea. After Joseph's death she denied that he ever taught or practiced plural marriage.

Smith, George Albert (1879–1951): Eighth President (1945–1951). He wrote *Sharing the Gospel with Others* (1948).

Smith, Hyrum (1800–1844): Second Assistant President[3] (1841–1844). He was murdered with his brother Joseph at the Carthage Jail on June 27, 1844.

Smith, Joseph (Jr, Jun.): Founder, Prophet, and first President (1830–1844). He allegedly translated gold plates into the Book of Mormon, received most of the revelations in the Doctrine and Covenants, translated the *Book of Abraham,* and wrote the Pearl of Great Price. He also wrote the Joseph Smith Translation and was the alleged author of *History of the Church.* He was murdered in the Carthage Jail with his brother Hyrum on June 27, 1844. (See Law, William, in this Appendix for more information on Joseph Smith's death.)

Smith, Joseph Fielding: Apostle (1867–1901), sixth President (1901–1918). He is usually called Joseph F. Smith to distinguish him from his son, Joseph Fielding Smith. He was the author of *Gospel Doctrine.*

Smith, Joseph Fielding: Son of Joseph F. Smith, Apostle (1910–1970), tenth President (1970–1972). He was the Mormon Church historian for over fifty years and the author of *Doctrines of Salvation* and *Teachings of the Prophet Joseph Smith.*

Snow, Eliza: When she signed the October 1, 1842, *Times and Seasons* article denying polygamy, she had already been one of Joseph Smith's polygamous wives since June 29th of the same year.[4]

Talmage, James E.: Apostle (1911–1933). He was the author of *Articles of Faith* (the book) and *Jesus the Christ.* He was instrumental in formulating much of the current Mormon Church doctrine.

Tanner, Jerald, and Sandra Tanner: Ex-Mormons, now Christians, they have made available to the public a wide variety of information on the past history and teachings of the Mormon Church. They run Utah Lighthouse Ministry, P.O. Box 1884, Salt Lake City, UT 84110.

Taylor, John: Early member, Apostle (1838–1880), third President (1880–1887). In 1850 he debated three ministers in France and denied that polygamy was practiced by the Mormon Church. At that time he had ten polygamous wives. When he signed the article in the October 1, 1842, *Times and Seasons,* he was married to, or soon to be married to, his first polygamous wife (second wife, total of two). He was an editor of *Times and Seasons.*

Whitmer, David, 1805–1888: One of the first members of the Mormon Church, one of the first three, of the eleven witnesses, alleged to have seen the gold plates, and an early leader (see the Introduction in the Book of Mormon). He believed that Joseph Smith drifted into error after he translated the Book of Mormon. He rejected the 1835 Doctrine and Covenants and many other teachings as not from God and left the organization he helped to start. He was excommunicated in 1838, though he claimed to have held on to his testimony of the truth of the Book of Mormon. He was the author of *An Address to All Believers in Christ.*

Widtsoe, John A.: Apostle (1921–1952). He wrote *Evidences and Reconciliations* and selected and arranged *Discourses of Brigham Young.*

Woodruff, Wilford: Early member, Apostle (1839–1889), fourth President (1889–1898). In 1890 he published the Manifesto (now called Official Declaration—1) ending the practice of polygamy in the Church of Jesus Christ of Latter-day Saints. While the practice was ended, the revelation allowing polygamy is still in the Doctrine and Covenants.

Young, Brigham: Early member, Apostle (1835–1847), second President (1847–1877). He clearly taught Adam-God doctrine from April 9, 1852, to February 7, 1877. He played a major role in saving Mormonism after the death of Joseph Smith.

Appendix 3

DETAILED CONTENTS OF CHAPTERS 3 THROUGH 7

3. Mormon Scriptures Compared

4. Mormon Presidents Compared

5. Changes in the Book of Mormon

Doctrine and Covenants Compared to the *Book of Commandments*

7. Absurdities in Mormonism

Appendix 4

RECOMMENDED READING

Helpful Books on the Bible and Biblical Christianity

Answers to Tough Questions, Josh McDowell and Don Stewart, San Bernardino: Here's Life Publishers, Inc., 1980, 197 pages.

The Bible and Modern Science, Henry M. Morris, Chicago: The Moody Bible Institute of Chicago, 1951, 1968, 128 pages.

The Canon of Scripture, F. F. Bruce, Downers Grove, Ill.: InterVarsity Press, 1988, 349 pages.

The Complete Biblical Library, 16 volumes, Springfield, Mo.: Gospel Publishing House, 1986.

Evidence That Demands a Verdict, Josh McDowell, San Bernardino: Campus Crusade for Christ, Inc., 1972, fourteenth printing, 1977, 387 pages.

An Expository Dictionary of Biblical Words, W. E. Vine, Nashville, Camden, and New York: Thomas Nelson Publishers, 1985, 755 pages.

How We Got the Bible, Neil R. Lightfoot, Grand Rapids: Baker Book House, 1963, 1983, 167 pages.

Jesus: A Biblical Defense of His Deity, Josh McDowell and Bart Larson, San Bernardino: Here's Life Publishers, Inc., 1983, 137 pages.

More Evidence That Demands a Verdict, Josh McDowell, San Bernardino: Campus Crusade for Christ, Inc., 1975, twelfth printing, 1981, 389 pages.

The New Testament Documents: Are They Reliable? F. F. Bruce, Grand Rapids: William B. Eerdmans Publishing Co., 1943, 1980, 120 pages.

Reasons Skeptics Should Consider Christianity, Josh McDowell and Don
Stewart, San Bernardino: Campus Crusade for Christ, Inc., 1981,
230 pages.
Strong's Exhaustive Concordance of the Bible, Nashville and New York:
Abingdon Press, 1894, thirty-second printing, 1974, about 1,500 pages.

Pro-Mormon Publications[1]

A Marvelous Work and a Wonder, (Apostle) LeGrand Richards, Salt
Lake City: Deseret Book Co., 1976 and 1979 editions.
The Mormon Experience, Leonard J. Arrington and Davis Bitton, New
York: Vintage Books, 1980.
Mormon scriptures, the *standard works:* see Appendix 1.

Critical Works

Those with a star (*) are suitable for the new and maturing student.

Adam-God, Craig L. Tholson, Payson, Utah: Publishment, 1991.
Adam-God Maze, The, Culley Christensen, M.D., Scottsdale, Ariz.: In-
dependent Publishers, 1981.
"And this is Life Eternal that they might know Thee, the only True God,"
?Adam? Melaine Layton, self-published, no date. The author's ad-
dress is 4383 Ruskin Rd., Rockford, IL 61101.
Answering Mormons' Questions, Bill McKeever, Minneapolis, Minn.:
Bethany House Publishers, 1991.
Beyond Mormonism: An Elder's Story, James R. Spencer, Grand Rapids:
Chosen Books, 1984.
By His Own Hand Upon Papyrus, Charles M. Larson, Grand Rapids:
Institute for Religious Research, 1985, revised 1992.
The Changing World of Mormonism, Jerald and Sandra Tanner, Chicago:
Moody Press, 1980. This is a condensed version of *Mormonism —
Shadow or Reality?*
For Any Latter-day Saint: One Investigator's Unanswered Questions, S. I.
Banister, Fort Worth: Star Bible Publications, Inc., 1988. This book
has a very good selection of copies from Mormon publications.

God's Word, Final, Infallible and Forever, Floyd McElveen, Grand Rapids: Gospel Truths Ministries, 1985.

How to Rescue Your Loved One from Mormonism, David A. Reed and John R. Farkas, Grand Rapids: Baker Book House, 1994.

Mormon Claims Answered, Marvin W. Cowan, Salt Lake City: self-published, 1984 and 1989 editions. This is also available in Spanish.

Mormonism, Mama, and Me, Thelma "Granny" Geer, Chicago: Moody Press, 1986.

Mormonism—Shadow or Reality? Jerald and Sandra Tanner, Salt Lake City: Utah Lighthouse Ministry, 5th edition, 1987. In our opinion this is the single best research book on what is wrong with Mormonism.

Mormon Polygamy—A History, Richard S. Van Wagoner, Salt Lake City: Signature Books, 1986.

Mormons Answered Verse by Verse, David A. Reed and John R. Farkas, Grand Rapids: Baker Book House, 1992.

No Man Knows My History, Fawn M. Brodie, New York: Alfred A. Knopf, 2nd edition, 1971.

On the Frontlines Witnessing to Mormons, Wally Tope, La Cañada, Calif.: Frontline Ministries, 1981 edition.

Speaking the Truth in Love to Mormons, Mark J. Cares, Milwaukee: Northwestern Publishing House, 1993. This book is recommended for its 185 pages on Mormon culture and terminology.

3,913 Changes in the Book of Mormon, Jerald and Sandra Tanner, Salt Lake City: Utah Lighthouse Ministry, no date. This is a photo reprint of the original 1830 edition of the Book of Mormon with all the changes marked to show different readings in the 1964 edition.

Where Does It Say That? Bob Witte, Grand Rapids: Gospel Truths Ministries, no date. This book provides a good selection of copies from Mormon publications.

Why We Left Mormonism: Eight People Tell Their Stories, Latayne C. Scott, Grand Rapids: Baker Book House, 1990.

Witnessing to Mormons, Jerry and Marian Bodine, San Juan Capistrano, Calif.: Christian Research Institute, 1978.

Note: There are many other excellent books on Mormonism and cults in general. Those listed above are some that we believe the average reader will find most helpful. A number of other useful books, booklets, and newsletters have been self-published by the various ministries noted below.

Ministries and Support Groups

Alpha & Omega Ministries, P.O. Box 47041, Phoenix, AZ 85086

Berean Christian Ministries, P.O. Box 1091, Webster, NY 14580. This is the ministry of John R. Farkas, an ex-Mormon and one of the authors of this book.

Christian Research Institute, P.O. Box 500, San Juan Capistrano, CA 92693

Comments from the Friends, P.O. Box 819, Assonet, MA 02702. This is the ministry of David A. Reed, one of the authors of this book, ministering primarily to Jehovah's Witnesses.

MacGregor Ministries, P.O. Box 73, Balfour, BC V0G 1C0, Canada

Mormonism Research Ministry, P.O. Box 20705, El Cajon, CA 92021

Personal Freedom Outreach, P.O. Box 26062, St. Louis, MO 63136

Utah Lighthouse Ministry, P.O. Box 1884, Salt Lake City, UT 84110

Utah Missions, P.O. Box 348, Marlow, OK 73055

Watchman Fellowship, P.O. Box 13251, Arlington, TX 76094

Note: Those listed above represent only a sampling of the many local ministries and support groups—primarily the largest, those staffed by former Mormons, and those most likely to be able to refer inquirers to sources of help closer to home. For a more complete list of such ministries and support groups, please see the *Directory of Cult Research Organizations*, published by American Religions Center, P.O. Box 168, Trenton, MI 48183.

The authors of *Mormonism: Changes, Contradictions, and Errors* have computerized listings of hundreds of contacts across the United States. If you wish to find help in your locality, or if you have questions or comments concerning this book, you may write John R. Farkas, Berean Christian Ministries, P.O. Box 1091, Webster, NY 14580.

NOTES

Chapter 1: Introduction to Mormonism

1. These were removed from the Doctrine and Covenants starting with the 1921 edition.

2. Membership data here and below are from *1993–1994 Church Almanac, Deseret News*, 1992, pp. 396–99.

3. Many Mormons are unaware of their Church's teaching on this subject.

4. The place where God the Father dwells, the celestial kingdom (*Mormon Doctrine*, Bruce R. McConkie, p. 416, item 3, and p. 116).

5. "In order of their precedence, beginning at the top, the general authorities of the Church include members of: The First Presidency, Council of the Twelve, the Patriarch to the Church, Assistants to the Twelve, First Council of the Seventy and Presiding Bishopric" (*Mormon Doctrine*, Bruce R. McConkie, p. 309).

6. Appendix 1 under "Scriptures" contains a brief description of these.

Chapter 2: The Basis for Evaluating Scripture Comparisons

1. From the footnote on page 324 and the text on page 341 of the reference, and D&C 57:1–3, we learn that Zion is in Jackson County, Independence, Missouri, where the new Bible was to be printed.

2. The exceptions are shown by also showing the JST wording.

3. See Appendix 1 for more information on the JST.

Chapter 3: Mormon Scriptures Compared

1. Mormon leaders had this to say about Adam-ondi-Ahman:

Though there is no uniform belief among Christian scholars as to the geographical location of Eden, the majority claim that it was in Persia. The

Latter-day Saints have more exact knowledge on the matter, a revelation having been given through Joseph Smith, at Spring Hill, Mo., May 19, 1838, in which that place is named by the Lord "Adam-ondi-Ahman. ..." (*The Articles of Faith*, [Apostle] James E. Talmage, p. 474, footnote)

When Adam, after being driven from the garden of Eden, went to Adam-ondi-Ahman to offer sacrifice. ... (*The Discourses of Wilford Woodruff*, [President] Wilford Woodruff, p. 18)

Garden of Eden and City Zion Same Place. In accord with the revelations given to the Prophet Joseph Smith, **we teach that the Garden of Eden was on the American continent** located where the City Zion, or the New Jerusalem, will be built. When Adam and Eve were driven out of the Garden, they eventually dwelt at a place called Adam-ondi-Ahman, situated in what is now Daviess County, Missouri. (*Doctrines of Salvation*, [Apostle] Joseph Fielding Smith, 3:74)

Since Adam called together seven generations of his descendants at Adam-ondi-Ahman, it can well be believed that there was his old homestead. **If so, the Garden of Eden was probably not far distant.** ... (*Evidences and Reconciliations*, [Apostle] John E. Widtsoe, p. 396)

2. This same lesson is also in *He That Receiveth My Servants Receiveth Me*, Melchizedek Priesthood Personal Study Guide, 1979, p. 81.

3. This revelation was not put into the Doctrine and Covenants until 1876, and not accepted by common consent until 1880.

4. It may be said that this was an apostate, a wicked person, saying this. But note that Alma, an alleged true prophet, did not correct this teaching. In addition, other Mormon scripture, as shown below, says the same thing.

5. As a reminder, when a biblical verse is used and the Joseph Smith Translation of the Bible (JST) is *not* shown, this means the JST has exactly the same wording or idea, even though the verse numbers may not be the same. If they are not in agreement, then the JST wording is also shown.

6. Most Mormons, and Mormon Church teaching manuals, say this really means the three Gods (Father, Son, and Holy Ghost) are "one God in purpose." This is their own interpretation as *no* Mormon scripture says this directly.

7. This verse and D&C 8:2: "Yea, behold, I will tell you in your mind and in your heart, by the **Holy Ghost**, which shall come upon you and which shall **dwell in your heart**," seem to have Mormon scripture saying that only the Holy Ghost can dwell in a person's heart.

8. Mormons *interpret* this as supporting ordinances for the dead. But Paul's intent is to support the *resurrection* of the dead. In all of chapter 15, except for

verse 29, Paul in speaking refers to "us," "you," "we," and "your," those in the Christian community. Only in verse 29 does he speak about "they," those outside the Christian community. Details on this are covered in our book *Mormons Answered Verse by Verse*.

9. Full details are covered in my (J.R.F.) unpublished paper "The Fulness of the Everlasting Gospel—What Is It?"

10. *The Evening and Morning Star*, April 1833, Vol. 1, No. 11, page 81, and the 1851 Pearl of Great Price, page 15, both have the Holy Ghost in this verse saying, "I am Jesus Christ," not "I am the Only Begotten."

11. The following is the immediate historical background of Joseph Smith's death:

> In the mean time Joseph, Hyrum, and Elder Taylor had their coats off. Joseph sprang to his coat for his six-shooter, Hyrum for his single barrel. . . . Joseph reached round the door casing, and discharged his six-shooter into the passage, some barrels missing fire. . . . (*History of the Church* 6:617–18, also see 7:31)

> . . . and pulling the six-shooter left by Brother Wheelock from his [Joseph Smith's] pocket, opened the door slightly, and snapped the pistol six successive times; only three of the barrels, however, were discharged. I [Apostle John Taylor] afterwards understood that two or three were wounded by these discharges, two of whom, I am informed, died. (*History of the Church* 7:102–3)

Webster's Deluxe Unabridged Dictionary says a martyr is a person who chooses to suffer or die rather than give up his faith or his principles. While we can understand why Joseph Smith would try to defend himself, the minute he did, he proved that he did not want to die. Hence he was not a martyr.

12. The Mormon Church now teaches that spirit and intelligence are not synonymous. Intelligence is eternal (*Doctrines of the Gospel*, Student Manual, Religion 231 and 232, p. 13), and spirits are procreated (*Gospel Principles*, p. 9). Joseph Smith and other early Mormon leaders for many years consistently taught that "spirits" are "eternal" and have "no beginning." Some examples follow:

> The spirit of man is not a created being; it existed from eternity, and will exist to eternity. Anything created cannot be eternal; and earth, water, etc., had their existence in an elementary state, from eternity. . . . If the soul of man had a beginning it will surely have an end. . . . Spirits are eternal. . . . the spirits of men are eternal. . . . Hear it, all ye ends of the world; for God has told me so. . . . The mind or the intelligence which

man possesses is co-equal with God himself. . . . I am dwelling on the immortality of the spirit of man. Is it logical to say that the intelligence of spirits is immortal, and yet that it had a beginning? The intelligence of spirits had no beginning, neither will it have an end. . . . That which has a beginning may have an end. There never was a time when there were not spirits; for they are co-equal (co-eternal) with our Father in heaven. . . . So with the spirit of man. As the Lord liveth, if it had a beginning, it will have an end. . . . I might with boldness proclaim from the house-tops that God never had the power to create the spirit of man at all. God himself could not create himself. . . . Intelligence is eternal and exists upon a self-existent principle. It is a spirit from age to age, and there is no creation about it. . . . (*The Teachings of the Prophet Joseph Smith*, pp. 158, 181, 208, 352–54. Most of these are also found in the *History of the Church* 3:387, 4:575, 6:310–11.)

This treatise on the "Regeneration and Eternal Duration of Matter," was written by Elder [Parley] Pratt while in Columbia prison, Missouri. . . . Matter and spirit are of equal duration; both are self-existent,—they never began to exist, and they never can be annihilated. * * * * Matter as well as spirit is eternal, uncreated, self existing. . . . (*History of the Church* 4:54–55, footnotes by B.H. Roberts)

13. The 1977 edition of the Book of Mormon says "foundation" instead of "preparator."

14. Many Mormons take great pride in the fact that their congregation leaders (ward and stake leaders) are not paid. Some even think the top leadership is not paid, but this is not the case (*The Mormon Corporate Empire*, John Heinerman and Anson Shupe, Beacon Press, 1985 pp. 87–89).

15. Brigham Young in a public meeting on November 2, 1856, appeared to put this revelation to use when he said: "If any man or woman complains of me or of my Counselors, in regard to the lateness of some of this season's immigration, let the curse of God be on them and blast their substance with mildew and destruction, until their names are forgotten from the earth. . . . I do not believe that the biggest fool in the community could entertain the thought that all this loss of life, time, and means, was through the mismanagement of the First Presidency" (*Journal of Discourses* 4:68).

16. We realize there are also what appear to be discrepancies in the Bible. Most of these are easily answered. We suggest the following books: *Encyclopedia of Bible Difficulties*, Gleason L. Archer, Regency Reference Library/Zondervan Publishing House, 1982; *Today's Handbook for Solving Bible Difficulties*, David E. O'Brien, Bethany House Publishers, 1990.

Chapter 4: Mormon Presidents Compared

1. For more on this subject see "Authority in the Mormon Church" in chapter 1.

2. In some cases we have used other top Mormon leaders (General Authorities) to provide additional information or even other sources when these are not available. All are identified in each case.

3. The "brethren" at conferences are the General Authorities of the Mormon Church. If what they say is "the mind of the Lord, the will of the Lord, the voice of the Lord, and the power of God unto salvation," then the sayings of the Prophet and President of the Church would be even more so.

4. This verse is used here as the Mormon missionaries use it, not as it is in context.

5. This and D&C 130:22 (the Father has a body of flesh and bones) should raise the question: How did God the Father get his body? The Mormon Church teaches that God the Father had a father. Each was a man. A Mormon Church manual used to prepare their members for going to the temple has: ". . . our Father in heaven was once a man as we are now, capable of physical death . . ." (*Achieving a Celestial Marriage*, 1976, 1992, p. 132). An LDS Melchizedek Priesthood Personal Study Guide has: "Man was born of woman; Christ, the Savior, was born of woman; and God, the Father was born of woman" (*Search These Commandments*, 1984, p. 152). The LDS Church today offers no answer for how the first man came about.

6. Also see D&C 27:11; 116:1; 138:38; Daniel 7:9, 13.

7. Dictionaries have the following definition for *omnipresent*: "Present in all places at the same time" (Noah Webster's 1828 *American Dictionary of the English Language*). A modern-day dictionary, *Merriam-Webster's Collegiate Dictionary*, 10th ed. (Springfield, Mass.: Merriam Webster, 1993), has a similar idea.

8. The 1986 edition of the Mormon teaching manual *Gospel Principles* and earlier editions had on pages 4 and 5 a picture of intergalactic space with the caption "Our Heavenly Father Rules the Universe." In the 1988 edition the picture and caption were removed, but the text remained the same. The current edition (1992) has been rewritten and all references to "rules the universe" have been removed. We can only speculate why this expression was deleted. Perhaps it clashed with the teaching on pages 289 and 290 about "exaltation", i.e., men progressing to become "Gods." In any case, the deletion brought this book into closer harmony with the current Mormon view of God, "Our Heavenly Father," as a more limited, finite being.

9. This "Doctrinal Exposition" in 1916 established the theology that Jesus was Jehovah, and God the Father was Elohim. There is no scriptural support

for this. Elohim is not in any of the Mormon Scriptures. It is a transliteration of the Hebrew word for God.

10. This 2 Nephi 19:6 quote is essentially the same as Isaiah 9:6. Because of this some Mormons might say: "Well, what is wrong with this? The Bible says the same thing!" What should not be missed is that Isaiah 9:6 and 2 Nephi 19:6 fit the trinitarian concept of God (see "trinity" in chapter 1, under "A Brief Summary of the Doctrine Taught by the Mormon Church") but do not fit the Mormon concept of three distinct and separate Gods (*Mormon Doctrine*, p. 317, under "God," and p. 278, under "Father in Heaven"). The Old Testament in several places in the original Hebrew says Jehovah is Elohim:

Hear, O Israel: The LORD [Jehovah] our God [Elohim] is one LORD [Jehovah]. (Deuteronomy 6:4)
. . . The LORD [Jehovah] he is God [Elohim]; there is none else beside him. (Deuteronomy 4:35)
For who is God [Elohim] save the LORD [Jehovah]? or who is a rock save our God [Elohim]? (Psalm 18:31)
And I appeared unto Abraham, unto Isaac, and unto Jacob, by the name of God [Elohim] Almighty, but by my name JEHOVAH was I not known to them. (Exodus 6:3)

See also Deuteronomy 4:39; 7:9; Joshua 2:11; 22:34; Jeremiah 10:10.

11. Keep in mind that according to the Mormon Church's teachings Jehovah is the premortal Jesus Christ, the Son of God, and Elohim is God the Father (Bible Dictionary, in the back of the LDS edition of the Bible, p. 711, under "Jehovah," and p. 681, under "God").

12. *Times and Seasons,* June 7, 1841, 2:498–99; *Times and Seasons,* August 2, 1841, 2:54; and October 1839, *History of the Church* 4:12 clearly show the enforcement of this. Members that sold or used "ardent spirits" lost their membership or were disciplined.

13. The words "Drank a glass of beer at Moessers" were removed from *History of the Church* 6:424. This is just one of the many changes made to "sanitize" Mormon history.

14. So what happened to Joseph Smith after he died? In the Mormon hymn, "Praise to the Man," about Joseph Smith, we learn that he is "crowned in the midst of the prophets of old." "Mingling with Gods, he can plan for his brethren" (*Gospel Principles,* p. 332). Brigham Young said: "Joseph Smith **holds the keys** of this last dispensation, and is now engaged behind the vail in the great work of the last days. . . . namely, that no man or woman in this dispensation will ever enter into the celestial kingdom of God without the **consent of Joseph Smith** . . . every man and woman must have the certificate of Joseph Smith, junior, as a **passport** to their entrance into the mansion where God and Christ

are . . ." (Brigham Young, at General Conference, October 9, 1859, *Journal of Discourses* 7:289). It appears that Joseph Smith's use of wine, beer, and tobacco did not affect his status in the afterlife.

15. An interesting admission since Mormons are taught that Jesus Christ was the alleged "founder of this work"; D&C 1:6, 30 says: ". . . my preface unto the book of my commandments, which I have given them to publish. . . . And also those to whom these commandments were given . . . the only true and living church upon the face of the whole earth, with which I, the Lord, am well pleased. . . ."

16. The kingdom of God is the celestial kingdom (*Mormon Doctrine*, p. 416, item 3, and p. 116).

17. Was blood atonement actually practiced? Yes, the above quote from Brigham Young shows that. And there is other evidence, but details are too complicated to include here. The Tanners cover this on pages 403, 404, 404-A of *Mormonism—Shadow or Reality?* On page 403 is described how Rosmos Anderson, a Danish man, was blood atoned for adultery. Several other examples are documented also.

The Mountain Meadows Massacre in 1857, where about 120 non-Mormon men, women, and children were slaughtered by Mormons and Indians, clearly shows that Mormonism, in Brigham Young's time, led men to do terrible things in the name of God.

18. This event allegedly took place in 1823. Some may point to the present-day D&C 27:5, which is dated August 1830, as added proof that the messenger was indeed Moroni. This name did not show up in this revelation until the 1835 D&C, 50:2, page 180. The original revelation in the 1833 *Book of Commandments*, chapter 28, page 60, had *nothing* on this subject. Oliver Cowdery in the April 1835 *Messenger and Advocate*, page 112, also named the angel as Moroni.

19. Published by (Apostle and mission president) F. D. Richards, Liverpool, 1851. This was the Mormon mission in England. Notice that the wording, except for the name, is the same as in *Joseph Smith—History*.

20. Joseph Smith was the editor of this paper, so it is not likely that this is a typographical error that slipped by. Note that he made this statement just two years before he died. For more on this subject see pages 136–37, 142-C of *Mormonism—Shadow or Reality?*

21. It is interesting to note that the Smiths moved to a town in 1818 that didn't exist by that name until April 16, 1822. The area that is now Manchester was Farmington until 1821. At that time it was named "Burt," and then it was named "Manchester" on April 16, 1822 (*Gazetteer of State of New York,* J. H. French, 1860, and *Gazetteer of State of New York,* Horatio Gates Spafford, 1824). *Joseph Smith—History* in 1:3 correctly recognizes that Palmyra at first was in Ontario County, then the name was changed to Wayne County (in April 11, 1823). Perhaps they didn't need to correct the name of the town they moved

to because they didn't move there until after the name change. This would be consistent with the 1823 date discussed below.

22. In his 1832 diary, page 3, he said he was in his sixteenth year.

23. Rev. Lane was not assigned to the Palmyra area until July 1824 and according to his own personal account the revival occurred in 1824 (*New Light on Mormon Origins*, Rev. Wesley P. Walters, pp. 8 and 9 and note 17 on p. 21; *Inventing Mormonism*, pp. 20–24).

24. These churches had revivals in 1824, but none during 1820 (ibid., pp. 15–41).

25. This was the first published account of this alleged event and is considered a significant milestone in Mormonism. It is written by Joseph Smith's scribe for the Book of Mormon. He was also one of the three witnesses of the gold plates, the "second elder" of the Church, and Assistant President of the high priesthood. It seems reasonable to expect he would also know the correct information about the First Vision story.

26. In other words, nothing unique happened to Joseph Smith in 1820, his fifteenth year, as in the Pearl of Great Price, *Joseph Smith—History* 1:14.

27. The official version of the First Vision story, which didn't reach its final form until 1838, seems to be based upon a typographical error. We speculate that Joseph Smith's scribe (James Mulholland) for the 1838 official version of the First Vision story, the one in *Joseph Smith—History*, used the December 1834 letter and missed the February 1835 correction. The first relating of the story has the revival occurring when Joseph Smith was in his fifteenth year. Two months later this was corrected to his seventeenth year in 1823. As the corrected age was not changed in following issues it seems reasonable to assume that Joseph Smith, who gave his approval for the history, agreed with the correction. Also, one would expect that the corrected date would have received a high level of investigation before it was made public. There is more on the First Vision in the item that follows in the main text: "Who or what did Joseph Smith see in his First Vision?"

28. The Mormon Church teaches that these personages were God the Father and his Son Jesus Christ. This event allegedly happened in 1820, but it did not get written up in this final form until 1838. This passage received wide use and eventually became scripture on October 10, 1880.

29. Abraham 3:18 also supports this teaching.

30. This is the present-day teaching of the Mormon Church. It also includes that our "intelligence" existed eternally.

31. This phrase is significant. According to this, Jesus Christ had a beginning; there was a time when he was not God.

32. Sometime after this, Joseph Smith may have tried to take Jane Law as a plural wife (*Mormon Polygamy—A History*, p. 57). Her husband, William Law, who had been Smith's second counselor, and a group of other dissenters in-

cluding his brother, Wilson, exposed Joseph's polygamy and political intrigues in the only issue of the *Nauvoo Expositor*, June 7, 1844. Joseph, through the Nauvoo City Council, had the press destroyed, an act that started a chain of events that led to his imprisonment and murder. A photo-reprint of the *Nauvoo Expositor* is available from Gospel Truth Ministries, P.O. Box 1015, Grand Rapids, MI 49501.

33. Hyrum, Joseph's brother, was the second and last person to be an Assistant President in the Mormon Church.

34. From a tract published by Apostle Taylor in Liverpool, England, in 1850.

35. Brigham Young University, Special Collection Library.

36. This was a pro-Mormon Church press.

37. Fannie Alger was probably Joseph Smith's first polygamous wife (*No Man Knows My History*, Fawn Brodie, pp. 181 and 458; *Mormon Enigma: Emma Hale Smith*, Linda King Newell and Valeen Tippetts Avery, Garden City: Doubleday, 1984, p. 66).

38. Brigham Young University, Archives and Manuscripts.

39. Although there was an 1844 edition of the Doctrine and Covenants, the revelation was not publicly revealed until August 29, 1852 (*A Comprehensive History of the Church of Jesus Christ of Latter-day Saints*, B. H. Roberts, 4:55–56), and was not added to the D&C until 1876. It was not approved by common consent of the Church until October 1880 (*Ensign*, December 1984, pp. 38–39).

40. *Mormon Polygamy—A History*, Richard S. Van Wagoner, Signature Books, 1986, is an excellent book on this subject.

41. For more on the post-Manifesto period see "Hannah Grover Hegsted and Post-Manifesto Plural Marriage," *Dialogue: A Journal of Mormon Thought* 26:3 (Fall 1993), Julie Hemming Savage, pp. 101–17.

42. This was in violation of D&C 58:21 and *Articles of Faith* #12, which claimed obedience to the laws of the land.

43. This appears to represent the present-day teachings of the Mormon Church (*Mormon Doctrine*, Bruce R. McConkie, pp. 799–801).

44. In 1849 a fourteenth Article of Faith (it was given number 11) was added. It said regarding the resurrection: ". . . the dead in Christ will rise first, and that the rest of the dead live not again until the thousand years are expired." This was dropped in the early 1880s (*Joseph Smith Begins His Work*, Wilford C. Wood, Vol II (1962), in the center of the book next to the picture of Joseph Smith; *A Mormon Bibliography 1830–1930*, edited by Chad J. Flake, University of Utah Press, 1978, p. 377, item 4771a, p. 624, item 7938; *New Light on Mormonism*, Mrs. Ellen E. Dickinson, 1885, p. 202, footnote).

45. Mormons take oaths not to reveal the temple ceremonies; hence most will not talk about it, even among themselves. General Authorities of the Mormon Church have not made public statements on the temple ceremony changes made in 1990, but it is clear that the changes were made with the approval of

the First Presidency and the Quorum of the Twelve Apostles (see *Salt Lake Tribune*, April 29, 1990, p. 2B). It is for this reason that we must use other sources.

46. More information on how the Mormon Church handles disciplinary action can be found in "The LDS Intellectual Community and Church Leadership: A Contemporary Chronology," *Dialogue: A Journal of Mormon Thought*, Lavina Fielding Anderson, Vol. 26, No. 1, Spring 1993, pp. 7–64. This issue also has more articles on this same subject.

47. LDS scripture has: "But neither teachers nor deacons have authority to baptize, administer the sacrament, or lay on hands; **They are, however, to warn, expound, exhort, and teach, and invite all to come unto Christ**" (D&C 20:58–59). **Note:** In the early Mormon Church teachers and deacons were adults.

48. Also see D&C 20:84.

Chapter 5: Changes in the Book of Mormon

1. See Appendix 1 under "Scriptures" for more information on this subject.

2. The Mormon Prophets have claimed the power to act in the name of God and to communicate with God for over 160 years; why have they, or their God, not given the Mormon people a Bible they can trust?

3. Martin Harris provided money to Joseph Smith during the translation process (JS-H 1:61) and paid for the printing of the first 5,000 copies of the Book of Mormon. For a short period he was Joseph's scribe. Martin talked Joseph into letting him borrow the first 116 pages of the handwritten manuscript of the Book of Mormon so he could show them to his wife. They disappeared while in the Harris home (*Truth Restored*, Gordon B. Hinckley of the First Presidency of the Church of Jesus Christ of Latter-day Saints, pp. 16–17).

4. The official position of the Mormon Church is that all of the Book of Mormon was translated from the gold plates by use of the Urim and Thummim (see Exodus 28:30 and the Bible Dictionary in the back of the LDS edition of the Bible) that Joseph Smith allegedly received from the angel Moroni along with the gold plates.

5. Why was this phrase "the Son of" added when other verses in the Book of Mormon still say that Jesus Christ is the Eternal Father? See Alma 11:38–39; Mosiah 16:15. Perhaps these were missed.

Chapter 6: Doctrine and Covenants Compared to the *Book of Commandments*

1. We feel that the last part of this verse was added to the 1835 edition of the D&C (and following editions) to prepare for the introduction of priesthood in the LDS Church. The foundational revelation on the Mormon Aaronic

Priesthood was allegedly received May 15, 1829, but it was not put into the Doctrine and Covenants until 1876 and not accepted "by common consent" of the membership until 1880. It is now D&C 13. It is the account of Joseph Smith and Oliver Cowdery allegedly receiving the Aaronic Priesthood from John the Baptist, who was allegedly acting under the authority of the Apostles Peter, James, and John (D&C 13 heading). This important event was *not* in the Mormon scriptures prior to 1876. Later on, these apostles allegedly gave Joseph and Oliver the Melchizedek Priesthood.

Some Mormons may say that priesthood restoration is also in JS-H 1:68–69, but this was not accepted as scripture until October 10, 1880 (see Introductory Note to the Pearl of Great Price).

2. The last paragraph of the Explanatory Introduction of the 1986 edition of the D&C says: "(such as discontinuing the unusual names beginning with Section 78)."

3. Kirtland, Ohio, was a Mormon town near what is now Cleveland. The persecutors probably were disgruntled Mormons fed up with Joseph's banking schemes (*Joseph Smith's Kirtland*, Karl Ricks Anderson, Deseret Books, 1989, pp. 205–6, 235–36). The first LDS Mormon temple was built there and is now owned by the RLDS.

4. The majority of Bible-believing Christians, however, believe that only Jesus Christ held the Melchizedek Priesthood, which is "unchangeable" and "untransmissible"; and that *all* true Christians, men and women, are a "royal" priesthood, who offer up praises of thanksgiving, because the blood of Jesus was sufficient to wash away the sins of the whole world.

5. These words were removed, the bold words were added.

6. Melchisedec is the New Testament spelling of the Old Testament Melchizedek.

Chapter 7: Absurdities in Mormonism

1. According to a letter to John Farkas dated February 4, 1993, from the Center for American Archeology, Kampsville Archeological Center, Kampsville, Illinois.

2. This is the end of the first group of Book of Mormon people, the Jaredites (2247 B.C. – 600 B.C.). Their extermination battle also allegedly took place on Hill Cumorah in New York State.

3. A chicken can actually run around with its head cut off because its legs can operate as a reflex action without signals from the brain; thus the familiar figure of speech "running around like a chicken with its head cut off." The human body does not function that way.

4. This does not include wives and children who were also present (Mormon 6:7).

5. In the Book of Mormon see 2 Nephi 5:15; Jarom 1:8; Mosiah 11:3, 8; Helaman 6:9, 11; Ether 7:9; 10:23.

6. The portion of this quote in italic bold letters was in a letter by the First Presidency titled: "Modern-language editions of the Book of Mormon are discouraged," *Ensign*, April 1993, p. 74.

7. The first and second cornerstones, as given by President Hinckley, are Jesus Christ and the First Vision story of Joseph Smith.

8. We recommend that all mature Christians studying Mormonism read the Book of Mormon.

9. *Gospel Principles*, pre-1986 editions, pp. 291–92.

10. Yet the Introduction of the Book of Mormon, first paragraph (1986 edition), says: "The Book of Mormon is a volume of holy scripture comparable to the Bible . . . and contains as does the Bible, the fulness of the everlasting gospel." In Mormonism the "fulness of the everlasting gospel" is that information (teachings and priesthood) from God the Father which, if accepted by a person and lived, will lead that person to exaltation in the top level of the celestial kingdom ("The Fulness of the Everlasting Gospel—What Is It?", an unpublished paper by John Farkas).

11. *Divergent Paths of the Restoration*, Steven L. Shields, Los Angeles: Restoration Research, 1990.

12. "Let my name be named upon it"—if this happened it was not visible in the several visits to the site I and others have made.

13. This phrase "as a city" is in brackets in *History of the Church*. It is not in Joseph Smith's diary, as shown in *The Words of Joseph Smith*, compiled and edited by Andrew F. Ehat and Lyndon W. Cook, page 166. This addition is one of the minor examples of how the *History of the Church* has been altered. More examples of these can be found in *Mormonism—Shadow or Reality?* pp. 5–13.

14. This historical information is from *Old Mormon Nauvoo and Southeastern Iowa*, Richard Neitzel Holzapfel and T. Jeffery Cottle, Fieldbrook Productions, Inc., 1991, pp. 150–53.

15. The remaining three apostles were ordained later: Parley P. Pratt on February 21, 1835, and Orson Pratt and Thomas B. Marsh on April 26, 1835.

16. A sample of 560 LDS blessings in the 1839–1899 period showed that six were told they would not taste death and fifty-seven were told they would remain until the Second Coming ("Patriarchal Blessings and the Routinization of Charisma," *Dialogue: A Journal of Mormon Thought*, Irene M. Bates, Vol. 26, No. 3, Fall 1993, pp. 9–11, 20, 21).

17. This group is the roots of the present-day Watchtower Society and Seventh-Day Adventists.

18. *Encyclopedia Britannica*, 1956 edition, 21:86–87.

19. The Mormon newspaper *Evening and Morning Star* (published in Independence, Mo.) of January 1833, page 64, featured an article heading "Re-

bellion In South Carolina." It described the political problems then occurring in South Carolina.

20. The "temple lot," as it is called, is in Independence, Missouri.

21. Apostle Orson Pratt, May 5, 1870, *Journal of Discourses* 13:362.

22. *The Complete Biblical Library, New Testament Study Bible, Matthew,* Springfield, Mo., 1989, pp. 531, 706.

23. For historical details about D&C 13, see chapter 6 under "Changes and the Mormon Priesthood."

Chapter 9: Is There Something Better?

1. Books on the Bible and biblical Christianity are listed in the Recommended Reading section of this book.

2. *The Church As Organized by Jesus Christ,* 1982; *The Falling Away and Restoration of the Gospel of Jesus Christ Foretold,* 1972; *Which Church Is Right?* 1982, pp. 9–18. All three booklets (tracts) were published by the Church of Jesus Christ of Latter-day Saints.

Chapter 10: Witnessing to Mormons

1. By mature Christians we mean those who know what they believe, why they believe it, and where to find it in the Bible. The opposite of mature Christians are baby Christians. These may be new in the faith or old-timers who have the same low level of knowledge and a fragile faith.

2. It is for this reason that we recommend that in general you ask only questions you already know the answer to and can document.

3. The Mormon may attempt to change the subject during the conversation, but the two of you must immediately get back to the subject at hand by saying: "We are talking about this now, we'll talk about that later." Then start a list for future discussions.

4. We have most of the references used. Copies of up to four pages of the references we have are free from Berean Christian Ministries, P.O. Box 1091, Webster, NY 14580. Send reference name and page number with a self-addressed, stamped (first class, two ounces), long envelope.

5. While we know that most Baptist churches do not have creeds, the Baptist church in Palmyra in 1820 set up at its founding in 1800 "Articles of faith and covenant." The record says, "In these articles the divine truth 'Ye are saved by grace' was prominently set forth" (records of the American Baptist Historical Society, Rochester, N.Y.; Wayne [County] Baptist Association Minutes, pp. 11–15). The succeeding American Baptists still accept this.

6. It cannot be found in the Book of Mormon or in the Bible. "The fulness of the everlasting gospel," according to Mormon leaders, is that information

and priesthood (as taught now by the Mormon Church) from God which, if accepted and lived, will let a person attain exaltation (becoming a God) in the top level of the celestial kingdom of God (from an unpublished paper, "The Fulness of the Everlasting Gospel—What Is It?", John R. Farkas, 1992).

Chapter 11: Authors' Testimonies

1. Mormons (males and females) who have been through the temple for their "endowments" are required to wear "temple garments" continually from that time forward. The original temple garment consisted of a one-piece white union suit reaching from the neck to the wrists and ankles. Shortened sleeves (like a T-shirt), legs to the knees, and separate tops and bottoms are now approved. The garments have four symbolic markings: a square on the right breast and a compass on the left, a stitched line over the navel and over the right knee. Masons have said that the breast markings remind them of the square and the compass pressed against the body in those locations during Masonic rituals.

Appendix 1: References

1. This information is a direct quote from the reference, and it is given here to show the claimed "authority," the pedigree of the reference.

2. When the position or office of a Mormon author (at the time of authorship) is not included in the reference, it is given in parentheses or brackets. When the position, or other description, is given on the title page of the work, parentheses or brackets are not used. These offices are given to show the authority of the author within the Mormon Church.

3. When only an initial is used in an author's name on the title page of a reference, then the full name is shown in parentheses.

4. Family home evening is the name given to the scheduled hours Mormon families spend together, usually at home, each Monday evening. No Mormon Church activities are scheduled for Mondays so this event may be held.

5. The preface in a reprint of the *Book of Commandments* reports the following:

> The typesetting on the book had progressed into the sixty-fifth chapter when a mob destroyed the printing house, scattered the galley sheets and type in the village streets, and threw the press into the Missouri River. Some church people gathered the five large galley sheets already struck (each having thirty-two pages—sixteen on either side—making a total of 160 pages, including the title page), cut and bound them, and tried to distribute them as widely as possible.

Perhaps as many as several hundred of these unfinished books, in various makeshift bindings, found their way into the hands of church people, and were used until 1835, when the First edition of the Doctrine and Covenants was released from the church press at Kirtland, Ohio. (Independence, Mo., Herald House Publishing Division of the Reorganized Church of Jesus Christ of Latter Day Saints, 1972)

Joseph Smith, and others, gave their testimony of the *Book of Commandments:*

In the second day's proceedings of the conference [November 2, 1831] it is recorded; "The revelation of last evening read by the moderator (this was Oliver Cowdery). The brethren then arose in turn and bore witness to the **truth of the Book of Commandments**, after which Brother Joseph Smith, Jun., arose and expressed his feelings and gratitude concerning the commandments and preface received yesterday." (Far West Record, p. 16.) (*History of the Church* 1:222, footnote)

With this, the revelations collected were approved by the top leadership of the Church at the special two-day conference. Also note that some of them had already been published in *The Evening and Morning Star*, the Church newspaper in Independence, Missouri. The fact that not all of the approved revelations were printed should not affect the alleged authority of those that were printed and distributed.

The page size of the *Book of Commandments* was 2 7/8" x 4 3/4" (as reported in *Joseph Smith Begins His Works*, Vol. 2, in the affidavit in the front pages).

Appendix 2: Mormon Writers and Personalities

1. *No Man Knows My History*, Fawn M. Brodie, pp. 181–82 and 457–59.
2. *Mormon Polygamy—A History*, Richard S. Van Wagoner, pp. 27–35.
3. Oliver Cowdery and Hyrum Smith were the only ones to hold this office.
4. *No Man Knows My History*, Fawn M. Brodie, p. 470, and *Mormon Polygamy—A History*, Richard S. Van Wagoner, p. 49.

Appendix 4: Recommended Reading

1. Appendix 1 contains a detailed list for the serious student. Those by the Church of Jesus Christ of Latter-day Saints, Deseret Book Co., Bookcraft, Inc., and Mormon leadership are pro-Mormon.

SUBJECT INDEX

SCRIPTURE INDEX

*"JST" denotes verses in the *Joseph Smith Translation* that have a different meaning than in the King James Version.

MORMON SCRIPTURES